NEW STRATEGIES
FOR MARKETING
INFORMATION
TECHNOLOGY

NEW STRATEGIES FOR MARKETING INFORMATION TECHNOLOGY

Edited by CHRISTOPHER FIELD
Writer, editor and publisher

CHAPMAN & HALL

London · Glasgow · Weinheim · New York · Tokyo · Melbourne · Madras

Published by Chapman & Hall, 2–6 Boundary Row, London SE1 8HN, UK

Chapman & Hall 2–6 Boundary Row, London SE1 8HN, UK

Blackie Academic & Professional, Wester Cleddens Road, Bishopbriggs, Glasgow G64 2NZ, UK

Chapman & Hall GmbH, Pappelallee 3, 69469 Weinheim, Germany

Chapman & Hall USA, 115 Fifth Avenue, New York, NY 10003, USA

Chapman & Hall Japan, ITP-Japan, Kyowa Building, 3F, 2–2–1 Hirakawacho, Chiyoda-ku, Tokyo 102, Japan

Chapman & Hall Australia, 102 Dodds Street, South Melbourne, Victoria 3205, Australia

Chapman & Hall India, R. Seshadri, 32 Second Main Road, CIT East, Madras 600 035, India

First edition 1996

© 1996 Christopher Field

Typeset in 11/13 Bembo by Photoprint, Torquay, Devon
Printed in Great Britain at the University Press, Cambridge

ISBN 0 412 61520 7

A catalogue record for this book is available from the British Library

∞ Printed on permanent acid-free text paper, manufactured in accordance with ANSI/NISO Z39.48–1992 and ANSI/NISO Z39.48–1984 (Permanence of Paper).

CONTENTS

Contents

Contents

CONTRIBUTORS

David Allenstein, Course Director, The Chartered Institute of
  Marketing (CIM)
John Armitage, chairman of Primary Contact
Andrew Barnes, managing consultant for Marketing Improvements
  Group
Peter Bartram, business writer and journalist
Graham Browne, Graham Browne Consultants
Natalie Calvert, director of Calcom Associates
Greg Cooper, Principal Consultant, Martrain Telemarketing and
  Database Consultancy
Colin Coulson-Thomas, managing director of Adaptation
Simon Daisley, marketing manager of Kerridge Computer Com-
  pany
Edwina Dunn, Dunnhumby Associates
Susan Goldsworthy, UK communications manager, Digital Equip-
  ment Corporation
Peter Hutton, MORI
Michael Juer, Workstations Limited
Nick Horley, Buffalo Communications
Chris Kaday, chairman of Hi-tech Marketing
Hugh Keeble, Interactive Group
Gordon Knight, director of Paragon Communications
Eric Leach, Eric Leach Marketing
Stan Maklan, ForeFront Consulting
David Mankin, managing director of SPY Design
Garrey Melville, chairman of the CSSA Marketing Group
Rob Pankhurst, Concept 20:20
Mike Park, Good Relations
William Payne, IT journalist and business analyst
Ian Ryder, Ian Ryder Associates
Jerry Sanders, editor of *Computing*

Contributors

Susan Scott Ker, marketing communications consultant for IBM
Michael Spring, head of communications, Oracle Corporation
Paul Stewart, Information Research Services
Merlin Stone, head of Avanti Consultancy Services
David Tebbutt, journalist and director of Press Here
Henry Trull, Henry Graham Group
Andy West, Text 100
Kevin Withnall, Spikes Cavell
Laurie Young, Avanti Consultancy Services

ACKNOWLEDGEMENTS

My thanks go first and foremost to the 35 contributors to this book. They share with me an enthusiasm for marketing and believe in its power to transform companies. No one paid me to get published and no one got paid to write.

Thanks to the Computing Software and Services Association's Marketing Group under the chairmanship of Garrey Melville. He gave me access to his network of members and they in turn helped me find other contributors.

Thanks to Ingmar Folkmans at Chapman & Hall who helped me see the wood for the trees and gave me encouragement when I began to believe that the whole project would not be completed.

Thanks to my wife, Philippa who put up with the lost evenings and weekends and who input so much copy when, along with disks through the post, came various viruses!

I am perfectly confident that this book will contribute to the creation of a marketing community that is so lacking in IT. Only by common agreement that marketing makes a difference and by the sharing of skills and experience will this community grow.

Christopher Field

PREFACE

Geoff Shingles, former chairman of Digital Equipment Corporation

The statement that a professional approach to marketing IT is essential should seem obvious to the point of being irrelevant. However, this industry needs to catch up with itself like no other; after all, it has become in 20 years what it took the automotive and aerospace industries almost 100.

IT is now becoming a commodity and it is all pervasive. Its hardware, software and services are used in all aspects of our life, when we work and when we relax. It is a vital part of the complete infrastructure of our lives, in our transport, communications, education and defence. Our financial institutions, shops and airlines would grind to a halt without it.

When IT was simply a product with limited professional application many of the major players, with some key exceptions, tended to be technology- or engineering-led. Today without professional marketing IT companies will struggle and their very survival may come into question. Marketing above all other disciplines is the one to focus on and it needs its own literature.

IT has not been sold or marketed well either internally, to the Board, or externally, to the end user. It has been proven though that when the Board saw the need to understand IT the whole enterprise benefited. On the other hand many Boards are convinced that IT has failed to deliver and additionally it can be argued that the current application of ill-conceived TQM (Total Quality Management) techniques are making its application worse. If this is true even to a limited extent it makes an even stronger case for a clear marketing approach to IT.

The traditional pyramid structures that we created over two centuries ago and which to this day pervade many of our current business organizations, will not serve us any longer. What has happened with IT is that we have taken a technology with the potential to support totally new enterprise structures and laid it over organizations based upon different and much more primitive technologies. It is no surprise it has not delivered and not met with our approval and satisfaction.

We still need to retain some clear command structure but it must now be much more flexible and adaptable, and make full use of fast communications and access to mass information. We must utilize the available technology to maximum advantage and adapted fastest and most completely. That is how the survivors will act.

Darwin deduced the success of those species who reacted in the same way when he went to the Galapagos. We can see it just as surely today in the companies which are adapting and transforming themselves fastest and embodying the full benefits of the new technologies and their application in communications, computing, video and audio. We have progressed through the mechanical, electrical and now to the digital implementation of these capabilities and a multimedia revolution is upon us. The fast adapters will survive and gain a stunning and unbeatable market advantage. TQM applied to these old feudal structures does indeed improve them in many ways but it only puts off the evil hour when the fundamental change must be made that brings those organizations the competitiveness needed for the 21st century.

If the IT company can explain to its customers how to use its wares, whether they are hardware, software or services, and allow them to implement a strategy and organization which gives a market advantage, it creates wealth for all stakeholders. This is the reason for this book.

IT is one of the major ways open to an enterprise to differentiate itself from its competitors. The IT company which markets itself and its wares to maximum advantage will survive in this world of ever increasing competition. The enterprise which differentiates itself and changes fastest will be the leader. We already see examples such as Compaq and Microsoft who have innovated in the IT world and Reuters, Marks & Spencer and British Airways who have embraced modern IT with devastating effect on the competition. Think back just ten years to the view we had of the last three companies compared to today; and who had even heard of Compaq and Microsoft?

The power of this technology is still not totally appreciated. It can create a company with a market capitalization larger than IBM and can help transform such a widely-disregarded company as British Airways in a decade. This alone should make the need for good IT marketing self evident. The need for quality IT marketing is fundamental to industrial competitiveness and progress now that the transition from the Nerdworld to the ubiquitous computer has quietly taken place. There is still one generation at least who claim to be fearful of computers and the dreaded keyboard. Yet these are the very people who use computers and benefit from them every day without even knowing it, in their cars, radios, televisions, dishwashers, phones and calculators. The modern car has greater computing power than the lunar excursion module which allowed Neil Armstrong his giant step for mankind onto the surface of the moon; you do not have to be a test pilot to drive that car.

The more invisible or normal and 'everyday' the computer becomes, the more easily it will be accepted, and we are already at the beginning of the period when IT becomes ubiquitous. It will be in every home and every workplace, integrated into our lives in every way. The companies that provide these IT goods and services across the spectrum `from the home to the great international enterprise will survive not simply on great products but on great marketing.

1

INTRODUCTION

Companies depend on information technology to help them keep up with the rapid and unpredictable changes that are affecting the way they do business globally and in the way they communicate.

However, the very industry that can provide these tools for change that companies so urgently require has made a poor job of promoting itself and the benefits its products and services can provide. Now it will have to. It will be a matter not simply of increasing turnover, but ultimately of survival.

This industry that stores, processes and transmits the information that is so precious to companies has grown to be the largest in the world, essentially on the back of chips, metal and plastic. But now everyone has caught on and they are all looking for margins that went out with the 80s.

Meanwhile, the market has also caught on. It now knows that the personal computer revolution brought no quantifiable rises in productivity; that the cost of owning technology is generally often higher than buying it; that astounding discounts are to be had for those with patience and cash; that a large part of the IT industry does not really understand its problems.

In short the market has matured. It has changed from being simply a passive consumer of technology products to an active specifier of technology services. Some IT companies have changed but the industry as a whole has not. The wind of change has been blowing for five years but only a few companies have felt it. It has even blown some away.

The giants of the IT industry were not as we thought indestructible – Wang, IBM, Unisys, Digital, Bull and others. A few have gone. A few such as IBM have undergone such a transformation that

New Strategies for Marketing Information Technology.
Edited by Christopher Field
Published in 1996 by Chapman & Hall, London. ISBN 0 412 61520 7

only their competitors could believe that they are remotely the same. And a few are at the cross-roads with poor prospects; only guess-work will say where they may end up.

The applause is now for the new giants such as Microsoft and Oracle, and yet even industry watchers are only prepared to make short predictions on their future. With IBM's acquisition of Lotus, Microsoft's domination of the desktop is no longer certain. Only change, constant and unpredictable, is certain. Companies are repositioning for change and the IT industry, slowly, is doing the same. But the implications for IT marketing, which is still trying to get the basics right, are worrying.

The future says that competition in the IT industry will intensify, it will be global, the rules will change, once sworn enemies will merge or partner. How will marketers market an alliance between a hardware, a software and a database company if the component companies' core competencies have been removed? Or market a service that can only be defined after the project is finished?

How will companies market to the customers of which they have little experience – the small office and home office buyer? Or the ordinary consumer who is now in the market for technology that was once confined to large organizations?

Soon there will only be room for companies that can use technology to solve business problems, create and reach new markets, and provide first class customer service. But to do this they must have a simple, accessible and very powerful marketing proposition, and to be able to say it very loudly through every type of media they can access.

None of this is new. Much of it was admitted by many companies during the last recession; some even vowed to do something about it when the good times came again. Unfortunately, with the good times came the money and once again marketing went back to its marginalized world of brochures and direct mail. It's true that companies have generally got better at marketing, but the future says that they will have to do a lot better than simply turning themselves into customer-driven, service-driven organizations. They will have to tell everyone as well.

SERIOUS MARKETING

This is a how-to book for people who know that how-to books do not work, that after the excitement of the management overview has waned, nothing actually gets done. It is a book for people who understand that marketing success often comes by accident, just as the means of determining the proportion of base metal in Hiero's golden crown came to Archimedes, just as gravity came to Newton from an apple on the head.

This is a book for people who understand that although planning, vision and research are essential to marketing, more human qualities such as inspiration, love and courage also play their part. Courage and the absolute certainty that marketing can do far more for your company than the products and services alone.

This is a book for people who are serious about a career in marketing, people who believe in marketing's power to transform companies, to build brand names and brand loyalty that can withstand change that is so rapid we may be never be able to document it, even years later. And of course, marketing's ability to give serious rewards in money, status and job satisfaction. The people who wrote this book are on their way there, why not you?

Christopher Field
Editor

Christopher Field is the editor of Retail Technology. He has recently launched 'Practical Publishing', a communications partnership that specializes in commercial writing, editing and contract publishing for companies such as IBM, Hutchison Telecom, Barclays and Esselte Meto. Chris also commissions and edits financial market research reports. He has worked for *Euromoney* and was commissioning editor for *Time* magazine's special reports.

PART ONE

LIVING IN THE EARTHQUAKE ZONE

Marketing strategy

INTRODUCTION

There are no end of books on marketing strategy and planning, some academic beyond the ken of mere mortal marketers, some full of advice that will only work if the entire board is tied up in the cellar, and some straight out of the door-stepping school of religious evangelism. The purpose of this chapter is to discuss some of the issues that are making strategy formulation a far more complex process than in the past.

Now companies must find out what their customers, each and every one, want before trying to condense their offering into one, neat, colourful package. Buying decisions are too often based on accidents and emotions and companies must come up with ever more varied, layered solutions in response. Already, solutions-driven companies have invented solutions only to find there was no market for them.

Strategy used to be based on various givens – that the world was exactly the way it appeared to be and would pretty much be that way in five years' time. Companies didn't question whether they would use the various classic techniques that used to define marketing, they would simply look at how much money they would commit to them, or what creative message they wanted to convey.

Now companies are having to lay the table in advance for a feast that may never happen, where the guests may be strangers and where the menu will be made up as the meal progresses. The only strategy that will work is the one that accepts that the only constant is change.

Laurie Young subverts the current thinking on service marketing. He says that companies will often seek to regain control of the very service they have outsourced because they feel that things are out of

New Strategies for Marketing Information Technology.
Edited by Christopher Field
Published in 1996 by Chapman & Hall, London. ISBN 0 412 61520 7

their control. One answer for suppliers is to involve them more closely in the process.

Henry Trull maintains that just as IT is too important to be left to IT professionals, so marketing is too important to be left to marketers. He says that marketing must be introduced throughout the company not just left to the marketing department.

William Payne looks at the battle between Microsoft and IBM for domination of the desktop and shows how marketing is making the difference for Microsoft.

Kevin Withnall aims at those readers who are looking for a brief guide to marketing planning.

Susan Scott Ker uses the example of IBM's VoiceType speech recognition to look at pre-launch software marketing and how much of the work is down to anticipating and managing unpredictable user expectations.

Garrey Melville takes his life into his hands and predicts how IT marketing will look in the future. The results are often surprising.

2

HOW TO *REALLY* MARKET COMPUTER SERVICES

Laurie Young

My colleagues and I recently won a consultancy contract with one of the big financial services companies. The project was to stimulate a review of strategy in the light of the radical new technology they were installing. The client had a specific need which had been clearly articulated to many suppliers, including most of the big computer manufacturers. His experience was interesting:

> They're all into services now so I asked them what they could do for me. They all said 'Anything. We provide a full service'. Of course that means nothing. They weren't telling me what they had to offer or why they are different.

He was very frustrated and had a strong perception that companies were trying to exploit the service theme because they could not make money out of mainframes any more. An indication that the IT industry does not yet have well developed service marketing skills is the fact that very few of their services are unique. The maintenance, desktop and consultancy services of the major IT vendors are so similar that they have allowed them to appear as commodities. This

New Strategies for Marketing Information Technology.
Edited by Christopher Field
Published in 1996 by Chapman & Hall, London. ISBN 0 412 61520 7

gives the customer very little choice in terms of features and forces them to choose on the basis of price. However, good service marketing would create a variety of services, differently priced, and better profits for all the suppliers. This chapter explores some of the techniques which make that happen.

It is not enough to try to sell services because the sales force need something to offer. There are some very special issues involved in bringing services to market which have to be addressed first. These have implications to the marketing of services which makes the approach different to the marketing of products. If attention is not paid to these issues, wasted expenditure, or worse, adverse customer reaction will occur. The service marketer must incorporate a number of principles in to the day to day service marketing programmes in order to succeed. They are:

THE PHENOMENON OF CONTROL

When a customer uses a service they give control to the service provider. The service provider is given the right to act on the customer's behalf and, in some cases, to do things to the service user. This happens in all services; from simple professional services such as hairdressing to complex business-to-business services. However, human beings do not like being out of control. Even though control is surrendered willingly, to gain some benefit, the customer will unconsciously try to regain control as they become more and more familiar with service process. Customers will therefore want to take over a variety of activities themselves from petrol filling and cash collection via bank machines to conveyancing and computer service. This one fact alone will hold up the development of outsourcing and cause some companies to take contracted services back into their organization.

This phenomenon invades the personal space of the service user in a way which products do not because most products are used after purchase by the customer. The customer then has complete control as to when and how to use them. They are even able to choose whether to comply with the manufacturer's instructions or not. This is not the case with services.

The act of giving control to a service provider induces stress in the customer. For example, the first time a person uses an airport is often a stressful experience. The customer has to ensure they allow plenty of time because they know that it will take a long time to get on board. They have to get to the right car park (most have heard horror stories of people being charged large amounts of money because they parked in the short stay car park by mistake). They then have to get to the terminal and find their way to the check in desk. Various people then want to check tickets, passports and boarding cards whilst they are making their way onto the aircraft. It can be confusing, bewildering and worrying. If there is a mistake in the signage or if an official says the wrong thing in the wrong way, the customer becomes alarmed and their stress increases. This alone can cause the customer to complain of poor quality.

There are several factors which can alleviate the stress caused by giving control to a service provider. The first is familiarity with the process. If a customer has used the service many times, they know what to expect and what the anticipated outcome will be. This ensures that stress levels stay low and any difficulties are seen as aberrations which can be corrected by excellent service recovery. The second factor is the individual performing the service. The character, reputation and professionalism of an individual can inspire confidence in the quality of the service to be received. In fact the individual can have such a strong reputation that it becomes a corporate brand, for instance Sassoons.

The corporate brand itself can allay the stress caused by giving control to a service provider. For example, the values of the brand 'Marks & Spencer' contain the promise of no hassle service recovery. Customers know that, if there is a problem with a purchased item, they can return it without any question or difficulty. This phenomenon has given Marks & Spencer a significant competitive advantage for a number of years because most people do not like to return faulty items. When thinking of complaining, they get stressed because they know that control is ultimately with the supplier.

Another obviator of the stress caused by giving control to a service supplier is the quality of the service process. If the customer experiences a clearly signposted service process, which meets their expectations as both an experienced or novice user, they will have much of their anxiety about the service outcome controlled. Advanced knowledge of the details of the service (via information supplied about the procedures that the service incorporates) will also allay stress by giving the customer a greater feeling of control.

The issue of control has implications for customer care, quality of service and service design which make the marketing of services different from products. For instance, the recent emphasis on customer care and the behaviour of front line staff has caused many people to assume that excellent service is primarily about training people to perform the service well on behalf of the customer.

However, if the customer is continually experiencing stress due to lack of control, they will be looking for ways to regain control. As a customer becomes an experienced user, they will look for ways to demonstrate their new expertise by taking shortcuts or performing service elements themselves. If the service supplier does not anticipate this, the customer will become frustrated and will have unnecessarily bad perceptions of the quality of service.

It follows that part of the phenomenon of control is the desire of the customer to take back control by undertaking self service. This means that it is possible to design processes whereby, as the customer becomes familiar with the service process, they can be included further into it. The supplier can design self service into the service system. This will reduce costs because some of the effort of performing the service now comes from the customer. However, it will also improve quality because the service performance is within the control of the customer and thus closer to their perceptions of timely delivery.

THE SERVICE PROCESS

Products are entities which are bought through a process but are independent of it. Services, however, have a process inherent in their design through which the customer must pass. The customer must first know how to access the supplier's service system. This has to be clearly signposted and designed to encourage both the novice and expert user. Educating the customer to access and use the supplier's process is, therefore, a critical component of service marketing.

Having accessed the service process, the customer must learn how to use it. For the novice user there must be clear direction and assistance from either people, signage or technology. The novice customer must be attracted to use the system and educated in the supplier's methodology at the same time. The customer must be made to feel that it is easily within their grasp to use the system. However, once the customer has a degree of expertise, there must be shortcuts built into the system that they can access easily. If this is not the case they will become frustrated and look for competitor service systems that will save them time.

The design and development of services must, therefore, pay particular attention to process design. In addition to making it easy for the novice and expert customer to pass through, there should be buffer systems set up to distinguish between erratic front line systems and smooth, production-orientated back office systems. There must also be flexibility built into the process which allows front line people to deviate from the norm on the customer's behalf in unusual circumstances. By designing a number of 'plan B' procedures, the company will improve the customer's perception of quality because the employee will be able to act when a problem occurs. However, the costs of such aberration will be kept low because there will be parameters in which to act.

INTANGIBILITY

Writers on services have argued that service marketing is different from product marketing because services are intangible and products are tangible. This is nonsense. All products are intangible concepts before they are brought to market. A proposal to bring to market a new service is as intangible as a proposal to manufacture a new product or to raise funding for a new business. Anyone who has tried to convince a board of a new product concept or potential backers of a new business idea understands that. The process of bringing products to market involves the creation of design concepts and the planning of packaging which appeals to the target market. In particular, the producer must plan a group of features which meet the benefits sought by the target customers.

A branded product remains an intangible concept when it is presented to a customer and earns added value revenue from its intangibility. A product such as Heinz baked beans is a combination of the following benefits: haricot beans, sauce, packaging, easy distribution and consistency of familiar taste. It is tangible in the sense that it contains physical product that customers can eat but the branded good remains a concept. Over years the company has invested time, money and skill in building the benefit concept in the minds of a group of customers. This is the fundamental principle of branding and it is what writers on service marketing have called the 'Fifth p' of service marketing: 'Presence'. But it is not, nor should be, limited to services. By emphasizing 'presence' they are simply reflecting the experience of marketers who create brands. The strategy and investment required to create a brand calls for long-term design and positioning work. It must be separated from the day to day operational communication programmes. It always was necessary to develop the 'presence' of products before handling 'promotion'.

There is no difference in building the benefit concepts associated with a product from those associated with a service. Products do not just comprise physical components. They have conceptual components and service components. For example a washing machine is bought because of the physical components, the design, the brand and the service support package. (It is also bought through the service system of a retailer.) Similarly a service not only has a service element. It must have a brand concept and some physical components. A computer service involves the physical components of the technology upon which it is built, the associations of the commodity service and the corporate name, in addition to the service provided to customers.

The major difference between product and service marketing is that there has been more of a history of creating branded goods than in the development of relevant, branded services. This is more because the skills of marketing have not been applied to many services than any major difference between making the benefit proposition more tangible before purchase. A key aspect of marketing services is, therefore, to create a presence for the benefits of the service in ways (similar to successful branded product marketing) which will make the intangible more tangible in the customer's mind. However, as the IT industry has not invested strongly in brand development to date, this will be a new skill in many IT companies.

Nonetheless, products are more physical entities than services and this affects the experience of the customer during and after purchase. It is not possible to taste, feel, see, hear or smell services before they are bought. Opinions may be sought before purchase and repeat purchase may depend on previous experience but the purchase is intangible and intangibility causes difficulty for some customers. (There are people who have no difficulty thinking conceptually. They can see a concept in their mind's eye and use that perception to their advantage. Such people find it easy to buy and use services. Others can only really appreciate a concept when it is presented tangibly in front of them. Such people find it hard to work on a concept until it is a reality. For them, the lack of a physical entity in service usage causes difficulty.) It is therefore important to manage 'post cognitive dissonance' very carefully.

As the purchase of a service is an emotional experience, the customer will be looking for reassurance that they were correct to purchase it. If they are presented with brand reinforcements after use (such as testimonials from others that have used it) they will tend to become an advocate of the service, increasing word of mouth communication.

In service marketing, therefore, it is not possible to neglect the development of a branded proposition in the way that the IT industry has tended to with its technological products. It is crucial to use every possible means to create a branded proposition before, during and after consumption. These include: the use of recognized branded communication to encourage purchase; the extensive use of brand, signage, brochure, and staff uniforms during the customer's experience of the service process; and the careful use of post experience communication to reassure the customer that they were correct to buy the service.

INVOLVEMENT OF THE CUSTOMER

The customer is intimately involved in the supply and performance of services. The degree of customer involvement is a key strategic decision in the design of services. Customers are not predictable. They use products and services in ways which suppliers do not expect. Service marketers must work in co-operation with customers as much as possible. In service propositions it is important to develop ideas and test innovations in conjunction with clients. As far as possible the service provider must allow the customer to do things themselves, or with the provider, rather than working on their behalf.

SIMULTANEOUS CONSUMPTION

A product can be bought and stored. It can then be used at a later date. Services, however, have to be used as they are bought. They cannot be stored. Quality cannot therefore be guaranteed in advance. This means that there is no opportunity to check, refine and hone the service until after it has been used. Quality of service and customer care are therefore as essential to the effective marketing of a service as are process controls.

Simultaneous consumption also means that the customer cannot check that service experience is consistent with the benefits claimed by the supplier in advance. The customer may seek reassurance by contact with other respected purchasers but will not really know what quality is to be received until the service is delivered. The contract between buyer and seller is therefore very important. As is the pre-purchase evaluation process.

EMOTIONAL INVOLVEMENT

There is normally more emotion in the process of consuming services than products. A manufactured product is a physical object about which purchasers can be detached and objective but the service user is more intimately involved in a service. (Possible exceptions are when a product has sentimental associations and when it has become a brand because consumers identify with the emotional characteristics of the brand. Also buying 'unmentionables' such as condoms, sanitary towels, toupees, etc. can be an emotionally charged experience!) However, as services are such an emotional purchase, research techniques for the design of services must get at the underlying emotional prejudices of the customer. Customer communications, particularly brand messages, must also be carefully directed at key emotional needs of customers.

THE IMPORTANCE OF THE CORPORATE BRAND

All marketers are familiar with the concept of brand and brand strategy. Companies have found that, by creating and developing both tangible and intangible product benefits, customers develop an emotional allegiance to a product brand which increases sales, profitability and longevity. Similarly, the corporate name and image of a company can communicate certain subliminal messages. This can be turned into a brand which inspires allegiance from customers. When aberration or stress occurs the customer looks to the corporate brand for reassurance.

Successful service products create customer allegiance more by the association of benefits with the corporate name than with the identity and benefits of the individual service products. Companies in other sectors have wasted vast sums by trying to create branded services which stand independent of the corporate brand. In service marketing, the values of the corporate brand are intimately tied to the individual service proposition in the customer's mind. It is fatal to divorce them.

This phenomenon means that the brand strategy for the successful marketing of services is different from that for products. In most product marketing it is possible to create a brand identity which is separate from the brand identity of the corporate name. It is not generally possible for services to succeed without the backing of the corporate brand promise. It is essential therefore for service marketers to establish and manage a corporate brand and then keep individual service brands in line with it. Brand management and corporate identity controls must be very strong in a service company.

THE INTERDEPENDENCY WITH CUSTOMER CARE AND QUALITY OF SERVICE IS MORE INTENSE THAN WITH PRODUCTS

During the 1980s a number of research reports were published which showed the effect of quality of product and quality of service upon profit. These were reinforced by some spectacular successes in certain industries, for instance the Japanese penetration of the world-wide car industry and the turnaround of BA by Lord King and Sir Colin Marshall.

There is a service quality evolution that companies and industries move through. It involves getting, first, to a standard of service which is the unwritten quality that consumers expect. This standard is created by the standards and experience of society. It is the 'par' performance quality. Consumers instinctively know what is above and below par.

Performance then moves through the proactive marketing of quality improvements onto real service differentiation. Finally companies make incremental revenue out of presenting 'added value' services to market which meet new needs.

The successful management of the development of a company's quality must interrelate the general improvement of service quality with the process necessary to bring new added value services to market. For example, BA worked on their general corporate branding and then their people's behaviour before launching club class.

It is difficult for companies to market added value services whilst their general quality of service is below par. Customers will not believe that they will receive a good quality added value service until the base quality is acceptable. Similarly, once companies want to create additional revenues by launching new services, they must clearly differentiate them from their core service. Once quality is acceptable and added value services are launched, there will be a continuous evolution as customers' standards continue to change and improve. Features which are added value to a customer segment one year become standard service the next.

Companies therefore have to understand both the interdependency and delineation between the general quality of base service and the opportunity to offer added value service. This is particularly important for IT services because the base service is often viewed as a commodity. Managers are therefore tempted to look for added value before bringing the general quality of service up to par or making the standard offer relevant to the market.

THE IMPORTANCE OF PEOPLE

People are not only important to the design and management of a service, they are part of the service itself. The motivation, behaviour, and appearance of front line people are part of the benefit package offered to customers. Managing the behaviour of people in line with changing customer expectations is a major focus and challenge for technical services. Managers understand that the body language, appearance and language of their front line people can cause customers to turn to or turn away from the service. Many have put real effort and resources into programmes designed to raise the impression caused by their people to a general quality. Few, however, have set out to discover the behavioural requirements and expectations of different customer segments and then design different people behaviours for those groups.

Companies who have large service functions are struggling with issues such as how to continue to motivate people to perform good service over a long period of time and what to do after the first few years of 'smile training' programmes. Others are experimenting with programmes to improve the behaviours of non employees who are part of the service such as dealers, subcontractors or self-employed people. Others are trying to maintain motivation in a climate of ever decreasing job numbers and job skills as the effect of new market forces and new technology undermines old job patterns. Yet the correct management of people in line with changing customer needs is a critical success factor for technical service firms.

SERVICE MARKETING – A DIFFERENT DISCIPLINE

These principles must be incorporated into service marketing programmes if IT companies are going to earn new revenues from them. The specific practical issues which IT companies should consider in marketing services are:

- Customer segmentation and analysis. There are different buying criteria and often different decision makers. These should be thought through carefully. A new segmentation should be postulated and which takes on board these different criteria.
- A service development process should be created. It is possible to successfully use product portfolio analysis for services and it is possible to adapt a product development process. However, this will only be successful if the unique issues of marketing services are built into the service design process. For example, there must be part of the process which explicitly matches the corporate brand values to the emotional needs of the customer. What most IT people call added value features of a service (e.g. quality) are in fact merely technical ways of augmenting the core service.
- Create 'product managers' for services. Companies will often have senior managers responsible for the creation and management of their key products. These should also exist for services.
- Turn the corporate image into a brand proposition which is relevant to the service needs of the target customers. Many IT companies do not even know the value of their corporate brand in a service environment, let alone using it as a source of added value as part of the proposition. Research the brand values and turn them into a design proposition at all points of interface.
- Pay fanatical attention to the service process and its development. Map out the process that the customer will move through. Make adaptations for the novice and the experienced customer. Create 'plan B' procedures for common aberrations and undertake relevant analysis of potential blockages using queuing theory. Finally, plot out the role of people and systems in the process based on customer preference.
- Understand the difference between the core service quality and the features of added value services. Plan the migration of these features into the core service over time.
- Communicate to the emotional needs of the customer. Do not neglect customer education as part of the communications process.
- Allow marketing skills to be applied to the quality programme.
- Vary the price.

In this way a range of diverse services will evolve that are unique to the supply companies and give the customer wider choice. The IT services market is currently like a car market where all the manufacturers produce the same car. The first companies to take service marketing seriously will therefore take market share by creating real value and variety.

Laurie Young is a specialist in services marketing and customer care. He is an associate with the Avanti Consultancy and runs his own services marketing consultancy.

3

COPING WITH THE EARTHQUAKE

From sales led to market driven

Henry Trull

> He's a man way out there in the blue, riding on a smile and a shoeshine. And when they start not smiling back – that's an earthquake.
>
> Arthur Miller, *Death of a Salesman*

An earthquake is a very unnerving experience, since it threatens our perception of reality. The ground is solid, it never moves, and neither do static objects. You don't have to think about it, that is how it is – until the earthquake. After the earthquake, you have to reorient yourself to the new reality – things have been rearranged, they are in different places, at different angles. Some things have been destroyed altogether. Our industry has experienced an earthquake, but we have not yet adapted our behaviour in this rearranged world.

Before the earthquake, all we had to do was to keep up a flow of good products and services, describe them in glowing terms, and hire some people to sell them. We could follow each other into new markets, we could talk the same language as our competitors and sell the same things in the same way. We could still make money, since

New Strategies for Marketing Information Technology.
Edited by Christopher Field
Published in 1996 by Chapman & Hall, London. ISBN 0 412 61520 7

in an ever expanding market there was plenty of room for every-body, and the ones who occasionally got in first could make a great deal of money.

Since the earthquake things have changed, and we keep bumping into furniture and falling into deep holes in the ground. In a maturing market, if everybody sells the same thing in the same way, the customers buy the cheapest. In a price war people lose money – the bigger you are (the more successful you were), the more money you can lose, so it becomes critically important to be different. Which is why everybody is suddenly talking about marketing, and why this book has been put together.

Obviously, the smart thing is to be different in ways that are perceived to be important by the customer, but that is easier said than done when you have never had to do it before. More mature industries who have already had to face up to this issue recognize that the key differentiators are often emotional rather than factual, which can be very difficult for us to accept. Buying is emotional – after all, nobody buys a BMW because it has a great engine, or a Sony TV because they have a fine appreciation of electronics. Consider the biggest buying decision that you or I ever made, and ask yourself when did you last actually buy a house based on a logical decision so that it was exactly like the house you set out to buy in the first place? Apart from the exploitation of fear, uncertainty and doubt, our industry has consistently ignored these emotional buyer values and will continue to do so at its peril.

We have tended to invent product or service concepts that suit the industry rather than to solve the customers' specific problems. For example, systems integration was invented in order for the large services organizations to generate more management revenues and better margins. In 1992 IDC did some research which showed that less than 3% of 750 senior non-IT business directors understood what systems integration meant, at a time when nearly all the major IT suppliers were telling the marketplace that they were leading systems integrators. In actual fact they were telling the IT community that they were leading systems integrators, since almost all 'IT marketing' until now has been concerned with supply, not with demand.

As an industry we have supplied our customers with a series of silver bullets, each one of which was the solution. The trouble is that the solution was usually for our benefit, to generate more business attacking the problem created by the last or last but one silver bullet. For example, hierarchical databases, data analysis, structured pro-gramming, structured design, structured analysis, relational databases, prototyping, CASE, I-CASE, re-engineering, systems integration, facilities management, outsourcing and masses and masses of hardware. None of these silver bullets has born any relation to the real needs of the business, but since IT wasn't a strategic issue it didn't matter. The customer had a vague idea that they were doing the right thing by being more modern and efficient as the computer churned out the invoices and did the accounts, and occasionally some interesting information surfaced, but IT was not really important. Of course there were increasing complaints about the cost, but we (the internal and external) IT experts were doing our best and becoming more 'professional'.

There is a strong irony in the fact that when we were successful and double digit growth was the norm for IT products and services, we kept trying to convince the world that IT was very important. Only a few years ago, the theme of the CSA conference, *IT Matters*, was devoted to proving it. But now, when most large organizations are trying to transform themselves from being large ships to being flotillas of small boats, IT has become critically important. It is the best chance of providing the glue that will keep the re-structured organization together and moving in the same direction. It has become a senior management issue, and as a consequence, far too important to be left to a bunch of technical people who speak incomprehensible 'gobbledygook' and persistently oversell their products and services and who fail to meet their customers' expectations. They may well need a client/server solution, or a network management tool, but that is not what they are buying, and certainly not what interests them, and so the customer is beginning not to smile back. IT is too important to be left to the IT professionals.

It is very important to recognize that this situation is not temporary; it is a historical transition that is directly comparable to other industries that have undergone a shift from initial dramatic growth towards maturity. A simple statement of the problem is therefore that in a more difficult climate we need to become much better at understanding the real needs and wants of the customers and their businesses. We have to learn to become more honest about we can do and what we cannot do. This is often expressed as moving from a sales approach to a marketing approach, however, as the title of this article suggests it is the market that matters, not the marketing function.

It is an extremely difficult transition to make, to transform the marketing function from a sales support function into a sales direction function. Many companies go about hiring professional marketers and PR agencies to 'do some marketing'. This is as likely to succeed as throwing some programmers at a user department is likely to result in some top-class business systems; the users find them incomprehensible, so they ignore them and let them get on with it on their own, with unpredictable results and predictable waste of effort. There is good PR and bad PR, and tons and tons of indifferent PR. Unless you have a very clear idea of what opinions are and who has them, and the changes in opinion that you want to make, then PR is likely to be a waste of money. All publicity is not good publicity, and a high media profile can be high risk as no doubt Ken Olsen and Gerald Ratner would agree.

There is a danger that marketing can become a giant carbuncle on the corporate posterior – it makes you feel very uncomfortable if you try to sit down and relax, but it does not really contribute anything to your performance. It is the market that needs to drive the business, not the marketing function, and the marketing function is doomed to failure if senior management fail to recognize that the organization itself has to make the cultural change. This is of course not unique to marketing, for example, making somebody or a department responsible for security immediately makes the security risks much worse, since everybody else immediately thinks – 'it's not my problem anymore'.

Marketing is like IT itself; it has its own jargon, its own specialists; it is not a solution in itself, and what senior management get out of it is directly proportional to the effort that they put into it. In other words, getting some marketing is not a silver bullet either. It has been stated in this article that IT is too important to be left to the IT function; for the very same reasons, for IT companies, marketing is too important to be left to the marketing function.

As you read through the rest of this book, look for ways to implement a marketing approach throughout the organization, rather than trying to buy in or build a central marketing function. It needs to be treated in a similar way to quality initiatives, and is of course closely related. The people closest to the customer have the best understanding of their needs and problems, not senior management or senior marketing executives. You will still need experienced and professional marketing people as well as the commitment of senior management to make it all work, but the role of marketing is to help, support, advise, protect the strategy and act as a catalyst, rather than having to be the people with all the smart ideas.

Of course, asking a marketing professional whether you need some marketing is like asking an insurance salesperson whether you need some insurance. But it is important to remember that marketing is not something that you can just buy off the shelf. Like quality, marketing is a circular process. It is more than just understanding what the customer wants now and will need in the future; you also have to work out how to change the organization to meet those needs better than any of your competitors.

After an earthquake, it is a good idea to find out what has changed and what has been rearranged, to identify where the hazards are – the holes in the ground. Then and only then is it possible to work out the best way to adapt to the new situation. As with any earthquake, there will be aftershocks as we try to adapt to the new situation without getting it right straight away. Change or die can be an uncomfortable choice, but without question, effective use of marketing will make the changes more pertinent and more manageable. And when the customers start to smile back again, maybe this time we will concentrate on keeping it that way.

Henry Trull is a partner in the Henry Graham Group, a new company that assists internal and external IT suppliers to make the transition from sales led to market driven. With 25 years in IT, Henry is a commentator on IT industry and has developed expertise on the delivery of software and services to business markets. He produces industry market research reports and has worked as a consultant for a number of well-known IT organizations in Europe and the UK.

4

THE LOOKING GLASS WAR

How IBM and Microsoft fought for domination of the desktop

William Payne

How does the largest computer company in the world lose the pole position in a crucial market to a company less than 15 years old? And how can it achieve this feat with a product that many claim is technically superior to its rival's? A claim that even its rival's chief executive appears to admit in public. Finally, having lost massive market share, and not a little credibility, how can the company ultimately turn the tables on its rival?

The answer, in the case of the long running IBM vs. Microsoft saga, the so-called 'operating systems' war, is marketing. Marketing at the strategic levels of both product and market definition. And marketing as a weapon to bring the war into your enemy's camp, and turn their strengths into weaknesses.

In the first round of this battle, Microsoft showed itself to be the clear winner, demonstrating an impressive strategic appreciation both of its market, and of the relative strengths and weaknesses of its Windows 3.0 product and IBM's rival OS/2 v1 operating system.

It is certainly true that Microsoft cannot have been hampered by the knowledge it gained as a result of largely developing OS/2 v1 for

New Strategies for Marketing Information Technology.
Edited by Christopher Field
Published in 1996 by Chapman & Hall, London. ISBN 0 412 61520 7

IBM. But that cannot excuse IBM's Armonk headquarters team for woefully misreading their marketplace. And this from the company claimed by both outsiders like McKinsey's Tom Peters and IBM insiders such as Buck Rodgers to be the supreme American marketing and sales organization.

'At IBM everybody sells!' claimed Buck Rodgers, self-styled 'supersalesman'. Perhaps. But clearly no one was doing much marketing in the late 1980s, and the result was that 'everybody' at IBM ended up trying to sell the wrong product, to the wrong set of people, at the wrong time.

Meanwhile, Microsoft cleaned up.

More recently, perhaps as a result of major management upheavals, as well as OS/2 v2's increasing stability and functionality, IBM appears to be displaying a surer touch, while it is Microsoft that could be in danger of losing significant market share.

Since 1989, the computer industry has been treated to the always enjoyable spectacle of two former allies falling out in dramatically public fashion. The growing antipathy between the two companies also became highly personalized between Microsoft chairman Bill Gates and IBM's head of Personal Systems, James Cannavino.

The turning point of the relationship between the two companies came in a garishly decorated conference room at the Comdex trade show in November 1989. Bill Gates and James Cannavino had reached an agreement. Before two dozen or so of the top executives in the PC software business, Cannavino would endorse the forthcoming upgrade of the Microsoft Windows graphical user interface software, while Gates would say that Windows was a low-end product and OS/2 should be used on more powerful microcomputers. Gates was also supposed to agree to focus Microsoft's efforts on developing OS/2.

While a noisy air conditioner droned on, neither Gates nor Cannavino went quite as far as they had committed to. When Gates refused to commit to OS/2, all the executives realized that Microsoft had declared war on IBM.

In essence, the row concerned not just a graphic user interface, but the future of the desktop PC itself, as defined by its operating system.

Both companies had come to the realization that DOS, the PC's original operating system, could no longer support the advanced graphic and integrated applications that users would demand in the 1990s.

Outside the PC environment, users could enjoy Apple's easy to use windowing environment, together with a high degree of seamless integration between individual products. And in the technical workstation marketplace, specialist users were beginning to use the very high resolution multitasking windowing environment developed for high speed Unix computers by the Massachusetts Institute of Technology: X-Windows.

In addition, new PC microprocessors were being developed by Intel that offered huge new capabilities, including 32-bit architectures, extended and expanded memories running to many megabytes, and multiple disk volumes, that DOS could simply not handle.

Both companies agreed upon the need for an operating system that could ultimately provide true 32-bit capabilities and take full advantage of larger computer memories. In addition such an operating system would also provide an advanced windowing environment with facilities for dynamic application linking.

The divergence between the two companies arose from a radically different perspective of the marketplace that went to the very top in both organizations.

As a result, the products of both IBM and Microsoft, in some way the result of the extensive co-development between the two companies, ended up being packaged and marketed in distinctly different ways.

Just as vitally, Microsoft deliberately created a marketing support programme – Transition – that was the direct result of Microsoft CEO Bill Gates' original marketing insight. Transition would prove to be vital to the runaway success of Windows 3.0, and the consequent failure of IBM's OS/2 v1 to capture more market-share.

IBM, by contrast, found it difficult to shake off the public perception that it was pursuing a hegemonist agenda in the PC hardware market via the OS/2 back door.

Certainly, the coupling of OS/2 with IBM's proprietary Micro Channel Architecture (MCA) did nothing to quieten fears that IBM was really intent on flattening its clone rivals.

Even worse, the imposition by IBM's top strategists of a subordinate role for OS/2 within IBM's grand SAA strategy compounded industry and public misgivings. OS/2 was being marketed by IBM apparently as simply a desktop Trojan Horse for the IBM mainframe. Departmental and workgroup users who had spent years shaking off the data centre's dictates, costs, and clunky, unfriendly centralized applications, faced having them reimposed by the deadly combination of SAA and OS/2. The only fly in the ointment for IBM was that when IBM launched SAA, it was a largely chimerical product, relying heavily on a combination of already available SNA products and an unpopular printer communications protocol, LU6.2.

Only the large banks, with their need for nationally distributed online processing to large central data processors, really bought into IBM's grandiose MVS to OS/2 via DB2 and SAA vision. For other corporate desktop users, it was a positive drawback.

Meanwhile, by its success at capturing market-share at the earliest possible opportunity with a markedly less ambitious, but more finished, product, Microsoft secured its domination of not only the PC operating system market, but also the incipient Windows word processing and spreadsheet markets. Word and Excel are now dominant in their respective spheres.

Microsoft has followed this success up by assailing the one major applications segment where the company had no presence: the database market. Here, its rival is predominantly Borland's Paradox product. Yet again, Microsoft has produced an inherently Windows product, Access, with a performance and degree of cross applications functionality that has delighted the marketplace, and left its rivals publicly wondering just how thick the 'Chinese Walls' separating individual development teams within Microsoft might be.

The difference in styles and approach between the two camps was starkly illustrated early on at the outset of hostilities between the two companies. This difference in marketing strategies was to prove crucial to the success of one product, and the relative failure of the other.

As early as 1989, one industry observer, Carole Patton, outlined what she perceived as the weakness in IBM's overall product marketing approach: 'Programmers wax poetic about OS/2 because they like the technology. But users never buy technology; they buy products. Besides, Windows 3.0 will have OS/2's multitasking and memory management abilities – and it will run DOS programmes. The only thing Windows 3.0 won't have is multithreading. People with industrial or engineering systems might be concerned about that, but secretaries and most professionals don't care a whit. Keep in mind that 90% of the people who use computers in offices are support personnel – and there's no such thing as a low-cost OS/2 workstation on the horizon.'

Even at this point, in 1989, it is clear that Microsoft has identified and focused on what it perceived as its main business market – non-technical desktop users and general office workers.

Specialists, Microsoft had already learnt, it could safely ignore. In the early days of the PC, programmers and systems houses came out heavily in favour of Digital Research's CP/M, then offered by IBM as an alternative operating system on the PC. It provided better functionality, multi-user computing, and a host of other features that excited technical users. Needless to say, it was the rudimentary DOS that succeeded in the business environment, not the more functional CP/M.

Other specialist users could be just as safely ignored. Technical, CAD/CAM, and scientific users were largely ensconced in the Unix workstation world, while design, publishing, and printing was very largely an Apple preserve.

These groups had always been completely peripheral to the success of the PC, whose appeal lay exclusively amongst the massive white collar desktop market. Yet IBM appeared to be marketing OS/2 v1 as a product to appeal to precisely these marginal groups, while ignoring the fundamental concerns of its core office desktop market for a simple to use product that was stable, even if less functional.

To many, it appeared as if IBM was not so much marketing OS/2 to the outside world, as involved in a wholly internal discussion. In many ways, this could be represented as the mentality and approach of the mainframe division in particular affecting the Personal Systems division. At that stage, perhaps, IBM's mainframe division could afford to view its world as painted blue. IBM's Personal Systems division could certainly not afford such a luxury, and paid the price in dollars.

An example of the different communications approaches adopted by IBM and Microsoft is provided by a conference held in London in 1991. Before 750 major corporate executives, IBM Personal Systems director, Tony Stefanis, and Microsoft's Bill Gates debated the future of the desktop, and the emerging trend towards rightsizing.

Stefanis chose to ignore any reference to the rift between his company and Microsoft and hardly gave a nod in the direction of user confusion over OS/2 versus Windows. Instead he elected to explain how IBM's Personal Systems division is organized – a subject of endless fascination for IBMers and any behavioural psychologists who happened to be in the audience, but of little value to anyone else.

In meticulous detail, Stefanis explained the organization of the division into advanced systems – file and input–output servers, multimedia systems and portable systems. Stefanis also described OS/2 as the foundation of the IBM desktop strategy. Buzz phrases were 'multimedia' and 'object-oriented' and Stefanis explained that IBM would provide tools to exploit these technologies across a variety of systems.

By contrast Gates' presentation was pithy and had more of a sense of vision – 'computers should be challenging to use in the same way that a well-made automobile is challenging to drive – the surprise is not in the oops but in the aaah '.

Gates claimed to have a scalable operating system, from Windows through to its multi-platform 32-bit NT development. The advantage, according to Gates, for business users was that the one basic operating system could span systems from the personal organizer through the notebook, the pen, the home, the multimedia and the office desktop system to the RISC server.

Reporting the event, Computergram International commented: 'While the Microsoft approach to object-oriented technology may be more credible in the short term, it is a far less ambitious project than that upon which IBM appears to be embarking and the stakes are, consequently, far lower. At present, Gates seems to have the advantage – the faster he can grow that Windows user base, the smaller the market for IBM's all-embracing object-oriented environment, which seems likely to replace OS/2.'

The strategy of bringing a more stable, albeit less ambitious product to market, and capitalizing on OS/2's teething difficulties, seems to have lain at the heart of Gates' plan for Windows 3.0.

In an internal Microsoft memorandum, published by *PC Week* in June 1991, Gates advised his staff: 'Other than usability, making sure Windows is the winning OS is our highest priority.'

OS/2 v2 represented a more ambitious project, Gates admits, and could be a significant long-term threat. 'If a customer buys OS/2 2.0, the problem for us is that they will expect to get [OS/2] Extended Edition and perhaps some [16-bit OS/2] applications that may not be on 3.0 so we may have lost that customer', the memo said.

Microsoft's opportunity lay in exploiting the market while IBM struggled with early teething problems: 'Our strategy,' wrote Gates, 'is to make sure that we evolve the Windows API and get developers to take advantage of the new features rapidly, while IBM has a poor product with poor Windows functionality.'

A key plank of Microsoft's original Windows marketing strategy was a migration policy to help non-technical business users rapidly achieve productivity. Gates had already identified these users as the key market for Windows, and was concerned lest the novelty of the new environment proved a barrier to Windows sales. He also recognized that the already launched OS/2 was suffering heavily because IBM did not have such a marketing strategy in place.

UK research company Romtec was commissioned to ask 300 IT managers and 300 users if they were happy with their new Windows environments. The results showed that the market was finding it difficult to make the move, and companies were finding desktop migration expensive. As a result, Microsoft launched its Transition programme.

The Transition programme combined product, training and consultancy, priced at a competitive level for corporate buyers. A separate scheme allowed legitimate owners of character based packages to buy the Microsoft Windows equivalent application for a trade up price of £99.

With the introduction of Windows 3.0's successor, 3.1, Microsoft introduced another marketing strategy. Under Microsoft's 'Windows 3.1 Ready to Run Program', vendors may offer Windows 3.1 pre-installed on their machines. By 1992, more than 90 hardware manufacturers had joined the programme.

The result of these initiatives, and of the differing marketing approaches adopted by the two rival companies, was stark: in the first month of its launch, Microsoft's second version of Windows, 3.1, sold 3 million copies. By contrast, IBM's sales of OS/2 v2, launched at about the same time, achieved only some 400,000 sales, although sales then picked up once Microsoft launched Windows 3.1.

In the first round of the OS/2 vs. Windows war, Microsoft emerged as a clear winner. It did this with a markedly less ambitious product, designed for the desktop, that was entirely complementary with the existing DOS operating system. OS/2, by contrast, was more designed as an ambitious client/server product, with multi-threading, full 32-bit addressing, and a stable seamless object oriented environment.

At the time of the two products' original launch in 1989, industry commentators suggested that Microsoft would enjoy an early lead. But as hardware developments progressed, and users' expectations rose, Windows would face an increasing threat from an increasingly robust and more competitive OS/2.

Although most analysts expected OS/2 2.0 to fail, and confidently predicted that potential buyers would purchase Microsoft's new 32-bit operating system NT instead, current trends actually suggest the opposite. However, when Microsoft did bring NT to market in 1993, the market's response was definitely lukewarm.

According to market research firm, International Data Corp, (IDC), Microsoft had managed to ship only 270,000 copies of NT by the end of 1993.

A number of reasons – both market and product-related – account for this stalling of NT. By 1993, Microsoft, not IBM, was perceived as the main industry monopolist. It was accused of abusing its position as both operating systems and applications software publisher. In addition, software developers appeared wary of an untried operating system of such complexity.

By contrast, IBM's increasingly stable OS/2 v2 had sold over 4 million copies by the end of 1993, with industry analysts predicting sales of up to 10 million by the end of 1994.

In 1994, with IBM's announcement of a less costly version, OS/2 2.1 For Windows, sales of the product have finally begun to take off. Priced at just $38, OS/2 For Windows allows users to replace DOS with OS/2 2.1 and still run their existing Microsoft Windows 3.1 code. Independent software vendors, waiting for Microsoft to deliver its long promised, and constantly delayed, 32-bit Windows 4 product, are now at last beginning to produce OS/2 versions of their products. IBM has also launched a new version of OS/2 aimed at small businesses and desktop users, OS/2 Warp, which bundles a large amount of business applications software and communications packages for CompuServe and Internet use.

Has IBM finally turned the tables on Microsoft? At the time of writing, it is far too early to tell. Microsoft has yet to launch its 32-bit version of Windows, Windows 4. However, most industry analysts have commented on its surprising similarity to the already available OS/2 v2!

Microsoft, as the world's most successful software company, is hardly beaten. But as new desktop processors appear, displacing the Intel 80×86 upon which Microsoft has built so much of its fortune, Microsoft may well find its control of the operating system market less sure in future than at present.

Meanwhile, IBM took a long-term gamble with OS/2 in 1989, hoping that the industry would fall in with its vision. However, poor communications and an unstable product left the market wide open for Microsoft's rival product. With an increasingly stable product and greater functionality, together with a corporate revolution that has transformed the company's marketing and sales, IBM looks set to establish OS/2 finally as a major desktop operating system. The days of one company monopolizing the desktop with a single operating system may finally be over.

William Payne is a business writer specializing in enterprise systems and international telecommunications. He is retained by Hewlett-Packard, Amdahl, X-Open, ICL, Cable & Wireless and Northern Telecom as a business analyst. He also provides economic analysis and process re-engineering consultancy for a number of UK trust hospitals.

5

A GUIDE TO BUILDING A MARKETING STRATEGY

Kevin Withnall

Successful traders with market stalls carry out their work while employing the marketer's skills. They know, through research, what their customers want and how much they are prepared to pay. They know that their pitch is good and that enough people pass by their stall. When customers arrive they sell to them, and they also happen to be pretty good at that too. But first and foremost they practise the art of successful marketing before developing their skills as traders.

And so it must be with organizations, be they large or small: the use of marketing skills prepares the way. It makes the right customers available, to allow sales to do what it does best. In the world of information technology, where the competition is fierce, where the margins can easily be eroded, where technological developments are rapid, where jobs are on a knife-edge, then the need for this marketing attitude or function is ever more vital.

Everyone, especially marketing, has to be accountable.

This article looks to examine the theory behind successful marketing within the IT context. But we will be doing more than discussing the concepts; crucially, we will be describing the practical steps marketing executives need to take in order to create successful

New Strategies for Marketing Information Technology.
Edited by Christopher Field
Published in 1996 by Chapman & Hall, London. ISBN 0 412 61520 7

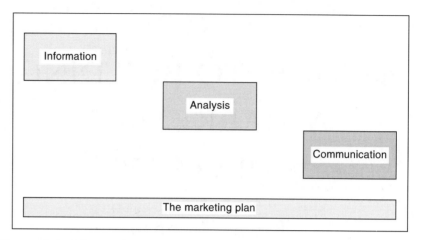

Figure 5.1 The marketing spectrum.

companies, and, incidentally, successful careers. The approach we will describe takes a holistic approach to the marketing concept, with information being collected, then analysed and with key messages then being communicated. This process is managed through the creation and development of the marketing plan. (Figure 5.1.)

INFORMATION

There are many factors impacting on an organization and how that organization presents itself to the wider market. By developing a means of collecting information, a company can begin the process of effectively presenting its products or services in a way which will prove attractive to the customer.

In order to start this process, it is necessary to understand who the customer is, what the customer is looking for, and how the customer will expect to have it delivered. The essence of this process can be centred on the Marketing Information System (MIS). An organization should not view the collection of information as an infrequent occurrence that is only undertaken when data is needed on a specific topic. If this is the norm, several risks would surface: opportunities may be missed, there may be a lack of awareness about wider issues, competitive information would be incomplete, marketing plans and decisions may not be effectively reviewed, information collection will become disjointed, and therefore of limited value, and therefore not used, and finally thought worthless.

This process of collecting information needs to be consistent and dedicated. It is essential for any organization, irrespective of size, to devise and employ an MIS fuelled by several key actions.

- collecting data from annual reports, from internal reports and from published sources;
- analysing the data and preparing the appropriate reports;
- disseminating the reports to the relevant decision makers within the organization;
- encouraging feedback and reaction to the reports;
- processing the feedback as part of the review;
- storing data for further analysis and comparisons;
- widening the information net to ensure all possible areas where the organization may meet its market(s) are covered;
- undertaking on-going data collection, analysis, dissemination and storage.

But the major part of this information strategy has to be the examination of customer needs, for it is from here that everything must start and finish. Without customers, any organization is dead. Without understanding what customers are looking for, then death will be all the more dispiriting because products or services will be offered without the knowledge that there is a need for the offering. 'Understanding customer needs' does not depend upon annual surveys conducted by market research companies with no inherited interest in your company other than as a source of revenue. 'Understanding customer needs' is dependent upon information from a variety of sources, both formal and informal, with a central point within the organization used to collect data. The points of contact between a company and its customer are many and varied. Equally, there are a number of places your customer can get information on you. Both elements need to be managed effectively. The information map drawn up by two companies 'working' together as customer and supplier is extremely complicated. Figure 5.2 indicates the typical points of contact. This is a simplified version.

In most companies there are more departments, and therefore more opportunities for dialogue, for information flow and for relationships to be supported or, dangerously, otherwise. Let us assume that there is a need to manage the information on customers. How should this be done? What are we looking to do? Who should take responsibility for it? When and where do we start? Is it really necessary? These are just some of the questions you should have at

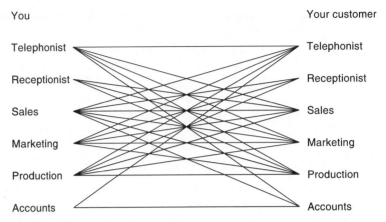

Figure 5.2 You and your customer: contact!

this point. There may be more. However, to deal with the ones given. Let's start at the end. Is it all really necessary?

Consider this scenario. Your company has spent many work-months putting together a proposal, beating off the opposition, and there comes that day when the contract is won and signed. When the champagne bottle is empty, and the hangover's long gone, the time will come when work will need to be done. To provide the service and/or product you have been contracted to give. At this stage, neither company wishes this relationship to stop. Both sides have invested a great deal of time and money in order to make sure the fit is right, that this 'partnership' will work. To add value. To improve revenue and hopefully, profits. From both sides. This relationship will not be discarded lightly. But the opportunities for disillusionment are great. There are lots of ways, as we have seen, that your company will interact with your new customer. This isn't just a marketing, sales or production issue. Therefore, everyone has to be aware of basic tenets (Figure 5.3) in order to be able to efficiently and effectively represent the company.

But this section is all about understanding customer needs, you cry! What does 'things every employee should know' have to do with that? The answer is that the communication process we will be describing here is two-way, and in order to be able to listen to the customer, the employee has to know what to listen for. The list in Figure 5.3 gives the employee the tools with which to understand. The most important tool, though, is management. So that when an issue arises, it is brought to the attention of the right people with immediate effect.

What the company does

Where the company is going

What the company is good at

Who its customers are

Who its current targets are

Who its partners are

Who deals with what

What their own role is

What their own objectives are

Figure 5.3 Things that every employee should know.

There are several ways that this can be brought about:

- End of term report: how did you do?
- Longer surveys: quantify how you did, and tell them you are doing it.
- Fast action facts: a quick response mechanism.
- Not happy, return money system: painful? Not as much as it might be!
- Focus group discussions with customers at which members of both parties, at all levels, meet to discuss new products or services.

In the information technology industry it is not always easy to get the customer to specify its needs when the language of the user and that of the supplier is not necessarily the same.

But if all the steps given above are actually carried out then your company will learn where to focus its efforts. The feedback will provide the organization with a great deal of information on what customers need, on how well your company is perceived, on what needs to be done, and on how to be successful.

But what counts is not simply the gathering of information. This is only the first step. The real test comes in deciding what the data actually means for your company and how you act upon it. And the function which must be in the vanguard of this cultural change has to be marketing.

ANALYSIS

The information has to be analysed to determine actions. There are three key areas of analysis that we will concentrate on:

1. Having looked at the market, how do we separate and group in order to maximize the marketing effort? This is market segmentation.
2. How can we measure our collective performance as an organization against the competition in order to determine how well we are doing? This is competitor benchmarking.
3. The measurement of customer happiness is important to determine improvement levels but what parameters should be measured and how should this be analysed? This is the practice of customer satisfaction auditing.

Market segmentation

If a market is the total of all possible consumers of a good or service, then by segmenting that market we divide it into bits that can be grouped together, because the members of each group share characteristics. To develop this target market requires three specific stages:

1. analysing consumer demand;
2. targeting the market;
3. developing the marketing strategy.

Analysing consumer demand

Determining demand patterns
Broadly, there are three types of demand pattern.

1. With homogeneous demand, customers have uniform needs.
2. In clustered demand there will be at least two segments or clusters to the market which have different needs and therefore need to be approached in different ways.
3. With a diffuse demand, consumer needs are so separate and diverse that no discernible pattern or cluster exists.

The next issue to address, once the demand patterns are understood, is to establish the possible methods or means of segmentation.

Establish segmentation
How you segment or cut up your total available market will depend on the product or service being offered and upon where the variations in the marketplace exist.

Identify potential market segments
The ability to identify those market segments correctly will give

Size
SIC code
Geographical location
IT platform
Application
Corporate culture
Function-led
Skills need
Nature of problem/opportunity

Figure 5.4   The corporate computer user: market segmentation possibilities.

your company the impetus to seek opportunity across a wide basis, but without having to interact, initially, with every customer prior to understanding the needs.

- Size of organization, standard industrial classification (SIC) and geographical location are the three most used segmentation methods.
- It will be no coincidence that the sales team is also likely to be organized in this way, because often we will find in this industry that marketing is a sub-function of sales.
- It is time for marketing departments to be more creative and intuitive in how they seek to get the messages across to the marketplace.
- Look at mixing the segments, for example SIC code with culture. It may be that building societies behave in a different way to the traditional lending banks and therefore have different needs. Or it may be that the market should be segmented by location and IT platform.
- It will depend upon the product/service being offered and the needs of the total available market.
- Your MIS should have given you enough information to determine which segmentation would best suit your organization in order to give you competitive edge.

Targeting the market
The second stage in a market segmentation strategy is to aim for your chosen market.

Select a target market approach
Use a **mass market** approach if your product or service had broad

based appeal, with a limited product/service set, with a wide distribution service, and seeking to appeal to a homogeneous demand via a single marketing plan. Such a technique was useful for Henry Ford and perhaps a floppy disc supplier, but is not useful for Porsche or BMW nor for any systems integrator.

The **niche marketing** method seeks to supply a narrow, specialized market and carve out a distinct area for a particular brand. Here the company is seeking to be viewed as a specialist and is unlikely to want to diversify. This is a good technique for small companies. The marketing programme would thus be highly specific with the right channels and the right media being utilized.

The third approach, **mixed segmentation**, is the most common, in global marketing terms, as it offers the large concern with a variety of brands the ability to approach a variety of markets with a different product or service. From the IT arena Microsoft is expanding its brands to include children's products. But in truth the software and services world is some way away from the highly sophisticated approach of segmentation analysis.

Selecting a target market or markets
Now, a decision. Which segment or segments offer the greatest opportunities? How many segments should your organization be pursuing? In deciding which segment is most promising, an organization should take the following elements into consideration:

- company strengths and weaknesses
- level of competition
- size of the segment and its rate of growth
- distribution methods
- company image
- ability to sustain a competitive advantage.

If the intended market has a high entry cost, for example the computing hardware market, then a new entrant would likely start with a concentrated marketing effort on the portable, desktop, or the home market depending on the parameters listed above.

Developing the marketing strategy

Position the company's offering in relation to the competition
Having decided which segment to attack, the company then has to position its product/service against the competition that already exists.

To compete against the entrenched PC suppliers, and there are a

Who they are

What they do

Which sectors they operate within

Who their major customers are

Who they partner with

What their competitive advantages are

What their weaknesses are

Figure 5.5 What you should know about your competition, part 1.

great many that try to, a new entrant would consider offering bundled software, on-site training, and full support.

Outline the right marketing mix
The last step in this target-marketing process is to develop a mix for each customer group the organization wishes to appeal to. One element that needs to be examined in conjunction with the segmentation possibilities is the performance of the competition. Just as no man is an island neither does a company operate without competition. Even in a nationalized industry, for example the railways, there will be competition, in this case from other means of travelling.

Competitive assessment

Competitive assessment or analysis identifies what you need to know about competitors and how to get that information. To start, there are three basic questions that need to be asked:

- What do you need to know about the competition?
- What are the main sources of information about competitors?
- How can you develop a good system for the analysis of competitors?

Figure 5.5 lists the information on your IT competitors which is relatively easy to obtain.

To gain this information is not difficult, despite the relatively closed nature of the industry. It requires systematic data collection across the whole of your organization, led by the marketing department. Why the marketing department?

- First, because there needs to be a central reservoir of data collection.
- Second, because as we have seen it is the marketing department

Market segmentation method

Organization structure

Sales per employee

Future strategies

Price rates

Motivation of key executives

Profit by market, product, customer

Future investment plans

Figure 5.6 What you should know about your competition, part 2.

that must have its eyes and ears open on the outside world; its antenna must be working for it to be effective.

- Third, because the marketing department needs to assess where the market is heading, where the competition is moving and therefore to recommend where your company should go in order to win.

But the competitive assessment requires even more in-depth information, information which is not so easily obtainable. Figure 5.6 lists what else should be known.

The key to successful competitive assessment is to fully document and continuously monitor the elements contained in both tables. And very few companies do. Yet if these areas are not known then this will result in poor competitive analysis which in turn will mean you will fail to see threats from the competition. Your company will not be in a position to anticipate any competitive moves.

The next task to consider is how to monitor this information. Do the following:

- Select only key competitors to monitor.
- Select individuals in each of your departments to collect information.
- Try to ensure sufficient time is spent on this task because information will need to be chased and evaluated.
- Ensure your information collectors give regular returns.
- When the collected data is analysed make sure the reports are circulated.

But once you have a series of reports, the next question to consider is what do you do with them. The last thing that any department must do is collect information which just lays fallow, because sooner or later this task will become pointless, waste time and will be dropped. The task has to have a central role in the growth of the organization.

	1	2	3	4
1. The project met the objectives as outlined in the proposal.				
2. Staff involved in the project demonstrated their knowledge of, and abilities in, the subject under consideration.				
3. The work was carried out with success and is clearly documented.				
4. The work was completed on time.				
5. Consultant contact and feedback was sufficient.				
6. The consultants were flexible in accommodating changes in direction throughout the process.				
7. Printed materials were well written, edited and presented.				
8. We would consider using for future projects.				
9. Any further comments.				

Scale:
1 = strongly disagree
2 = disagree
3 = agree
4 = strongly agree

Figure 5.7 Customer satisfaction questionnaire.

Customer satisfaction

Your organization and the competition are only after one thing . . . customers. We have talked about how you decide which customers (segmentation) and we have talked about how you assess the competition. In this section we need to understand how to keep your customers. In our view, there is only one way – keep them happy. You do that by providing them with what they need at a price which they can see is value for money. Having done that you need to invest time and money in making sure you are continually meeting your customers' needs. The best way of doing that is a formal customer satisfaction process. Figure 5.7 gives an example of a customer satisfaction questionnaire.

The questionnaire should:

- be easy to administer;
- be highly structured yet have space for comment;
- have a four point scale to avoid average scoring;
- be administered in person;
- be regularly carried out after the completion of every project/ piece of work;
- enable cross-response analysis to take place;
- ensure your organization is aware of the results of the continuous monitoring;
- make sure that direct action follows the analysis;
- feed back to the clients the effect the surveys are having on your company's performance.

The concept of measuring customer satisfaction has been taking hold throughout the service industry, but the resources attached to the task within the IT software and services sector is not as expansive as seen within other sectors. We can think of no reason as to why this is other than the fact that the IT services industry until recently has not felt it necessary to utilize customer facing practices. And as we have seen a key element of the customer satisfaction process is the communication of the message, both within and beyond your organization.

COMMUNICATION

By now we have examined customer needs, we have segmented the market, we have assessed the competition and we have measured the levels of satisfaction we achieve with our customers. In carrying out all this work, we will be generating messages about our company, its hopes, ambitions and achievements. These messages are of value to the market and to the organization. There are several questions that need to be asked:

- What messages?
- To whom?
- How?
- When?
- What next?

Figure 5.8 indicates the variations that take place when setting down the communications track. It can be seen that the possibilities are wide and it follows that care must be taken to ensure the optimum communications tool is used. The chart also indicates that while great effort in most companies is spent in sending and receiving messages from customers, the shareholders and, most importantly, the employees receive relatively little communication. And we remember that communication is a two way process which gives us even further reason to be concerned.

The approach which we would advocate is to consider the employee audience at the same level of importance as the customer. In this way, employees can be used to 'rehearse' the messages. There are many advantages of this approach but perhaps the two best are:

1. The employees are aware of what's happening, have opportunities to influence what's happening, and can therefore 'buy in' to the direction. This will cut down attrition and create a more positive and motivated team.
2. The opportunity and need to 'rehearse' is vital, should be seen as part of the process but rarely is. By spending time in preparation, the organization will increase the chances of success. The ability to improve the likelihood of success is an advantage that very few companies can choose to ignore.

Table 5.1 lists each variant in the communications plan and provides guidance on the strengths and weaknesses of each approach.

By using the tables presented here, we can see that there are various routes to achieving the aim. If we believe that the bottom line in marketing terms is to:

1. improve our understanding of customer needs;
2. manage the marketing effort in such a way as to maximize the opportunity for meeting customer needs;
3. ensure continuous improvement in the meeting and managing of customer expectations;

then by careful manipulation of the communication tools at our disposal, all these aims can be met. If this is done with employee and customer involvement then the success can be maintained. But throughout this methodology, we have stressed the importance of careful management. The final element of this document deals specifically with the handling of the marketing process, i.e. the marketing plan or what might be termed planning the plan, or then again, might not!

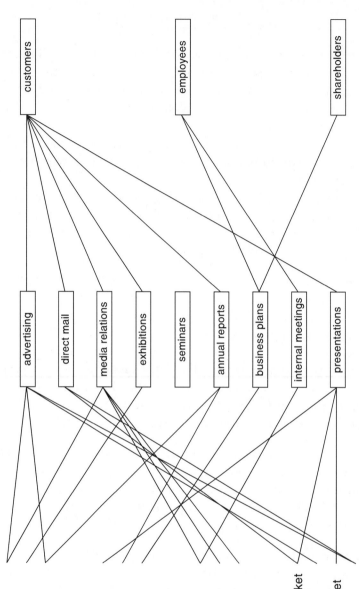

Figure 5.8 Communications chart.

Table 5.1 Strengths and weaknesses of each variant in the communications plan

Medium	Strengths	Weaknesses
Advertising	brand awareness, corporate identity, 'feel good' factor	needs careful targeting, difficult to judge impact, 'random' readership
Annual reports	opportunity to impress, can unite the employees, long shelf life	'worthy', historical performance, consolidated approach
Business plan	provides direction, opportunity to unite company, valuable business re-engineering tool	often left on the shelf, distant from employees, confidential – not for customer consumption
Direct mail	lands on the desk of the 'needer', handled in-house, response-oriented	floods of the stuff, needs follow-up, must have specific target/offering
Exhibitions	good to be 'seen', product/service new offerings, large audience	random audience, competitive presence, possible only limited marketing success
Meetings	excellent for in-depth discussions, valuable for customer or employee feed-back, controlled environment	expensive, limited audience, need careful and experienced management
Media relations	good for corporate awareness, individual growth and exposure, valid marketing tool	need constant management, need employee co-operation, difficult to measure impact on bottom line
Presentations	excellent for in-depth discussions, valuable for customer and employee feed-back, controlled environment	expensive, limited audience, need careful and experienced management
Proposals	customized and specific opportunity, promotion of partnerships, corporate branding opportunity	opportunity only to reinforce company messages, limited marketing potential, expensive tool
Seminars	invited audience, new product/service announcements, corporate messages.	limited exposure, demand excellent presenters with good material, need careful management

THE MARKETING PLAN

The key to success is good planning, management and execution. The key to that key is the marketing plan which describes where the marketing effort is headed, keeps the marketing ship on course, and describes the actual results against the planned objectives. For the marketer, change, and adapting to change is vital, but the plan allows the marketer to anticipate, to regulate and to control the elements of change rather than allowing them to happen.

The evidence exists that quality plans do have an effect on an organization's success. There is also evidence that too often they are observed rather than ingrained. The advantage of a carefully constructed marketing plan is that it too will induce a quality response but the demand will be for a cultural response rather than the knee-jerk reaction of an 'in the manual' attitude which too often serves within the quality community. In other words this is real and actual not theory.

When the marketing plan is integrated, all of its constituent parts are unified, consistent and co-ordinated; and a total quality approach can be followed. Such a plan is composed of seven key elements:

1. **Clear mission**: this describes in simple terms the organization's commitment to the market. This mission must not be a cliché but must be real and alive to all within so that it may be accurately communicated (there's that word again) to the outside. But this must not be a static statement that does not change over time, it must be continuously appraised and reassessed. Is this what we want to be? Is this what we are? Is this where we are going?

2. **Long-term competitive advantages**: for advantages to be maintained, the customer must believe that there is a specific, positive difference that your company has over the competition. But more, that difference must be linked to a capability gap that the competition will have difficulty closing. Finally, the advantage must be linked to a customer need which will not disappear but will endure.

3. **Precisely defined target market**: where it is understood in fine detail just what the customer needs. Such needs will fluctuate depending on external and other circumstances. Not all such needs will remain the same and therefore they must be carefully and constantly monitored to ensure there is a response to change. Common factors such as price or quality can grow or diminish in importance depending on circumstances or customer. Catching the right tone is the key to communicating to the target market.

4. **Compatible long-, medium- and short-term marketing plans**: which really means making sure the whole picture fits and that while the long term gives the broad picture, the medium is

directed towards the long-term goals but with more detail, while the short term defines today's actions which, again, are driving the organization towards the medium and long term. It follows that in arriving at these plans the route should be in reverse, hence one determines the long-term horizon, and then the medium-term milestones and finally the short-term steps which will get us on the right track.

5. **Co-ordination among the strategic business units (SBUs)**: the SBUs are part of the whole and the whole must be greater than the sum of the parts. In order for this to happen the units must be co-ordinated, all following in the same direction in terms of culture, attitude, goals ('to be the best') and procedures.

6. **Co-ordination of the marketing mix**: which may seem a ridiculous thing to say but it is the case that the mix (product, distribution, promotion and price) needs to be consistent with, and supportive of, the organization's mission statement. This can be easily checked. Examine a company's stated goal, available in any published material or annual report, and get the meaning and the long-term aims thoroughly isolated. Now take the elements of the mix that can be readily viewed. Let's say we are talking about a piece of shrink-wrapped software. How far does this item match, support, correspond with and underline the key strategic messages that you have already isolated? This is the test. Try it with your own organization. Often in the software and services industry the marketing function is there to support the sales team. This is important but cannot be the sole reason for a marketing department's existence. Indeed, we would question if, in organizations where marketing has this subordinate role, the full use of the discipline can ever be accomplished. The key is co-ordination with the mission statement. If this happens then the mission statement will mean something, the marketing package will add value and the company has a chance of moving in the right direction as a unit. But this is a test. Is it working in your company?

7. **Stability over time**: one difference between a marketing-led culture and a sales-led culture is that the former looks at the longer view while that latter concentrates on the short-term opportunities. Hence, when things get rough, companies will by default seek quick turnround contracts in order to get revenue flowing through the books. Of course, if such actions were not taken there may not be any books for the revenues to go through, so the balance is fine. Nevertheless we are firm advocates of the consistent view, as you will have seen, which

means that the marketing plans must have some element of stability in order for the whole process to work. This is not a quick fix, but a slow and co-ordinated view of the future.

But a plan is not a plan if there is no objective measurements and if on-going achievement against the plan isn't recorded. Thus with analysis of the marketing plan, actual performance against expected performance is measured.

Having set up the marketing plan for the next twelve months, this should describe specific objectives for each element of the marketing mix. Such objectives need to be measurable, achievable and desirable and the whole of the organization needs to be made aware, on a regular basis, of how the marketing function is performing against the target. But what target to take? Measuring marketing effectiveness is a notoriously difficult thing to assess, but it is vital, particularly in an industry where the use of marketing skills is still limited.

There are two main methods to measure marketing effectiveness:

- analysing sales;
- undertaking a marketing audit.

Sales analysis

This is the detailed study of sales data in order to determine the success of a marketing strategy. By deciding which organizations, sectors, markets, constitute the greatest percentage of sales, companies can recognize which companies/sectors/markets are likely to yield greater rewards. In other words by finding out where the sales are coming from, effort can be spent on those areas rather than on ones which are yielding limited rewards. This technique or method is the 80/20 principle, i.e. 80% of the revenue coming from 20% of the customer base.

There are drawbacks to this method.

1. The link between marketing spend and sales success is not always causal, may often be coincidence, and is always difficult to prove.
2. The analysis perpetuates the vicious circle. Hence, the argument goes, concentrate on the small percentage of the market that provides sales and spend much less time and resources on the major proportion. But in so doing the marketing thrust will not be working in an area (i.e. the major proportion of the market)

that requires help and so this area will always yield only limited success and hence will remain as the 20/80 element.

The second technique, the marketing audit, looks in contrast at the dynamics of the marketing plan and describes through various means the scale of its success against the plan.

The marketing audit

A marketing audit is the systematic review of the goals and policies of the marketing function, including a review of the structure, methods, practices and personnel tasked with the objective of implementing those policies and achieving those goals. In effect, it is really taking the marketing function and applying those marketing principles to the management of the marketing department itself, as it were turning the spotlight inwards. Thus customer satisfaction audits are a key part of the process. Such an audit then should be conducted on a regular basis, at least annually with the results made known to the whole of the company. The audit would involve the following steps:

1. **Decide who should do the audit**: the audit has to be undertaken without fear or favour and therefore should not be seen as an 'inside job'. A company manager or an external consultant would be the best resource.
2. **Decide timing and frequency of audit**: there are two recommendations here. First; it should be done at the same time every year, in order to be better able to compare results, and second; it should be conducted at least once a year.
3. **Horizontal and vertical audits**: should be used with the horizontal audit, the overall marketing performance being measured while the vertical audit is an in-depth analysis of the key elements of the mix.
4. **Develop the audit questionnaires**: list the topics to be covered and these should be completed by chosen respondents through dialogue with the auditor.
5. **Conduct the audit**: care needs to be taken on timing and on whether the organization is to be told of it proceeding.
6. **Presenting the results**: this needs to be done to senior management in order for them to carry out any resultant actions.

By conducting such an exercise on a regular and consistent basis, companies can judge for themselves the progress that is being made towards becoming a truly marketing-led organization with a desire to delight the customer. That in itself is the end result of having the right marketing attitude.

Kevin Withnall is an ex-teacher and ex-actor and for the last 15 years has been a marketing consultant, currently with Spikes Cavell. Previously he was Director of Marketing with Data Logic and before that a marketing consultant with BIS Strategic Decisions.

6

NEW PRODUCTS
Managing the market, managing expectations

Susan Scott Ker

In March 1994, IBM launched a revolutionary speech recognition system, called VoiceType Dictation, to PC users to make use of their voice to type rather than their hands. The system is over 95% accurate and at under £1000 was the first truly viable speech recognition available. IBM felt that a normal consumer product launch that attempted to sell large volumes of product to all computer users would fail in the long term. The company believed that a relatively new and untried technology needed a different approach. Here I look at some of the strategies that we used leading up the launch.

Although speech recognition had been the goal of technologists since the fifties and although various products had been launched over the years, the results had tended to be interesting more for their technological advance than their business benefits. VoiceType however was positioned as a software productivity tool first and foremost, supported by advanced technology. It was announced as a tool that would overcome the main barrier that many employees have in interacting with computers, the keyboard.

IBM had worked on speech recognition for 20 years but only recently did it feel that it had a marketable product. Companies of such a size and pre-eminence are always judged extremely harshly by

New Strategies for Marketing Information Technology.
Edited by Christopher Field
Published in 1996 by Chapman & Hall, London. ISBN 0 412 61520 7

press and public, so the product had to be very good indeed. It also had to fit in with IBM's image as a solutions provider. Solutions combined with great technology, but solutions the main priority.

Moreover, we had to take into account the environment into which VoiceType would be launched. New products are today judged not simply on their own merits but their ability to work with different hardware platforms and their ease of use. A new product will always sell to a small group of people who are enthusiastic about technology, and then go no further. Solutions marketing means you have to provide a solution to lots of different groups of people, each with their own ideas of what equals success, and all of them looking for significant productivity benefits. Thorough market research is therefore essential.

The problem was that we could see that there were almost no limits to the number and type of people who would welcome speech recognition on their desks. At the same time, if we were to try to reach all these people at once, we would probably end up reaching none of them very successfully. Moreover, although the concept of speech recognition is simple and extremely attractive, it was almost completely untried by the market at which it was aimed. It was important that we chose the market carefully and managed their expectations even more carefully.

We also felt that there were limitations to the way that most software is promoted. Computer users never use the full capability of their software packages, in fact it is more likely that they will use as little as 15%. They typically learn all they need to fulfil the task in hand but never move on. They then start to judge the software by their own standards. They may even start to judge the operating system as responsible for not giving them enough functionality because they have seen a colleague get more out of software on another platform. What they don't see is that the other platform may be inferior to theirs but that user is getting the maximum benefit out of the software.

All in all, we knew that VoiceType would be subject to these vagaries of judgement. Another irony with breakthrough technologies is that the better they are, the quicker users will try to knock them down. They will swallow all the benefits at one gulp and then look for what the software cannot do. One pilot user of VoiceType at a large City firm of solicitors was critical because VoiceType would not run on his portable. Actually, it did and we proved it but, up until that point, we had only be talking about desktop workstations. We had to cover off all the angles and get the users' requirements satisfied before launching. If you are not ready to satisfy a particular user's requirements from day one of the launch, be sure that you will be able to later. Many a software product has died because it was not or could not be developed. Users won't wait any more for companies to have another go at getting it right.

THE STRATEGY

The core of the launch strategy was to educate the market by finding influential individuals and groups who would try the product and endorse it. These opinion formers on the one hand were people who were enthusiastic about technology and would want to test the software to its limits, and on the other people who had avoided computers for a variety of reasons and would only be convinced by real benefits.

We chose various companies to start with but in the end they chose us. The main opinion formers were and still are, the head of radiology at the Belfast City Hospital, an IT director at the Bank of Scotland and a group of lawyers at Masons Solicitors in the City of London. Over a number of months, these users tested VoiceType in their everyday work lives. The work they were doing and which was a common thread between them, was dictating reports. They had all been used to dictating to a machine or a secretary but the change to dictating directly to their computers was quite different. Initially, it required patience and persistence so that the computer could become accustomed to its master's voice.

It is in these initial learning stages that a software product, good or bad, is most vulnerable. If users take a dislike to some small aspect, then they are likely to judge the whole system negatively. We knew that if we worked closely with our users they would judge the system on its merits and give us the feedback we were looking for. In fact, most of them were evangelical for VoiceType. One reported that we had overcome a fundamental barrier to interacting with computers. Others said that speech recognition would in time be common to all computers. The users were given no incentives to say nice things about VoiceType; they were all paying the going rate for the work we were doing with them.

THE PRESS

Journalists were of course targeted as important opinion formers and VoiceType in its original guise of IBM Personal Dictation System, received a great deal of positive press coverage. Again, our concern was to get ongoing endorsement from the initial product launch onwards so that we would have a convincing body of written testimonial to show to customers.

Compared to the way that, say, car manufacturers launch new models, there does not seem to be anything new in this, but in IT, this is not a common approach. The normal approach is to launch software to journalists and the public at about the same time, or even with a short gap. The risks of taking this approach are simply too great. As software becomes more powerful and therefore more beneficial to users, it had better work or the first buyers will be merciless in their criticism. And there is no more merciless a critic than the press! Fortunately, IBM had a great product.

We initially matched the press to our pilot groups, so chose legal, medical and banking magazines. We also concentrated on national newspaper journalists and subdivided them as we had done with the pilot users, into technology and general journalists. We wanted the press to use VoiceType in their own business and make personal judgements on that basis. From there we moved onto all other press and missed no opportunity for coverage, including radio and TV (BBC, independent, local, cable, satellite). Computers are notoriously unphotogenic and also do not make great radio copy, so we put our users forward and the press organized shoots and recordings at the hospital in Belfast and the firm of solicitors.

Remembering that it was essential to cover all the angles in advance, one proposed piece of TV coverage served us well by never appearing! A TV production company wanted to do a story on the product using the 'technology puts secretaries out of work' angle. It never went ahead. The production team were unable to find a secretary that would endorse what it was trying to say. We couldn't engineer this positive result for ourselves of course, but we had to be aware of the very worst that anyone with an unrelated agenda would try to say about it.

What actually came across in the press was that secretaries were cock-a-hoop about being let off the heavy typing part of their jobs, giving them more time for rewarding tasks and in many cases for taking on a more executive role. At one of the trial sites, Masons Solicitors, the secretaries are using spreadsheets and presentation packages to turn the raw, dictated text into something more appealing. They are shaping the company's work and making a more visible contribution.

SEMINARS

Before the official launch, demonstration seminars were an important way of showing the software off to corporate buyers but mainly to demonstrate speech recognition not as a stand-alone, blue sky product but as a business tool working alongside existing business software applications. We had a relatively small marketing team with which to promote VoiceType, so 'group selling' to educate the market was an effective use of resources.

These seminars were organized into a roadshow that went about the UK, inviting local company representatives to attend. One criticism we heard about seminars is that they are always very impressive and therefore less than completely believable. The critic said that the software was only given information to process that it could do easily, that the demonstrator was usually highly polished and evangelical so that it was often hard to think up a question to ask at the end because all the angles appeared to have been covered.

We made sure that the seminars were well-presented and impressive but not so staged that the audience would not ask questions. The balance is not easy to achieve. Users expect high quality presentations and technology has enabled this to happen. Our stand at Document 94 at Earl's Court featured a presenter and two computer users each with a PC representing different departments of a company. The purpose was to ape a real company and show how business applications including speech recognition and data could be integrated into workflows.

PRICING

There are formulas for setting prices for products. I would suggest that they are hardly ever used. Common sense told us that once we had 'packaged' speech recognition, we would have to take general packaged software prices into account and price VoiceType in that area. Some voice systems in the past have been priced at some tens of thousands of dollars, possibly in expectation that the manufacturer did not really believe he would sell big numbers. However, some of these voice experimenters were small start-ups with venture capital putting pressure on them to deliver fast results.

With a new technology, patience and investment are essential. Some software manufacturers were lucky. They launched poor products but marketed them extremely well, listened to customers and then brought out a decent product. Other manufacturers, thinking that existing customers would stay loyal whatever was offered to them, found out the hard way. Their competitors forced them to shrug off their complacency and change their products completely. Now manufacturers have to get it right first time around. No one will queue up for version two and three if version one is too complicated or difficult to use.

COMMUNICATIONS PHASE

While spending a lot of time and resources out in the market, we also worked hard internally. IBM is a large organization and unless it knows about a new product it cannot act as a salesforce. It was essential that we all said the same things about VoiceType, so we spent time on internal marketing in order to get cross-company endorsement. We communicated in particular with groups that sell solutions into which VoiceType fitted neatly, with the Software Enquiry Desk group and with IBM dealers.

All this activity went on before the actual launch date and included various existing customers, key press, our opinion formers and those who had attended the seminars. In this respect, the actual launch date was more of a formality than the event on which some companies depend entirely on for success.

The post-launch activity included the general press, potential customers through seminars, direct mail and advertising and a continued focus on our opinion formers and new endorsers.

ON RECORD

At the launch itself, we made sure that there was a lot of promotional material available. We kept a verbal, written and visual record of everything that our opinion formers had done with VoiceType. These were condensed into a series of reference fliers, press articles and a promotional video. Interestingly, IBM's not insignificant resources were not a factor in the amount of money that was spent. VoiceType is just one product and probably cost us no more than a small start-up ought to spend if they have a similar product.

ON AND ON

In order to maintain excitement about VoiceType and to emphasize IBM's commitment to speech recognition, we kept up the activity.

We launched language models in Spanish, French, German, Italian and US/UK English; a PCMCIA card for portable computer users; a version for Windows; and specialized language dictionaries for medical and legal users.

TEN TIPS FOR MARKETING NEW SOFTWARE

1. Set not one but many targets that you can achieve throughout the pre-launch period. It is easy to get distracted and even put off when the end target fades from sight, which it will inevitably do from time to time. By setting lots of smaller targets along the way, you can also measure your success.
2. Research everything, all the time. Look at the potential size of the market, divide it up into segments and work out what activity is needed for each group. Ask potential users if they would use what you are proposing and don't just look for positive feedback. Measure results throughout the campaign.
3. Build up a solid foundation of endorsement for your product before you go public. If that endorsement is not forthcoming, don't launch. In the 80s you would have been good for a few thousand copies sold, but with today's margins, competition and smart users you will be dead in the water. Take your time to get third party endorsement so that you have already anticipated the best and worst that people can say about you.
4. Invest in presentation and design that complements your product and use classic marketing techniques such as advertising, public relations and direct marketing. Having a sensational product is no excuse for forgetting the basics.
5. Be flexible enough to change your pitch according to your experience. So work with you early adopters to decide what will work promotionally and what will not. Take everything that everyone says into account and so avoid embarrassment later on.
6. Keep a full record of all pre-launch activity. If you are humble enough to make changes in direction as dictated by your opinion formers, then recorded information can be extremely useful.
7. Get answers for every question you are ever likely to be asked before you are asked. However, if you have no answer, say so, don't bluff.
8. Remember that product price is often set by accountants who look at the investment and work out the number of units that

need to be sold based on the price of similar products. Take other factors into account – if you have the best product in your category, you can consider charging more than everyone else; if you are too cheap, people may not take your product seriously; is the price so high or low that the channel cannot handle it? And so on and so on.

9. Find marketing consultants that have experience of fmcg (fast-moving consumer goods) promotion. They may work in IT but it may be worth taking a chance with a supplier that knows more about marketing cornflakes and soap powder.

10. Finally, don't let the launch date affect what you do before the launch. It can take real sang froid to do this, particularly if you suspect that a competitor is up to something. But in the long term, there is no substitute for taking the time to get it right first time.

Susan Scott Ker is Communications Advisor for IBM UK Software. She has worked in public relations consultancy in both New Zealand and the UK and specializes in information technology and telecommunications industries. Her role with IBM comprises internal and external communications for IBM's software business on data management, applications development, transaction systems, networking and systems management, workgroup and speech recognition software.

7

IT MARKETING IN THE YEAR 2000

A view of some of the developments in store

Garrey Melville

Forecasting is difficult at the best of times, but when you are asked to address an issue as complex as marketing and how it might evolve in the IT industry over the next five years, the challenge magnifies several times over. At first thought you may think how can you even consider forecasting such an issue given the many variables that can impact marketing in our industry. Your thoughts are absolutely correct. However, what you are about to read in this chapter will provide you with what I believe to be an overview of what can only be described as an indication of some of the developments that will take place across our industry over the next five years in the field of IT marketing. In reading this chapter, therefore, I hope to provide you with some new marketing practices you can consider in your current approach towards business.

INTRODUCTION

The future of marketing within the IT industry rests upon many different criteria. Foremost among them are those factors that drive

New Strategies for Marketing Information Technology.
Edited by Christopher Field
Published in 1996 by Chapman & Hall, London. ISBN 0 412 61520 7

the development of the IT industry and the various customer groupings that we serve. It is well beyond the scope of this chapter to attempt to present how the customers for IT services and products will change over the next five years and, indeed, how the IT industry will evolve. However, in looking at how and why marketing will change, I cannot fail to make reference to industry trends.

It is worth mentioning, at this stage in this chapter, that I will not only comment on the different roles of the marketing department and the skills and activities performed, but will make some comments about the relevant support services that we as marketers so heavily rely upon.

THE MARKETING CHALLENGE OF THE 90s

IT marketing has improved considerably over the past decade as IT companies have sought to embrace the fundamentals of business, and respond to competitive forces and recessionary circumstance. Throughout this period of transition, clear groupings of IT companies can be identified as organizations have sought to both understand marketing and to implement it effectively for the benefit of the company.

A clear transition scale can be drawn as an organization progresses its customer orientation and focus, from the introductory cycles through to a mature or expert understanding and application of marketing. In comparison to other industries such as Retail, Financial Services, and Pharmaceuticals, most parts of the IT industry are at the introductory phases of marketing, with all but a few organizations understanding and applying what can only be described as 'mature' techniques.

At one end of the scale we find the 'learners' – those organizations who in 1994 find themselves with inexperienced marketers. The typical symptoms that point to this are:

- no idea of how to measure marketing effectiveness;
- wrestling with channel management issues;
- do not understand the risks of not conducting market research;
- have limited control over market perception; and
- struggle to understand the basis of segmentation.

There are many IT companies in this situation and, unless things change, I would question their survivability.

At the other end of the scale, we have the 'leaders'. They have a completely different approach towards business. They are worlds apart. From experience, these organizations have encompassed the marketing approach and invariably have marketers on board who have applied their skills in other markets, providing the company with an additional edge in the market. How do these companies operate? Quite simply they have evolved a clear meritocratic business style where their culture, values and operating style are one and the same. They encourage and encompass innovation in every sense of the word and ensure that innovation and change is rewarded. Why the emphasis on innovation you may ask yourselves. Because innovation is the competitive differentiator of the 90s in an industry that is commoditizing fast.

The 'leader' will practise marketing fully, where the marketing department(s) will have the resources both financial and material to deliver competitive edge. The CEO will fully understand marketing, and will rely upon his or her marketing director to guide the organization forward and to focus the sales operation. The 'leader' will be around as a clear player in the year 2000. Today, I can only identify a handful of IT organizations that fit the profile of a marketing led company. In my view, one organization stands above them all – they will dominate the industry and set the trends for the future. It is not IBM!

So, in summarizing the state of marketing in the IT industry today, I see a number of challenges facing the industry if it wishes to control its own destiny. There are four areas where change will take place. All four areas are widely recognized as the barriers to good marketing practice in our industry today (Figure 7.1). For marketing to improve it must address all four quadrants. Poor IT marketing is rarely due to problems in one quadrant alone; it is normally a combination of two or more.

Senior management require a better understanding of good marketing practice and in line with this require to be exposed to good marketing practice. Only when this takes place will we see management commit more to marketing in our industry.

From a marketing perspective, our industry requires to see an improvement in marketing personnel through better skills and, in turn, results. For this, we require the role of marketing to broaden and grow in IT companies.

The sales perspective is in many respects similar to management. The sales operations require a better understanding of marketing and in that sense will then place different demands on the department. Leading from this, we will find the expectations from the sales operations to be fundamentally different. The sales operation will respect marketing considerably more.

Rarely a single factor

Management	Marketing
Understanding	Experience
Experience	Marketing skill
Commitment	Role definition

Sales	Other factors
Understanding	Research agencies
Demands	Delivery groups
Expectation	PR companies

Figure 7.1 Barriers to cross.

Finally, the support functions. There are many good marketing support organizations within our industry who are worthy of comment, however, for every good organization there are two poor organizations who have stepped beyond the bounds of professionalism to provide misguided advice in many areas such as PR, research and strategy. Such organizations require to be driven out of our industry as they are doing the marketing profession an injustice, misleading management and damaging the IT industry as a whole.

THE STRUCTURE OF THE MARKETING OPERATION IN 2000

The structure of the marketing operation is a common question that is raised in our industry. Clearly the structure of the marketing operation will depend upon the structure and nature of the organization it is servicing and its customers. As I speak to managing directors and marketing directors of IT companies, I find that today marketing is either centralized, distributed, integrated or a mixture of all three within a company. The size of the organization together with the market offerings are but some of the factors that dictate how and where marketing should sit within the organization. What about the year 2000? Well, I believe that we will continue to see all four positionings. The centralized marketing operation provides many benefits, not least a clear company strategy, centralized customer ownership through precise database management and relationship marketing techniques, brand ownership, economies of scale through single agency usage, and so the list continues.

The decentralized department provides similar benefits and for some organizations, it is appropriate to have smaller central departments spread across the company. The smaller distributed marketing functions provide a number of additional benefits, not least the fact that marketing becomes closer to the customer and therefore is better able to respond, forecast and of course, innovate.

Decentralized marketing is also viewed as fragmenting marketing skills into centres of excellence such as market research, media planning, strategy, promotions, direct mail and business development. I believe that we will see less of this activity by the year 2000, for the simple reason that the marketers of the 21st century will be required to understand all of these activities and will be using these skills daily.

Fragmentation of the marketing profession reminds me of a company I once worked for. As a new employee to the company, I found that people had been engineered into the marketing processes to the extent that it proved impossible for me to get anything done in a reasonable period of time. There were people at agency briefings who quite frankly new nothing about the customer, the company offer, the market conditions or the competition – I found myself briefing both the internal staff who were meant to be managing the agency and the external agency. I found the internal 'experts' were not so expert. The cost of marketing was unacceptable, decision making was slow and basic business operations were lacking. Nobody knew any better. It was very sad really. It didn't take long for this to be recognized by management and for changes to take place.

Certain decentralized marketing disciplines will disappear in the 21st century as marketing matures and IT companies recognize that marketing is about customer intimacy, change and profit. I believe that marketing will become fully integrated into IT companies, as business managers are forced to understand marketing techniques and apply them to their business. For many organizations this will prove a vital differentiator, and as a result many marketers will become business managers. Many business managers will return to sales management roles. The market offering, the company structure and the nature of the market you are servicing will help to dictate the pace of this change.

THE ROLE OF THE MARKETING OPERATION

It comes as no surprise to hear that the role and importance of marketing will increase tenfold by the year 2000. The IT industry is becoming more competitive and, as a result, we will see the demise of many of today's existing players in all of the key sectors, from systems integration to database provision to hardware and maintenance. The demise of these organizations will in most cases be due to poor marketing. For some organizations the writing is already on the wall. Next to poor financial control, bad marketing is the most common reason for company failure. The IT industry like others have had their fair share of bad marketing. The next five years will see this change as marketers prove their worth to their organizations.

The marketing operation of the 21st century will be the driving force of the organization, forecasting how the market will evolve over the next 1, 3, 5 and 10 year periods and using this knowledge drive the organizational change programme. Marketers will service, support, drive and direct many different parts of the business. They will be the conductors of business development. These roles in their own right pose a major issue for the IT industry. It is a sales oriented business. Good marketing skills are viewed as a threat to many people in the company as their business acumen is exposed. The goal is to educate and partner senior management so they do not feel threatened, and then let marketing take the lead. The challenge for some executives, however, is to establish whether they have a good or bad marketing person at the helm. In so many cases they only find out when it is too late to turn the ship around.

THE MARKETING INFORMATION WAR

The marketing operation of the 21st century will practise what can only be described as competitive marketing tactics. All of these will revolve around information, innovation, creativity and solid marketing practice.

A marketing information war is already underway across the IT industry to the extent that if you are a medium or large player and you are not aware of it, I would strongly suggest you are not part of the future of the industry. The marketing information war is about the different levels and different types of information that are required to make marketing decisions. This has focused marketing departments on customers, competitors, trends, company performance, marketing metrics, KPIs, and so the list continues. Technology plays an important part in the process, as of course do the skills of the marketers.

I am still amazed at the complacency of senior management in certain organizations when they say they don't spend much on market research, or they don't know the strength of their customer relationships. This is made more ironic when I find myself in situations where competitors know more about a particular company's market positioning than the company itself. Enough said!

The marketing information war will lead to a number of key industry developments. Specifically:

- a shake out in the IT information services industry leading to better service and new players;
- the wider use of marketing technologies across the IT industry;
- better business decisions including acquisitions and mergers;
- head to head competition in considerably more markets;
- differentiation will force the IT industry towards classical marketing;
- marketers running IT companies.

DELIVERABLES OF THE MARKETING OPERATION OF THE 21ST CENTURY

The maturing of the marketing information age in the 21st century will mean that most organizations will be information rich. They will differentiate on a number of factors which the marketing operation will orchestrate.

Branding
This will become a real issue for marketers in our industry. Accordingly, the attention paid to this subject will increase a hundred fold. Brand image and brand mapping studies will become common practice as the science and art of branding are better understood. IT organizations will actively seek to understand their brands and their contribution to their business. Creativity and innovation will come to the fore once again. The marketing operation will own, drive and build the brand, a name that personifies the companies culture and total market offering. Branding is a differentiator.

Planning and analysis
This will be the key behind all marketing activity. The seat of the pants marketing decisions of the 80s will be long gone. In the

information rich 21st century, one of the many key skills of marketers will be segmentation. A marketing director who does not know how to segment a market, will force the business down the wrong track. When I refer to segmentation, I do not refer to the naive methods used at present to arrive at a horizontal or vertical cut. I am referring to lifestyle analysis, multiple groupings of customers based upon common key values and attributes, together with the evolution of cultural profiling across customer organizations that ensures a cultural fit exists between the buyer and supplier. But there is more to planning than segmentation. The planning processes will be rigorous, the marketing plans all encompassing, and the direction and focus they provide will be well thought through.

The marketing plan will play an additional role in the 21st century if not before. Customers will evaluate prospective suppliers and partners based upon the integrity of their marketing plans. The driving force behind this is the fact that a marketing plan provides a glimpse of the future; it is a key indicator of the financial health of a company. As a result, key partners and customers will actively contribute to IT companies' market planning processes, as the bonds between customer and supplier strengthen.

New functions of marketing will evolve within our industry to support the way in which customers procure, and to reflect the information they require to analyse strategic IT solutions and to aid the decision making process. The introduction of an 'IT economics department' in the leading IT companies will become an important component of IT marketing in the 90s. There is already strong evidence to suggest that several of the lead players in the IT industry are moving down this track, and they will shortly announce new developments in this area. I will cover this subject in more detail later in the chapter.

Promotions

Branding has already been mentioned in this chapter, however, as branding is but one consideration in the promotional cycle, it is worth raising a few of the other developments that will take place in this area. Marketing information, creativity and innovation will continue to be the key components behind successful promotional campaigns, which in my view will remain much of a muchness. Perhaps the major difference I would expect to see in this area is the quality of campaigns, the planning behind them and the measurement of the results. We can expect to see significant improvements in all three areas.

The promotional side of the IT business will see wider use of competitive loyalty programmes. The loyalty programmes could have catastrophic consequences for many markets and companies and of course, do wonders for others. In the year 2000 if not sooner, I would expect to see better margin management of core products and services and from this, the wider introduction of loss leading campaigns put into place to allow companies to win and retain custom. Take the software industry for example. Software companies could deliver services at cost or cost minus X in order to retain software margins, retain customers, gain market share, and ensure their core business software is protected. Depending upon their strategies, they may well offer free information services. All sorts of loyalty and bonus schemes will evolve that will provide customers with better value. There is no question about it, certain segments of, and players in, the IT industry will disappear very rapidly through the introduction of competitive loyalty programmes as the lead players jostle for survival. I believe the training and maintenance markets will become very interesting over the next 2–3 years as loyalty techniques are used to distance the lead players from the second division players.

The success of all of these promotions, and an organization's ability to develop competitive campaigns, will be based upon a detailed understanding of the core triads that make up the IT industry together with information on the market.

Relationships

The acquisition and merger activity that will take place globally, coupled with the fallout of many of the current top thirty players, will lead to a polarization at the top end of the IT supply market. The frenetic industry change will lead to significant organizational change and in turn staff movement across the industry. Collectively, these factors place a very high emphasis on customer relationships as the continuum that many parts of the industry must manage if they hope to survive. I have already commented on customer loyalty, customer intimacy through information and customer focus through planning. These factors represent some of the key components in the sphere of relationship building and relationship retention. Customer and organizational relations will provide marketers with both the greatest opportunities and in turn the greatest risks. The ability of marketers to manage and leverage these relationships to the benefit of their organization will be key strategic issues over the next five years. Customer information, customer loyalty, customer understanding and customer intimacy will be core components of the marketer's plan.

Although marketing can play an important role in the relationship building process, it is the person to person contact that can have the greatest impact. Cost will play an important role in the one to one contact, as will technology, both of which are expanded in more detail in other chapters.

Selling IT

As an industry that sells complex products, salespeople will continue to have an important role within the many parts of the IT industry. The multiple driving forces that will lead the sea change on the sales front include the cost of sale, reductions in margins, staff availability, new technologies with 'window' opportunities to market, relationship management and administrative overhead. Collectively these factors, together with industry trends will force a shift in the way the sales operation is managed and the role of sales personnel. Changes will include:

- an increase in the use of part time sales staff;
- an increase in the number of women in IT sales roles;
- the contract sales force will become a common tactic in new product launches and be a key marketing weapon;
- the sales force will receive more direction and support from marketing;
- the sales manager will spend more time managing the sales force and less on central company wide issues;
- sales staff will be more focused and skilled, and be encouraged to spend less time in the office and more time with customers;
- IT suppliers will have many different types of customer facing personnel, all of whom will bring value to the customer in one form or another;
- sales staff will work more closely with the IT economists who will advise customer organizations on the economics of IT solution procurement and implementation.

Many of the above approaches are already in place in forward thinking companies; over the next 2–3 years they will be more widespread as IT companies better manage their sales channels.

MARKETING CHANNELS

Those organizations that are wrestling with marketing distribution channels today have a lot of catching up to do if they want to be around in the 21st century. Distribution and support channels are fundamental to marketing. If a company cannot work out how best to service and support a customer in 1994 when things are simple and competition is not that fierce, I would question their survivability by the year 2000 when competition is tough.

There are multiple distribution options available to marketers, each demanding one or a number of supporting activities, and each in turn carrying a set of costs and delivering different margins. The leaders in 1994 drive their business down multiple channels, providing complex support packages and deals for each member company, all of which is geared to profit. These organizations monitor channel trends carefully and adjust their offerings often on a monthly basis to ensure that they optimize their investment in each channel.

Marketing channels in the IT industry include partnering activities, promotions, pricing, selling and many other components of the mix. I have separated channels out for a simple reason: the IT industry struggles with marketing, and anything that can make it easier for people to understand has to be good for business. I could compile a lengthy list of changes the IT industry requires to make in the field of channel management when compared to other industries. However, rather than doing so, I have highlighted some of the more strategic developments that have still to emerge across the board.

- Channel member organizations will drive the 'poor performing' supply company channel strategies whereas the lead supply companies will drive the channel. One grouping of supply companies will flounder, one grouping will flourish!
- Channel member companies will spend more time analysing channel support packages and product offerings to allow them to negotiate better deals. Improved marketing and the requirement to compete will be driving forces behind this approach.
- Channel support will increase dramatically for top performing channels members. Poor performing members will struggle for support.
- The lead IT companies will invest in 'professional business consultants' who will advise channel member companies on better marketing and business practice to ensure their partners grow and prosper. This will be real advice and not just ½ day workshops or co-op marketing spend.
- Truly competitive channel strategies will be common practice as companies measure their business performance by channel type, channel focus and channel profit and loss.
- Channel management will mature within the IT industry over

the next five years as trade marketing managers from the retail sector clean up the PC industry, and swiftly move into other marketing positions within the industry.

Channel management, motivation, selection and measurement techniques are fundamental to good marketing practice. Without a firm grasp of channel techniques, organizations will struggle to survive. There is ample room for improvement in many sectors of the IT industry and multiple opportunities for organizations to develop lead strategies.

IT MARKET RESEARCH

We are in the mid 90s and directors of large multimillion pound companies continue to make business decisions with very little market information on which to offset the risk of failure. The consequences are visible across the industry. Marketing decisions in the year 2000 will be based upon solid market and customer information. This in its own right will see an increase in the budget set aside for market research. However, before every market research agency rubs its hands with glee, I would add that the IT market research industry in its current form is in for a rude awakening. At a recent CSSA marketing group meeting a number of critical points relating to IT market research were raised. IT market research in large customer organizations is very close to saturation point as far as the customer is concerned. This has a number of concerns for IT marketers, namely:

- increasing cost of market research;
- reduction in the quality of the research;
- concerns on the sampling front.

All in all this could have disastrous consequences for future marketing decision making as marketers rely upon research to support and help define their strategies.

As a result of this, the CSSA marketing group is currently looking at a number of initiatives on the market research front to help marketers. They are as follows:

- the compilation of a list of MRS recognized IT market research agencies;
- the production and promotion of a CSSA code of practice for market research agencies;

- the identification of new market research services required by IT marketers.

Alongside this, the CSSA marketing group will look to reclassify the different types of research supplier to the IT marketing community.

The problems that have arisen in the field of market research have revolved around telesales and PR companies who have decided to conduct market research with limited understanding of the problems and pitfalls that exist. The outcome for marketers has been reports that have been badly written or recommendations based upon questionable information. There are, however, many exceptional companies who take a professional and ethical approach to research, and as a result deliver valuable information. Organizations such as IDC, Romtec, Input, Dataquest, to name but a few, are well qualified to take on and respond to the toughest market research challenges and deliver high quality work.

IT INDUSTRY ANALYSTS

When I first moved into the IT industry, I conducted an unofficial audit of the different practices used by the major industry analysts. Having examined their practices in detail, I believe there is room for improvement in this sector alongside the research sector. The IT industry analysts are very good at technical product evaluation and technical trends, however, when it comes to offering advice on competitive strategy from a marketing perspective many of their assumptions fall down. IT industry analysts have an important role to play in the marketing community; however, to use their work as the single source for business decision making is a high risk strategy. The analysts' views should provide a secondary view of how issues are evolving.

As with the market research agencies, I believe we will see a number of developments amongst the analysts, as they re-profile their services to reflect the needs of the IT marketing community and to counter competitive challenges from other information providers.

All in all, we as marketers will find that our marketing information requirements will be better serviced in the 21st century.

MARKETING BUDGETS

It will come as no surprise to most of you that in line with the changes that I have forecast in this chapter of the book, there has to be some mention about the marketing budgets within our industry. In line with the increasingly competitive nature of our industry and in parallel with the development of other markets, marketing will without question become the differentiator for the 90s. For marketing to add real value to the business, however, the relevant resources require to be channelled into the department.

The marketing budgets across the IT industry currently range from 1 to 5% of company turnover. I forecast a significant increase in marketing budgets in the IT industry. They will be wider spread to reflect the different strategies of IT companies, with the figures ranging from 2.5% through to 10% of turnover. In looking at the higher scale of marketing budget, I would clearly expect the marketing director to be using the full mix of marketing tools and techniques available.

I always look back to the days when I was a product manager in the pharmaceutical industry ten years ago, when I managed a budget of £¼ million. At the time it was a run of the mill marketing budget, however, it allowed me to add real value to the company, and significantly increase the profits of my product lines. I was able to perform my job effectively and deliver real business value. Ten years on, as I talk to people in a different industry, I find that there are but a handful of IT marketing managers who feel they have the financial resources to allow them to add value to their business. They are resource constrained. This must change!

CRITICAL QUALITIES FOR THE FUTURE OF IT MARKETING

This short chapter has sought to provide a commentary on some of the marketing developments that will take place over the next five years if not sooner within the IT industry. Many developments have been listed, and some several times over. In concluding this chapter of the book, I would like to visit what I believe to be some of the key qualities that every CEO should be looking for from their marketing operation in 1995; they are criteria that will be vitally important if their organization wishes to make it to the 21st century.

If what follows is in place today, all that has been read in this chapter will seem logical and will reflect some of your plans for the future. If not, perhaps it is time for a change.

With such a variety of tasks to manage and develop, the success of marketing rests firmly on the quality of the individual marketer. Good marketers have one common trait: the correct attitude towards

- Creative
- Responsive
- Analytical
- Flexible
- Open-minded
- Communicative
- Outward-looking
- Thorough

Figure 7.2 Critical qualities in IT marketing.

business with an ability that firmly underpins this. They can be superb salespeople but not always – some can be better at some aspects of marketing and not so good at others; some will be mediocre at everything. Each has their strengths and weakness. A good management team recognizes this and builds skills accordingly. The management team that ignores and undermines professional marketers does so at their peril.

Marketers are individuals with receptive minds who listen to customers, analyse market trends and spot business opportunities. They have creative flair to help differentiate their company from the competition and to apply creative thoughts to the business, leading to proposals for revenue generation and innovative promotions. Marketers have an analytical approach towards business and markets, and can provide a detailed insight into a customer's real needs and requirements. They should demonstrate a good understanding of competitor activity, their strengths and weaknesses.

Marketers have a flexible working style that allows them to respond to sudden changes in customer requirements and to handle difficult market situations. They have an open mind that welcomes change. They listen and readily acknowledge ideas and proposals from all quarters of life. They bring thoroughness and rigour to bear within their organization and, in doing so, can clearly evaluate and demonstrate their real contribution to your company and your customers. Marketers are individuals who will communicate freely within the organization and openly share information about their market and customers. They will own the problems and challenges that require to be addressed by the company.

Marketing is a critical business discipline for IT companies. The people that apply good marketing practice today should not be concerned about the future; their attitude and skills will carry them forward. Those that do not apply marketing will find themselves continually missing financial targets, cross questioning the abilities of the enterprise and, generally, be in a position where things never seem to work. Good marketing falls firmly into the hands of good businesspeople. I look forward to the 21st century.

Garrey Melville is the UK Marketing Manager of the Systems Integration Group of Bull Information Systems and the founding Chairman of the Computing Software and Services Association's Marketing Common Interest Group. He has held marketing positions with several leading international organizations including the Sterling Winthrop Group, Ernst & Young and Deloitte Haskins + Sells. He specializes in the use of relationship marketing in the IT industry and has developed methodologies for channel management and improving marketing effectiveness.

A FUNNY THING
HAPPENED ON THE
WAY TO THE FORUM
Markets

PART TWO

A FUNNY THING HAPPENED ON THE WAY TO THE FORUM

Marker

INTRODUCTION

Markets are what marketing is all about. They are simply groups of customers identified by the seller to share a potential interest in what is offered to them. If all IT marketing was built around markets then this definition would not have to be made, but much of it is so removed from the customer that it cannot really qualify to be called marketing at all.

Once marketing decides to redirect itself at the market, the next problem arises. How to define the market. Soap powder manufacturers aim for markets of hundreds of thousands of consumers and can both use and afford blunderbuss media such as television. Many IT companies are more likely to discover that their market numbers less than 50 customers. The small customer base is an invention of IT and yet the techniques to target and capture these micro–markets are only now being recorded.

An understanding of the actual rather than the wished-for is essential. And from there, knowledge of the individual customer and their needs must be built up. After all, how often is time and money spent bidding for business from a company about which very little is known?

The next problem is, how to get information about the customer when the salesperson is standing firmly in the way. Salespeople can guard their customers in the same way an animal will protect her new-born. Jealously and fiercely. Most marketers faced with this obstacle will fall back on the sort of bland, scatter-gun research that says, 'There's a huge market out there just waiting for you to call. We're not sure exactly who they are but our figures show that the whole market will grow by $x\%$ in five years!'

One mailing list I cleaned up a few years ago for a major hardware

New Strategies for Marketing Information Technology.
Edited by Christopher Field
Published in 1996 by Chapman & Hall, London. ISBN 0 412 61520 7

manufacturer contained no less than five dead people, 35 employees that had moved company and many that were no longer in positions with purchasing power. The list was reduced from 4000 to 350 names. I never found out if it worked, but at least the direct mail costs plummeted.

Professor Merlin Stone says that companies must understand the way that high-tech markets evolve and focus on them more closely. He shows up the limitations of the traditional approach and proposes new guidelines.

Graham Browne says that the traditional market has been by vertical sector and by size of company. He proposes new ways to segment markets based more firmly on the needs of the customers.

John Armitage says that there are many ways to qualify a prospect long before the opportunity for business from them arises. When it does, you will be ready.

Andrew Barnes, managing consultant for Marketing Improvements Group, says that salespeople are often guilty of not selling to the user base, particularly to those customers that may not have spent much in the past. They do not want to be existing account managers because it can lack the excitement of new business. Barnes looks at marketing to this user base and shows just how profitable this can be.

8

FOCUSING ON KEY MARKETS

Merlin Stone

IT companies often fail to make the most of marketing because they do not understand the dynamics of high-technology market evolution or the implications of this evolution for successful, focused marketing.

This chapter provides a straightforward guide to achieving success through focused marketing. It shows:

- why and how IT markets evolve, and how the requirements for success evolve with them, including the requirement for competitive focused marketing;
- what IT companies can do to ensure they achieve this focus.

The example of systems focused on supporting customer service, sales and marketing is used to illustrate how to manage focus. It draws on Avanti's experience as a focused supplier itself, as a business partner of many of the larger companies operating in this area and through the large number of marketing, sales and service system evaluation projects Avanti's clients have required.

THE EVOLUTION OF IT PRODUCTS AND MARKETS

Most IT markets go through a cycle which is more or less as follows:

New Strategies for Marketing Information Technology.
Edited by Christopher Field
Published in 1996 by Chapman & Hall, London. ISBN 0 412 61520 7

1. **New product concept**: a new concept (e.g. hardware, software, services) is developed and launched by one or a few companies. It leads the market, either because of sheer technical performance (e.g. speed, volume of data managed, graphics quality) or because of quality of service (e.g. facilities management). Price is usually (but not always) high, depending on whether the supplier follows a market penetration (low price) or market skimming (high price) strategy. Here, the advantage goes to suppliers who are able to deliver the new concept to the market reliably.

2. **Competitors emerge**: they copy the original concept. Price is driven down. Here, the advantage goes to suppliers whose price/performance ratio is ahead of the market.

3. **The search for added value**: suppliers seek to protect themselves from price erosion by adding value to the core product by additional features. The concept is still a general concept, valid for any market. Here, the advantage goes to suppliers who are ahead of their competitors in anticipating required additional features. This advantage often derives from working closely with customers in adapting the concept to their requirements.

4. **Ways of adding value are also copied**: wherever added value is based on additional features, they are easily copied. Here, the advantage goes to the company which gets to market quickest with a comprehensive package of features.

5. **Market focus**: suppliers identify patterns to added value and start to match combinations of features or services to particular markets, supported by in-depth understanding of those markets and the specialist skills required to sell to and service them.

6. **Back to new concept**: a new concept comes along, so far in advance of what is available on the market, that focused suppliers are either undermined by it, or adopt it very quickly and convert it to fit the requirements of the markets they have focused on.

The commercial implications for this cycle are as follows:

- As the market evolves, physical market share gets shared amongst an ever increasing number of suppliers, but may get reconcentrated when Stage 6 arrives.
- However, a supplier who manages to outpace all others can maintain market share for a long time, although in practice this is rare.
- Although the market share of the core concept diffuses, successful suppliers find that their revenue per customer rises, as they sell

first more features to all customers and then more customized
features to customers in their focus markets.

- If suppliers hit upon a general or focus market which is
  expanding – either because of demand in its own end–user market
  (e.g. for air travel) or because the general concept they are selling
  is so attractive (e.g. it is an excellent substitute for other inputs
  such as labour, or it changes the ways customers add their value),
  the growth rate in the overall market may allow most suppliers
  to achieve rapid growth although their market share is falling.

Put simply, unless a supplier is certain that it can stay ahead of all of
its competitors with its core product concept or come up with a
succession of core concepts which undermine the focused marketing
positions of its competitors, every supplier should plan to use
focused marketing. Even if a supplier reckons that it can stay ahead
on the core concept, some involvement in focused marketing will
bring the benefit of a very close working relationship with customers
– a relationship which can provide clues as to the next core concept.

The larger the company, or the larger its desired volume of
business, the greater the number of focus markets required, and the
larger the average size of each focus market. Because large suppliers
find it hard to manage too many different areas of focus, they often
seek business partners (e.g. value-added resellers) with whom to
achieve focus in lower volume markets, and reserve their own efforts
for larger focus markets. These may be defined in many ways, such
as by market sector, e.g. financial services, retailing, by function,
e.g. inventory control, manufacturing, and by organization type,
e.g. multi-branch businesses.

ACHIEVING FOCUS – WHETHER AND HOW

In the rest of this chapter, a straightforward recipe for achieving
focus is presented. At each stage, examples are drawn from the focus
market to illustrate the point.

Step 1: defining the market

Market definition is a creative task. From a competitive point of
view, if a target market segment is easily identifiable to every
potential competitor, be sure that the market is likely to be crowded
(e.g. the financial systems market). The market is not just defined by
application, but by a combination of factors such as:

- typical size of projects
- scope of projects
- involvement of different levels and types of manager
- customer's familiarity with the application
- links to other applications.

For example, some suppliers of Computer Telephony Integration have defined power and telephony utilities as one of their focus markets for the 1990s. The utilities are faced with the move from a monopoly (in some cases serving only one region) to being one of many companies able to supply power or telephony to anywhere in the UK. Their old customer-management systems are not suitable for this task, and will need to be replaced. Similarly, suppliers of billing systems are targeting this market, as each utility will be supplying a variety of services to each customer, rather than a single service. The associated systems acquisitions are all large project which are the subject of major tenders, involving very senior utility management, and involve a complete rethinking of the commercial aspects of data processing.

Avanti has defined its target market as systems projects which lie at the interface between competitive marketing and customer service, where the client is looking for a system which will help it win new customers, retain existing customers and allow improved customer communication, care and service.

Step 2: is the market right for you?

This is not just a question of market size, except for the very largest companies. It is more a question of whether you have the right products, skills and resources to be a credible supplier in this area – or else whether you can bring them together, either in your employment, as business partners or as a consortium leader.

Step 3: making the commitment

Put simply, a market is only right for you in practice if you make the right commitment. In focused markets, credibility is all, and credibility does not come without commitment. Potential clients are also asking for reference sites, where they can see what you did and whether it worked.

Here are some examples of the results of commitment:

- ICL's commitment to investment in retail point of sale created a credible team selling credible systems, and resulted in the establishment of one of their most successful businesses.
- Data General's acquisition of the right to sell Brock Activity Manager software running on their fast Unix minicomputers, together with the development of a sales team with the appropriate skills, gave Data General the credibility to attack the market for telephone-based customer handling systems.
- CACI's strong positioning as a supplier of customer data, when combined with externally-sourced billing system software, gave it the strength to attack this market.
- IRI Software's pedigree in market research has stood it in good stead in the marketing of Express, its marketing data analysis package, which dominates its target market.
- Infolink has built its marketing data services on the back of a very strong position in the market for consumer credit data.
- In order to deliver its Customerize initiative in practice, Unisys recruited a very strong team of management consultants, who can deliver the promise of producing the required high quality of analysis and recommendation, to help their clients improve how they work with their customers.
- Avanti built its credibility by adding to its very strong marketing systems expertise the additional dimension of marketing and customer care strategy, by the recruitment of two nationally known senior consultants specializing in this area.

Step 4: making the commitment known

Once you have made the commitment, you must make the commitment known. If your company is large, you do this through marketing communications which follow the time-tested principle of concentration, domination and repetition. The Unisys Customerize communications programme is probably the best example of this. Backed up by a research programme, to which Avanti contributes in the UK, Unisys gets its message across very strongly, not only in its house magazine *Business Solutions* (for which it hires top business journalists to write up case studies and reviews), but also in the marketing and customer service specialist press, its own press and industry sector conferences, its sponsorship of customer service competitions and publications, and so on. House journals are also used by Infolink and IRI Software to channel new concepts to their clients, who then return to these suppliers for ways to implement them.

As a smaller business, Avanti keeps its name and ideas in front of the marketing and service systems community by seeking business partners who will expose it to their customers. Its partners over the years have included British Telecom, EDS, Unisys, IRI Software and Infolink. It also maintains a continuous programme of research into marketing and customer service systems and the strategic issues that drive them, sponsored by the above companies. In addition, Avanti ensures that it places several serious articles each year in the marketing and customer service media.

Step 5: controlling the market

To be the leading focused supplier, you must find ways of differentiating yourself from your leading competitors. Ways of doing this include:

- being a constant source of new ideas for clients – as Infolink and IRI Software are, through their house journals;
- providing access to peer experience – or networking, practised by most companies in the marketing and customer service market;
- creating an exclusive client club – so clients can learn from each other – best done by Unisys in Nice;
- implementing with the very highest quality – BS5750 is becoming commonplace, so new measures may need to be developed, e.g. staff and customer satisfaction, rather than the process-oriented BS5750;
- responsiveness to change – a question of the closeness of management to clients;
- exclusivity on relevant sourced software or hardware;
- ability to integrate the services of different suppliers seamlessly – a strength that EDS plays upon.

If you achieve a lead in this way, you will come to be regarded as one of the few suppliers – and ideally the only one – worth talking to in your focus market. This should always be your ambition.

Step 6: tailoring the option competitively

Of course, there must be a hard commercial edge to your proposition. You must be able to quantify the benefits of what you offer, and also provide it competitively. The key here is to establish a methodology which suits your focus market, and adjust it to client requirements.

You must also, of course, establish a cost base that suits your clients. Specialization should bring with it economies of scale, because your projects have common components across different clients. You should not aim to take all of this as profit, but explicitly share the benefit with clients. That way, your position will be almost impregnable.

Step 7: keep an eye out for change or, better, create it yourself

New concepts are always appearing in focus markets. A few years ago, database marketing was key. Today, although many clients still need to get their basics right in this area, customer care and customer loyalty have come to the fore. You must not wait until new concepts come to the fore, but instead help create them and shape them. You must therefore have at least one or two people in your organization who are happy to work at the conceptual level with clients, develop new concepts and then work with technical people to turn them into solutions.

If you do this, then you'll never be caught out in your focus market!

Professor Stone is a partner in Avanti Consultancy Services, specialists in strategies and systems to support marketing, customer service, customer care and loyalty. He is a nationally known expert on customer care, customer loyalty and customer information systems. He is also a leading researcher on the use of information systems at the point of contact with customers. His research is commissioned by Unisys, and co-sponsored by BT, IRI Software and Infolink. Current clients include British Telecom, Corporate Executive Search, Infolink, Insurance Courier Services, IRI Software, Motorola Cellular Systems, Sainsbury's Homebase, Unipart, Unisys and Volkswagen–Audi. He is the author of nine books on marketing and customer service, including the bestselling *Competitive Customer Care and Database Marketing*. He is also co-author of *How to Market Computers and IT* and of the forthcoming *Designing, Developing and Implementing Customer Information Systems*. Until 1993, he was Dean of the Faculty of Human Sciences at Kingston University, where he still teaches part-time.

9

EFFECTIVE MARKET SEGMENTATION

A commercial imperative

Graham Browne

The IT industry has not entirely ignored market segmentation but its application has, at best, been crude. For some years now, the industry has used the term 'vertical markets' to describe the segmentation of the customer base by industry sector and some distinction has been drawn between the sales approach adopted for large and smaller customers. However, such segmentation as existed was introduced as much for administrative convenience as a response to the perceived structure of the market.

Although it is easy to deride this simplistic approach to the market when compared to the sophisticated target market strategies practised by more mature industries, it did represent a rational response within an industry that was once used to high growth and substantial margins. Then, substantial opportunities existed for all competitors, both established and new, and there was comparatively little need to differentiate products and services to meet the needs of targeted customer groups. However, the onset of a level of market maturity has resulted in a significantly more hostile environment in which the assumptions of the past have lost their validity.

My principal hypothesis is that, far from being of purely theoretical interest, effective market segmentation has now become a

New Strategies for Marketing Information Technology.
Edited by Christopher Field
Published in 1996 by Chapman & Hall, London. ISBN 0 412 61520 7

Table 9.1 European IT market growth rates

	Percent	
	All IT	Software and services
1982	18	21
1983	21	22
1986	16.8	18.4
1989	15.8	17.5
1991	3.9	9.3
1992	4.2	9.4
1993	2	5.6

commercially essential element of the strategic thinking of the IT industry. I will highlight the impact that the existing lack of target marketing is having on the market development and profitability of key areas such as the IT services business. I will also discuss the practical problems that exist in attempting to segment the customer base and offer as an example the practical utilization of a well established model as a tool with which to define a coherent view of the overall market.

However, first it is necessary to clarify the application of the term 'maturity' to the IT market. The adoption of sophisticated marketing techniques can be justifiably considered as an expensive irrelevance within a rapidly expanding market in which the established competitors can consistently deliver a high rate of return on the capital employed by their investors. The requirement to invest in marketing only becomes imperative in an environment in which growth has slowed, margins have declined and competitors are forced to identify and satisfy the needs of the market in order to provide a source of competitive advantage which is not dependent on cost leadership. There is no doubt that all these factors have been evident during the first half of the 1990s. Table 9.1 illustrates the decline in revenue growth that has occurred in the European marketplace and the problems experienced by IBM, Digital and other computer manufacturers provide ample evidence of the squeeze on margins that has been experienced.

The key question, of course, is to what extent these problems will prove to be short term? There is a school of thought which suggests that future growth will exceed that of the gross domestic product of the major economies which, almost by definition, implies that

Table 9.2 External expenditure growth forcast, United Kingdom

	Percent
1992–1993	4.7
1993–1994	5.8
1994–1995	3.8
1995–1996	3.4
1996–1997	2.2
1997–1998	2.3

the industry has not yet matured. Indeed, it would be generally accepted that the market for particular technologies or services will exhibit high, perhaps even spectacular, growth: the potential assigned to the development of 'information highways' is one obvious example. However, forecasts from IDC (Table 9.2) indicate that, certainly as far as the UK economy is concerned, growth in external IT expenditure will be severely limited for the remainder of the 1990s. It must therefore be considered dangerous to assume that the industry will return to high growth and suppliers must therefore adapt their strategies to the current, slow growth phase of the life cycle.

THE EXISTING PROBLEM

The implicit assumption that has historically applied throughout the industry is that market segmentation equals vertical markets. Some thought was given to the scale and size of the customer but this consideration was usually limited to deciding the point at which the third party channel was utilized rather than the direct sales force.

Within the current climate of reduced growth and profitability, the excessive reliance on industry sectors as a means of segmenting the market has two major flaws.

In the first instance, the majority of products and services supplied by the industry are infrastructural in nature and are purchased across the entire spectrum of the market as can be seen from the conceptual representation in Figure 9.1. The principal point to note from this model is that the only categories of product and service which are unequivocally linked to the industry sector of the customer are strategic and principal business applications. Computer-aided manufacturing is obviously supplied exclusively to manufacturing indus-

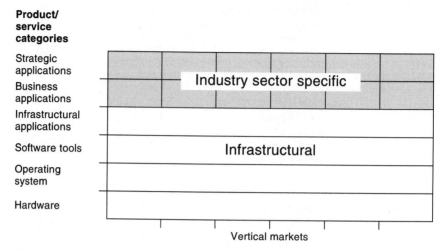

Figure 9.1 The limitations of vertical market segmentation.

try in the same way that point of sale applications are largely confined to the retail and wholesale sectors.

However, applications which form part of the organizational infrastructure, such as payroll systems, electronic mail and desktop packages, are sold to all categories of organization, in the same way that the demand for hardware and software infrastructure components is generally unrelated to particular industry sectors. Database engines, for example, are used throughout British industry and commerce and although banks, for instance, have a requirement for databases capable of handling transaction intensive applications, the same requirement also exists in a variety of other business areas.

Although the use of industry sectors will continue to be regarded as a valid marketing tool, its finite value as a means of segmenting the market must be recognized. Several examples exist within the industry of organizations that have successfully adopted a considered approach to market segmentation resulting in a clearly defined target market strategy. One example of such a company is Granada Computer Services which primarily targets its third party maintenance business at companies with a large installed base of mini and mainframe computers from a range of suppliers.

The second and most critical flaw in current practice is that the excessive reliance on industry sectors as the primary means of segmenting the market has resulted in a severe lack of product and service differentiation among suppliers. At a time when the market was growing extremely rapidly, the adoption of largely undifferen-

Table 9.3 Network management services purchasing criteria

	Percent
Priority 1	
Cost	14
Track record/experience	13
Technical ability	10
Reliability	7
Priority 2	
Cost	26
Location	5
Quality of service/response	4
Speed of response/operation	4
Priority 3	
Cost	25
Company stability	4
Quality	4
Reliability	3

tiated marketing strategies on the part of the major players helped to structure the marketplace and give it a recognizable form. However, in a more mature environment the lack of coherent target market strategies and consequent product differentiation is having the effect of accelerating the evolution of a given market into a price sensitive, competitive and low margin business.

Nowhere is this more evident than in the IT services market, which has been characterized during the first half of the decade by the adoption of service product concepts such as 'facilities management' and 'outsourcing', terms used to describe the provision of long-term contracts designed to place responsibility for the management of elements of the IT infrastructure with a third party. Despite the fact that suppliers of such services are keen to demonstrate the extent to which they can provide added value to the customer, the market for such services has very rapidly assumed a high level of price sensitivity as the example of network management services contained in Table 9.3 clearly illustrates.

A partial explanation for this level of sensitivity can be attributed to recessionary pressures within the economy but the extent to which suppliers have adopted these concepts without targeting the service to meet the requirements of defined groups of customers has undoubtedly had an adverse effect on the development of the services market as a whole.

The market for externally supplied network management services provides a clear example of this situation. The term 'outsourcing' has been adopted by the industry to describe a wide range of service offerings. However, in the minds of the customer the expression is increasingly being used to describe a large contract, negotiated at board level, and which involves the transfer of IT staff to the supplier's headcount. Comments from IT managers such as '[the role of the IT department is] to provide a more efficient service than external competitors', illustrate the response of internal IT departments to this development.

It is clear therefore that the service supplier must target their services either at the board or at the IT department. The type of service offered, the perceived benefits of the service and the language used to describe the service must all be designed to meet the needs and allay the fears of the target customer, a basis of segmentation that is of far greater commercial relevance than maintaining a largely artificial vertical market split.

The requirement

It is clear that the lack of attention that has been given to the issue of market segmentation is having a negative impact on the commercial performance of the industry as a whole. However, providing a workable model that offers a base from which suppliers can develop appropriate target market strategies presents a very significant challenge.

It is generally recognized within the industry that IT marketing can draw on the experiences and expertise of more mature industry sectors: the recruitment of marketing professionals from such sources provides an obvious example of this realization. However, it can be argued that simply aiming to catch up with other industries will not provide an adequate solution. Unlike almost any other area of business to business marketing, the IT industry represents a combination of technical complexity and universality of application, which the market segmentation techniques practised by, for example, the automotive industry, cannot hope to address. In addition to the complex and increasingly business-critical nature of the technology and the services that underpin it, the way in which the technology is applied within organizations, the role of the IT department and its relationship with its internal customers all contribute to an extremely complex marketing environment.

The challenge facing the industry therefore is to develop segmentation models that take account of the complexity of the environment and which can be used by individual suppliers to differentiate their products and services by meeting the needs of defined target markets.

One well-established model that offers the potential to provide a coherent basis from which to segment the market is the 'stages of growth model'. First postulated by Nolan and Gibson of Nolan, Norton and Company in 1974,[1] it has been extensively analysed, revised and refined by academics to the present day. The original model was based on the hypothesis that the development of IT usage within an organization could be defined in terms of four, subsequently revised to six, stages of maturity. Much of the work that has been done on the model has been designed to meet the practical requirements of the IS manager attempting to develop the use of IT within the organization. However, from the perspective of the supplier the model clearly offers a tool to define the complex characteristics of the market.

The version of the model utilized within this chapter is the one developed by Professor Galliers of the Warwick Business School with A. R. Sutherland.[2] It defines a set of common responses of organizations within six stages of IT evolution against seven defined organizational and management factors derived from McKinsey and Company's 'Seven Ss'[3] as follows:

- Strategy
- Structure
- Systems
- Staff
- Style
- Skills
- Super ordinate goals (the shared values or culture of the organization).

The six stages of IT evolution are defined as follows:

1. **Ad hocracy**: the term is used to describe the uncontrolled and ad hoc approach exhibited by organizations in the initial stages of IT usage.
2. **Starting the foundations**: the first stage of the ascendancy of IT within the organization.
3. **Centralized dictatorship**: this term characterizes the move to a comprehensive system of centralized planning as a reaction to the uncoordinated approach adopted during stages 1 and 2.
4. **Democratic dialectic and co-operation**: a move towards co-ordinating and integrating the IT function with the rest of the

Table 9.4 The stages of growth model (*source:* Galliers & Sutherland)

Stages of growth	1. Ad hocracy	2. Starting the foundations	3. Centralized dictatorship	4. Democratic dialectic and co-operation
Strategy	Acquisition of hardware, software etc.	IT audit to find out and meet user needs in a reactive way	Top-down IS planning	Integration, co-ordination and control
Structure	None	IS function, often subordinate to accounting or finance	Centralized DP shop with end users running free at stage 1	Information centres. Office automation in same information services unit
Systems	Ad hoc, unco-ordinated operational systems concentrating on financial applications	Centralized operational systems, mainly financial, with many gaps and a rising load of maintenance	Mostly centralized on a database with end user computing out of control, despite most business activities being covered	Unco-ordinated decentralized approach with integrated office systems and some ad hoc decision support
Staff	Programmers/ contractors	Systems analysts, DP Manager	IS planners, IS managers, database administrators	Chief information officer, business analysts
Style	Unaware	'Don't bother me, I'm too busy'	Abrogation/ delegation	Democratic, dialectic
Skills	Low level technical expertise	Systems development methodology	Project management. IS knows best what the user needs	IS knows business. Business knows IS (in their area). IS staff learn business management
Shared values	Obfuscation. Limited sharing of knowledge	Confusion	Senior management concern. DP defence	Co-operation

organization as a response to the conflicting forces that emerge from stage 3.

5. **Entrepreneurial opportunity**: the emergence from a supporting service to a function offering strategic benefits in its own right.

6. **Integrated, harmonious relationships**: a term used to describe the sophisticated use of IT within an organization within which IT has become deeply embedded.

Table 9.5 The revised stages of growth model – applied to outsourcing attitudes (*source: IT Outsourcing, The Changing Outlook*, IDC/Warwick Business School)

Transition from stages	1–2	2–3	3–4	4–5
Business – IS issues	Business efficiency	Costs and control	Getting the IS function to work closely with the business	Using IT to obtain significant strategic advantages for the whole organization
Business attitudes to IS function	Emerging concern about what they do and rising costs	Disappointment at lack of DP credibility	Retrain, replace and make them more business oriented	They are beginning to become part of the solution instead of part of the problem
Business attitudes to outsourcing	More likely to insource	Could be a way to get rid of the problem	Could provide some short cuts to get rid of problematic bits of the IS function	Likely to consult with the IS function for their advice
IS attitudes to business	We know best	Defensive	Variable depending on whether they have accepted the new drive for co-operation	Very keen to identify and develop strategic opportunities for IS systems
IS attitudes to outsourcing	Not relevant	Major threat to be resisted	In most cases as a threat or by some enlightened staff as a way of getting rid of some DP slums	An opportunity to get rid of some of the legacy systems
Outsourcing drivers	None	Cost and opportunity to get rid of the problem	To speed up the IS transformation	Free up resources to devote more effort on strategic systems
Possible outcomes	Likely to insource – nothing to outsource	Lock stock and barrel deals. Maybe also long contracts	Part outsourcing of legacy systems and getting rid of intractable IS problems	As 3–4, but the IS function takes a stronger role as adviser and manager of the external relationships

The full model provided in Table 9.4 incorporates the critical assumption that the relative maturity of an organization as an IT user has a fundamental impact on the key factors that influence the purchasing decision, such as the position of the IT manager within the organization, the perception of IT within the organization as a whole and the level of integration that has been achieved. It also offers a coherent attempt to encapsulate the complexity of the market within a framework that has been the subject of a substantial level of academic scrutiny over a long period of time.

In order to provide an example of the way in which the model provides the opportunity to segment the market by the relative maturity of the user organization, Table 9.5 illustrates a version of the model, modified by Henry Trull of IDC, which examines the possible demand for outsourced services from organizations in transition between stages. The clear conclusion to emerge from this analysis is the wide variety of types of services that are required by organizations as their use of IT evolves.

CONCLUSION

The purpose of this chapter has not been to provide a prescriptive lesson in market segmentation but to highlight the problems that are being encountered as a result of the lack of attention that it has received within the industry. The Stages of Growth Model presents a clear example of a possible approach that can be applied in practice but it is intended as an example of the type of technique that can be considered. It is certainly not being presented as a complete answer to the industry's problems.

In addition to the view that effective market segmentation has assumed fundamental importance to IT suppliers, the key conclusion of the chapter is that segmentation and the resulting target market strategy provides a critical source of differentiation. Adding value to meet the needs of defined target customers rather than imitating the products and services of the market as a whole provides a commercially attractive alternative to a highly competitive, price sensitive market served by undifferentiated products and services. Market segmentation as a source of product and service differentiation is rapidly becoming a commercial imperative.

Graham Browne is an independent consultant and runs his own strategy and marketing consultancy practice providing specialist services to the UK IT services business. He is an associate consultant with IDC. He has over 12 years' experience within the IT industry which, in addition to his consultancy work, has included a variety of managerial, technical and project management roles gained within a major equipment manufacturer and a leading software and services company. Graham is a partner in the Henry Graham Group, a new company that assists internal and external IT suppliers to make the transition from sales led to market driven.

10

WHY WASTE MONEY ON MARKETING COMMUNICATIONS?

John Armitage

There is no way of generating regular sales without a good product at a price which provides the customer with perceived value for money. But not every such good supplier actually gets a fair share of a competitive market.

To get a high market share it is also essential to build awareness of the product and its benefits and a good corporate image for its supplier among all decision-makers well ahead of any decisions to buy. Well-known and reliable companies will be approached early in the buying sequence: others may not be.

Today any IT company that doesn't tailor its products and services to customer needs is doomed, and cannot be saved by spending money on such marketing tools as advertising, PR, promotions or direct mail. No genuine commitment to a real marketing philosophy and to customer-directed innovation in a fast moving world means no sales and mega-buck losses.

Customers don't just want the latest hi-tech things with 'bells and whistles', they want solutions – that means good advice plus reliable products and systems that do the (often very fundamental) IT tasks

New Strategies for Marketing Information Technology.
Edited by Christopher Field
Published in 1996 by Chapman & Hall, London. ISBN 0 412 61520 7

that their companies need. And good service and technical back-up is a 'given' – it has to be there.

THE ROLE OF MARKETING COMMUNICATIONS

Once we have got the products, services and back up right, we need to persuade our customers and potential customers that this is so and we have got to re-establish this idea every time something new happens in our ever-changing marketplace. So we have a constant and ongoing job for marketing communications.

A recent study of a large IT company's business indicated that when sales were below budget, profitability was negatively impacted, not just by increasing overheads, but more importantly by shrinking gross margins. In order to get closer to their targets, the company's representatives were discounting their prices to get sales. And, in this particular case, the turnover of the company was so big and the cost of advertising so relatively tiny, that it was possible to demonstrate that any measurable positive effect (however small) would be cost-effective.

But it is still quite possible to waste money on marketing communications and to get no return, because campaigns have to be properly conceived, planned and executed to be effective. Just as every good marketing plan is developed to achieve specific business goals, so every good communications plan must be developed to help to achieve the specific objectives and strategies of the marketing plan.

THE DECISION-MAKING PROCESS

The secret of developing a successful and effective marketing plan, and of defining the tasks and action standards for the communications plan, is to understand the 'decision-making process' in your part of the market. Buying decisions for major commercial or industrial projects will inevitably mean that a large number of people will be consulted or directly involved.

The process will probably go through up to eight definable stages – each of which offers your company an opportunity to influence the decision (Figure 10.1).

An important point to note in this example is that the outside supplier is unlikely to know that a potential customer is actively in the market until the fourth stage of their internal 'decision-making

1. Identification of need. The branch office – 'We need pricing information daily, how about a new ISDN link?'

2. Authorization of search. Chief Executive – 'Go ahead, within a budget of *x*.'

3. Specification. IT management – 'Remote access LAN link which can work with our existing network.'

4. Search for suppliers. Purchasing Department – 'Do you wish to tender to this specification?'

5. Choice. All the above – 'OK, let's go with this one as the best compromise.'

6. Authorization of expenditure. Finance Department – 'Are you within budget?' Specialist Adviser – 'Are there any overall corporate implications in this choice?'

7. The order. Purchasing – 'We accept your proposal subject to the following.'

8. Monitoring. Specifiers and users – 'Did we get what we want? Is it working properly?'

Figure 10.1 A possible decision-making sequence for a major IT contract.

process' is underway – and may even find out too late to be included in the list of suppliers asked to tender.

PLANNING THE MARKETING COMMUNICATIONS STRATEGY

No effective marketing action can take place until the supplier has defined the target markets, their stages of decision-taking, the membership of their DMUs (Decision Making Unit), and the information they need at each stage. In some cases, strategic market research will be needed first.

However, given agreed targets, it should then be clear where marketing communications are necessary and what their task is. This will clarify the most appropriate techniques for each stage.

Table 10.1 shows that the complete communications task cannot be achieved effectively by one technique on its own, however much money is spent or however creative its execution. Almost all successful marketing campaigns integrate several techniques.

For example, advertising is excellent at creating among all

Table 10.1 How marketing communications can influence a buying decision

Buying sequence	Role of advertising and promotion at each stage	Candidate activity (Marketing/ Advertising/Promo)
Stage 1 Identification of need	To highlight the need amongst target audience – and to demonstrate the problem and the solution	• Advertising • POS • Direct Mail • Cross-selling • PR
Stage 2 Decision to search	To build brand awareness – 'a good company to approach' because of reputation and relevant products	As Stage 1
Stage 3 Requirement or specification	To get on shortlist because product/service meets the perceived need	As Stage 1
Stage 4 Shortlist/comparison	To build confidence in the company – and to provide all necessary information and assistance	As above plus: • Literature • Personal advice • Self help
Stage 5 Decision to purchase	To maintain top-of-mind awareness – and to make decision to purchase simple and attractive	As Stage 4
Stage 6 Checking the decision	To maintain awareness and confidence among target audience and among all possible advisors	As Stage 4
Stage 7 Purchasing	To make purchase as quick and easy as possible	• Fast, friendly response • Simple order/ application form • Simple clearance procedure
Stage 8 'Did we get what we wanted?'	To give reassurance that decision was right – and to build a desire to recommend to friends and contacts	• Advertising • Follow up calls • PR

members of a DMU awareness of a product and its major benefits, reinforcing the reputation of its supplier and reassuring buyers after the event that they have made a wise decision. Public relations activity can reinforce these particularly with specific and influential sub-categories of the target. Direct response can help identify buyers at the time when they are actively searching for information. But to match a product to its potential customers and make the sale itself, personal contact will usually be needed, backed up by literature and interactive techniques such as telephone help-lines. By their nature and cost, these techniques must be targeted very narrowly to potential buyers at the point of decision.

Each market will be different, and different suppliers in any market will need different strategies, to the extent that they will be aiming their products at different segments of the whole.

SUMMARY AND CONCLUSIONS

To be successful in all parts of today's competitive and fast-moving IT market a company must be totally committed to a marketing (customer-orientated) approach. And a company that adopts strong marketing communications as part of their way of doing business will gain a competitive advantage over those who don't. They will gain from stronger company reputation, and from higher awareness and better value perceptions of their products and services. They will also gain from higher motivation of staff and sales force.

My own company has built up a portfolio of over 100 case histories – many of them in IT. We find that advertising and other marketing communication activities are (or can be made) highly effective, and that if so, they will almost always prove more cost-effective than many other highly-regarded sales-builders such as price-cutting.

For example, research shows that:

- Goods and services which are seen as higher quality justify and get higher prices.
- Salespeople who are well-supported sell more – and discount less.
- Relatively small increases in volume and especially price often have a substantial effect on net profits.

Let me finish by referring back to my opening paragraph, which points out that there is no way of generating regular sales without a good product at a price which provides the customer with perceived value for money – but that not every such good supplier actually gets a fair share of a competitive market.

Dynamic companies use marketing communications to make sure that their share is as large as possible – and they know that the promotional spend is highly cost-efficient, and not a waste of valuable money.

John Armitage is Chairman of Primary Contact, the specialist 'Business-to-Business' agency of the Ogilvy Group in London. Prior to this he was a Director of Ogilvy & Mather Ltd (1971–85), handling a wide range of accounts such as American Express, British Tourist Authority, The Woolwich, Bernard Matthews, Golden Wonder, and the Milk Marketing Board.

11

THE CHALLENGE OF MARKETING TO THE USER BASE

Andrew Barnes

For many IT companies, the 'user base' is made up of historical customers who have neither attained major account status nor are deemed strategically important by virtue of their being members of key industry groupings. Left trailing in the wake of apparently more exciting sales opportunities, the 'user base' is frequently regarded as second-class, fit only to be 'swept' for upgrades when the quarter-end figures are looking soft.

This is extremely dangerous – research by Miller Business Systems showed that 68% of companies that changed suppliers, did so because they felt that the supplier had lost interest in them, compared to only 5% stating 'competitive reasons'!

Combine that fact with the results of other research showing (a) the cost of selling to existing customers to be around one sixth of that of attracting and gaining new business, and (b) that just a 5% improvement in customer retention can boost profitability by 85% (*Harvard Business Review*), and the economics of selling to new, rather than old, accounts starts to look extremely precarious. The user base is clearly a major marketing asset – so why do so many IT companies appear to ignore it?

New Strategies for Marketing Information Technology.
Edited by Christopher Field
Published in 1996 by Chapman & Hall, London. ISBN 0 412 61520 7

I am convinced that existing customers represent the major opportunity to achieve low-cost, volume sales for vendors that can respond to the challenges of:

- identifying high–opportunity users;
- creatively segmenting the user base;
- mounting effective and efficient marketing campaigns.

In many cases, we find that the challenges are amplified by a dearth of useful information about these customers. Indeed, there usually is plenty of information available on technical problems and billing history, and generally a five-year-old sales file. We rarely find up-to-date organization charts, or any information on buying processes and criteria, or on the business or market issues facing the customer.

Faced with a low level of available sales and marketing resource, as most priority is generally given to major accounts and vertical markets, and faced with virtually no useful information, it is hardly surprising that this valuable source of sales opportunities is frequently left to wither on the vine. Attempts at segmentation are made, but normally emerge as a classification of 'dead' accounts.

Perhaps the IT industry's persistence with calling its customers 'users' (rather like British Rail's 'passengers') gives the best clue to this neglectful treatment of a major asset. Users (like passengers) are a nuisance. They complain about service, wrong bills, and want bugs fixed. New customers, by contrast, sign orders, take delivery, and buy new products. They carry no baggage. Users are a pain; new customers are exciting.

The alternative view is that users, by definition already customers with known contacts, who will meet to discuss opportunities at (hopefully) short notice, are the only real friends that vendors have. Why treat them like lepers? If a consultant offered you such a contact list, would you buy it? Of course you would! Only a fool would turn down the chance to get in front of proven IT spenders. It is surprising then, that so many vendors are prepared to consign existing users to the dustbin. Dead accounts, killed not by malice, but by neglect.

A large user base will almost certainly contain a number of accounts who will spend a very large amount of money on computing products and services next year – with somebody! The problem lies in identifying them, without the associated massive expenditure of resources, which means a sales visit to each and every existing customer.

Reliable identification of high opportunity customers, based on little information, and constrained resource is, of course, impossible.

Identifying likely high-opportunity customers is, however, relatively straightforward, once some useful information is gathered about 'the customer base'. Companies that, for example, have in place IT strategies compatible with the vendor's product philosophy, and significant wherewithal to buy and pay, are obviously attractive and an investment of marketing resources is likely to be rewarded. Fortunately, information on the IT strategy, and size/growth/ profitability of existing customers is not difficult to obtain. At Marketing Improvements, we have developed a methodology for deciding on the level of marketing resource that is appropriate to each customer, or group of customers.

We normally start with a situation whereby our client (the vendor) has very little information on each of a large number of existing customers. Step one is to decide on, and gather, the minimum information on each customer necessary to carry out the first 'cut'. This cut is based on the minimum likelihood of the vendor getting significant IT spend from the account. Thus – data on customer size, growth, attitude to the vendor, etc. (all easily and cheaply obtained), can be used to identify those accounts which will receive the lowest level of marketing resource – e.g. direct mail twice a year, one invitation to a seminar, etc.

The remainder of the non-strategic accounts are then assessed in two ways – firstly as an individual account, and secondly as a potential member of one or more segments. In both cases, information on each account needs to be collected (and of course maintained).

Individual accounts that score very highly on a rating scheme composed of 'highly attractive, highly likely to spend' factors are designated as primary accounts and are allocated a relatively high marketing resource spend (e.g. the attention of the direct sales force, invitations to corporate sponsorship events where they meet the key accounts).

The remaining third group of customers are then the subject of a segmentation exercise. In our experience, vendors are often ignorant of major sales opportunities because of their concentration on product based segmentation framework. All IT companies would benefit by looking at their existing customers in terms of their membership of real, need-based market segments – not their SIC code, installed CPU or geography (just about the only segmentation variables the IT industry has used in the last 10 years) but creative, useful segments that can sustain focused, intensive marketing campaigns. Segments that reflect issues that are important to the customers, rather than a stodgy classification framework.

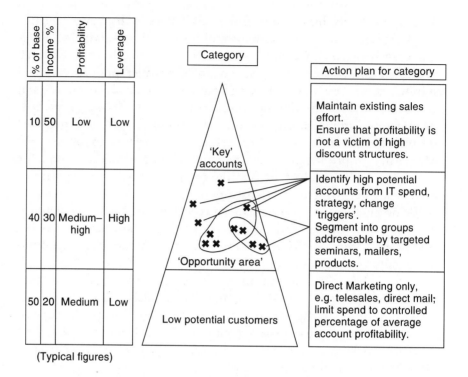

(Typical figures)

% of base – Number of accounts in category as % of total customers
Income % – % of sales contribution by category
Profitability – Relative profitability of sales to category
Leverage – Relative sales return from increased sales marketing effort

Figure 11.1 Diagram of account 'pyramid'.

Figure 11.1 shows a traditional IT vendor's account 'pyramid', divided into three categories: the 10% of key accounts, the 50% 'low potential' accounts, and the 'opportunity area'. This comprises the 40% of customers who are either high potential because of, for example, their size, IT spend, and favourable change indicators such as recent acquisition activity or a new management team, or are members of attractive segments.

The critical factor is the different levels and types of marketing activity accorded to each category. Key accounts are sales, rather than marketing targets. Dedicated sales resource is usually applied to such accounts, but the resultant high costs of selling and large negotiated discounts often cause key accounts to be of low profitability.

Marketing to low-potential customers is crucial if accounts are to be developed or at least retained, but the average level of marketing activity must be consistent with the profits gained from such customers. This will dictate the type of marketing activity – low cost telemarketing, direct mail, etc., with leads passed to the direct sales force only when qualified.

The opportunity area comprises individual high potential accounts, who justify at least some level of direct contact, and segments that can be the subject of highly focused events, such as seminars.

Of course this is a simplified model – in practice, several more bands of customer category are designated and varying amounts of marketing resource allocated to each – but the principle remains the same: stay in touch with all customers, but decide on the appropriateness and cost of the marketing activity first.

Recent work with a major client involved us in implementing a programme for continuous identification and exploitation of segments comprising existing customers: segments such as 'Suppliers to Central Government', 'Impacted by new environmental legislation', and 'Members of the shipbuilding supply chain'. Other, similarly creative segments will provide major marketing opportunities.

Not all segments are attractive to a particular vendor, so a prioritization process has been developed by MI to reflect compatibility issues.

Such segments provide opportunities for effective and efficient selling. It is effective because the matters addressed in seminars or other promotional activity are of great interest to members of the segment if it is defined correctly, and the 'right' customers identified.

It is efficient because the campaigns can be instituted quickly, and generally at low cost, and because several prospective buyers can be addressed at one session.

Crucially, the segmentation process is geared at identifying actionable customer groupings. Marketing departments are often accused of not knowing who their customers are, and failing to deliver what the salesforce needs – qualified leads. All too often, segmentation is a long-range planning exercise, targeted at senior management. The IT industry has enough strategy papers; now is the time to get the salesforce moving, by directing them at attractive segments, differentiating their offering, and delivering the goods – the three 'D's of marketing.

Once identified, high-opportunity customers can then be the subject of client development programmes, emphasis being placed on consultative selling and relationship management techniques with the objective of growing the ugly duckling user into a major account. Indeed, the much maligned 'user base' could well be best appreciated when seen as a nursery or hot-house for high-opportunity accounts, 'testbedding' of new salespeople and new marketing techniques such as direct marketing, and also for growing new industry sector groups.

Creative, proactive, and energetic exploitation of target segments can revive a dead-end sales section. Campaigns can be run like fashion shows – have a 'summer collection', a 'winter sale', a 'spring show' – have three campaigns running, three being exploited and another three in preparation. The days when vendors could afford to produce unfocused, unimaginative, tired marketing programmes have now gone forever.

The future belongs to those vendors who don't just talk about marketing strategy and produce long-range plans, but to those who realize that supply now exceeds demand, that selective, targeted marketing is essential, and of course also get out there and actually do it!

Andrew Barnes is Managing Consultant in Marketing Improvement's IT Marketing Division. After graduating in Physics from London University, he joined the computer industry in 1968, initially working in technical roles with suppliers. He moved into marketing in 1982, and started his consulting career in 1985, first with Logica, then Coopers & Lybrand. He has been with MI since 1992.

PART THREE

THE LONELINESS OF THE LONG DISTANCE SWIMMER

Channels

INTRODUCTION

Although IT companies talk as if they had discovered channels, most manufacturers of premium products have been doing it for years. They look for outlets that will allow them to get to as many people as possible, but not so many that the brand name and image are devalued. For some, it must only be boutiques, for others it must be mail order. Once the brand has become mass market, it can safely be sold in supermarkets. Once devalued with one sector, it can become valuable to a new one. Pierre Cardin is a classic example of an exclusive label that is now anything but. Manufacturers are so good at channels that they can plan the birth, life and death of a product.

Unfortunately, there is little such planning in IT. This is a particular problem in IT because IT products and services are dependent for their success on channels and there is so much wrong with channel marketing at present. Each member of the chain has its own sales targets to reach and it is common that marketing effort is duplicated. The manufacturer, distributor and reseller may all be targeting the same customer and not using their relative strengths. On the other hand, although the manufacturer may be doing national advertising while the distributor does local direct mail, the two campaigns are not co-ordinated, and each tells an entirely different message about the same product.

Meanwhile, co-operative marketing schemes where the manufacturer promises resources to the distributor are either not taken up or operated only at the level of direct mail printing.

Stan Maklan asks, 'Are you a member of a value chain or is your independence blocking you out of the big business?'

New Strategies for Marketing Information Technology.
Edited by Christopher Field
Published in 1996 by Chapman & Hall, London. ISBN 0 412 61520 7

12

CHANNEL MARKETING IN THE INFORMATION INDUSTRIES

Stan Maklan

Distribution is rarely the glamorous part of marketing and in most texts usually merits only a small article under a review of the traditional four Ps. However, in the information industries, channel strategy is often the fundamental marketing decision facing a company. Where the company positions itself on the distribution chain will determine who are their customers, partners, competitors and the services they must sell.

The information industry led the industrial world in the delayering of large, vertically integrated giants into smaller, specialized companies who partner and compete with each other according to the needs of individual companies. In turn, this has led us into a world of customer-driven markets, choice and value for money. Despite this progressive attitude to delayering, companies in the information industries have not always understood the marketing implications of the new world they created. In consequence, ForeFront's research finds turmoil and confusion in the distribution and value chains.

Over the past year, ForeFront interviewed senior executives in charge of marketing, channel management or strategy at successful computing and telecommunications companies in the UK. Compan-

New Strategies for Marketing Information Technology.
Edited by Christopher Field
Published in 1996 by Chapman & Hall, London. ISBN 0 412 61520 7

ies included leading computing vendors, distributors, systems integrators, value added resellers (VARs), retailers, international telecom suppliers and local telecom operators.

We found that all players along the distribution chain have gravitated to a similar positioning strategy: 'Partner with me, I offer a total solution to your needs'. Surely not every supplier at every level of the distribution chain can offer the total solution and long-term strategic partnership to every customer? Companies are in conflict between their heads, which leads them to commit to open systems and partnering with competitors where client needs justify it, and their hearts, which desire to own the end customer and provide the total solution.

ForeFront believes this delayering of distribution will continue with the following consequences for the 1990s:

- Companies will continue to contract out sales, marketing and service functions to focus on their unique competencies and maintain a competitive cost structure.
- Some companies will learn to share ownership of the end customer to remain credible with customers, retain important distribution partners and avoid needless marketing wars.
- Those who traditionally have not been perceived as solution sellers will develop more sophisticated marketing and selling skills to communicate their competencies both to customers and the rest of the distribution chain. VARs, local telcos (telecom companies) and cable TV companies could become, in their industry, as Sainsbury and Tesco are to consumer goods.
- Technology and deregulation will assist delayering in telecommunications so that it increasingly resembles the computer industry. Telcos will need new skills and cost structures to compete.

ANALYSIS

Breaking up the market leaders

Pre-1980s, computing was dominated by vertically integrated systems sellers and telephony by national public operators (PTTs). Technology helped break their dominance. Systems' intelligence moved from large central sites to big company sites, to the desks of corporate managers and is now moving into homes and small businesses. The democratization of intelligence created opportunities for new competitors in hardware, software, communications, systems design and services.

Computing saw a migration from large mainframes, through minicomputers, to client–server architecture. Each change was led by successive new companies in a cycle of David and Goliath encounters. Similar changes are occurring in telecommunications where the most sophisticated customers boast of better international network management systems than do most telcos. The pace of change has been slower than in computing, and this could be due to continued government regulation in many key world markets (e.g. Germany).

The interviewees came from newly deregulated telecommunications companies and market leading IT companies prominent in the new forms of computing.

Changes in distribution – the computing model

The companies interviewed did not have the marketing, distribution and servicing resources of the integrated vendors they challenged. They built their businesses through a pyramid shaped distribution network that developed the market, trained the service engineers, sold the solution packages and often staffed the help lines (Figure 12.1).

In the late 1980s, the large vendors interviewed took a conscious decision to move closer to the customer and take responsibility for marketing. Their products were becoming industry standards and they felt that existing distribution arrangements limited their

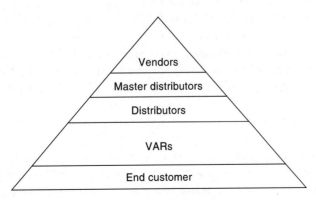

Figure 12.1 1980s computing channel structure.

volumes to the capacity of the distributor. These vendors increased channels to market, margins in the channel fell and distributors reduced marketing investments behind those products.

Successful vendors managed this transition by:

- Compensating for the declining marketing investment of the channel by adding their resources. They communicated effectively with the leading users of IT to influence the agendas of the largest corporate users: teams of industry specialists were often sent to partner with senior managers at user sites.
- As much as possible, they ensured that business was generated through the distributors, whose role was defined as logistics and cash flow management.
- Installation and maintenance of complex technologies were left in the channel. To ensure channel, partners delivered the targeted level of service, vendors built extensive dealer certification and training programmes. Novell is an outstanding example of this policy.

One of the most profound effects of the above was to build a complete network of distributors, VARs, service operators and systems integrators able to serve customers at least as competently as the traditional large systems suppliers. This layered value chain is built to serve a decentralized computing world and is inherently more flexible and cost effective than the structures it challenged for market leadership.

As channel margins fell, the distribution network was compelled to enhance its offering beyond its vendors' products, and sell it on as added value. Some of the distribution partners interviewed are trying to become sophisticated marketing organizations capable of being branded services independent of the major vendors.

Customers are now offered a wide range of choice of both brands and the partners to help them implement new technologies. This report suggests that end-customers will first determine who will be their prime partner: the vendors' brand of hardware or software, the VAR who can deliver and service the final solution, or the systems integrator who can create competitive advantage through technology.

Thus, customers determine their purchasing strategy after their overall information strategy. Vendors now operate a channel policy that allows end customers to buy their goods according to customers' purchase strategy and not on the old push-down model. The rest of the value chain must react in a manner that supports the customer decision and avoids duplication of effort through the chain.

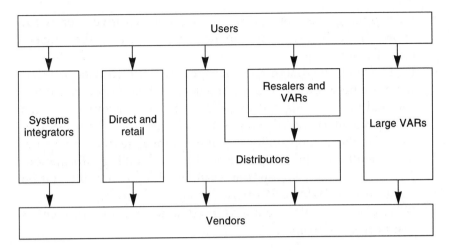

Figure 12.2 Modern computing channel structure.

Modern computer channel management might therefore look like Figure 12.2.

Telecommunications

This article suggests that telecommunications (telecoms) will follow the computing model. However it should be noted that there are two historical factors to account for:

1. Governments still restrain competition, although this will abate.
2. Telecoms has a completely different starting point to computing. Voice telephony began as a system of real time, desk to desk communications operating through universal standards. Whilst the system's functionality was very limited, the telephone industry had achieved some of the computer industry's goals many years ago.

Nonetheless, those interviewed felt that leading corporate customers are driving the industry into part of a larger, integrated information industry. As a consequence, computing's progress exposes the limitations of the PTTs and their traditional public switched networks:

- Functionality offered to even sophisticated users over the public telephone network was limited to the lowest common denominator to ensure ubiquity of service.

- PTT pricing was not sufficiently volume sensitive, nor is the evolution of the price/performance curve matching the efficiencies of computing.
- PTTs could not design and manage international data or infrastructure networking across countries for their customers. International negotiations had to be done by the customer between every two international end points in the network. The customer took on the responsibility for international network management, fault reporting, repair procedures and billing information. PTTs failed to develop the systems design and integration abilities of an IBM, CSC or Andersen.
- PTTs traditionally were not as good at account management as computing companies.

The first delayering of telecoms was to multinationals building private networks over leased lines. This allowed for the high speed data transmission their computers demanded, controlled costs and permitted customers to develop the international network management that national telcos were not organized to build.

Some of the largest private networks are now international telecoms companies in their own right and are competing with national telcos, where permitted, for other customers' business: e.g. MDIS (McDonnell Douglas Information Systems), GEISCO (General Electric Information Systems Co.), SITA, CEDAL and SWIFT. One telco executive commented that SWIFT and SITA look more like telcos than like the banks or airlines that respectively own and run those two organizations. This view was strongly endorsed by a SITA executive who felt that SITA's 200 country network and specialized applications in travel and related services provides SITA with a long term and defensible position in the market.

Deregulation in the UK is creating the next layer in the chain. Like their computing counterparts in the early 1980s, new competitors like Mercury did not have BT's resources and direct access to millions of homes and small businesses. Mercury formed relationships with cable TV companies to deliver and service hundreds of thousands of residential customers cost effectively. BT has largely retained the fully integrated supply structure that proved so costly for large computing companies.

A senior Mercury executive commented that a successful channel strategy is one that changes the basis for competition in the industry. As delayering takes hold in telecommunications, the channel mapping looks like the diagram in Figure 12.3.

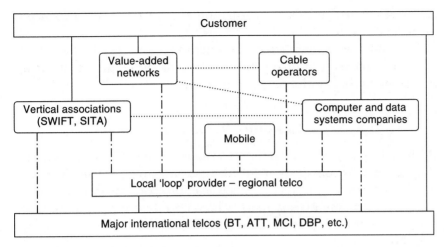

Figure 12.3 Delayered channel structure.

Like computing, customers have increased choice of whom to select as their prime contractor for all or some of their telecoms. Layers of distribution are developing into sophisticated marketing organizations offering solutions to customers that were once the exclusive territory of the PTT.

The vertically specialized players like SITA, SWIFT and value added networks like CompuServe offer specialized applications, software, security and cost sharing benefits that the major international telcos are hard pressed to match. To compete for that business with the customers, the telcos would need to develop the systems and software capabilities of computing services companies like Andersen, CSC and EDS and it is questionable whether they can.

Data network suppliers like IBM, Digital, Unisys and large companies' in-house resources have traditionally been limited to interconnection of computers. Deregulation and technical changes will likely allow them to add voice, image and video to their established networking skills, making them very serious competitors with traditional telcos. These companies understand corporate networking better than the old PTTs. Modern deregulated telcos are investing in acquiring these skills and see data network suppliers as a key competitive threat.

Interviewees in the telecommunications industry suggested that the telecom share of large companies' total information budget is 10–20%. In a deregulated world of free-flowing digitized information, customers are more likely to turn to computing companies for integrated voice and data information system design and management.

The cable companies offer a broader range of service possibilities than telcos have traditionally been allowed to, although restructuring and deregulation is blurring the distinction.

Customer domination

Both industries are becoming customer-driven. Choice, technical change, internationalization of business and government deregulation have been key drivers in this transition from the domination of the integrated systems suppliers. There is no reason to assume those key drivers will change in the next few years.

In both industries:

- Vertically integrated monopolies or near-monopolies are eroding.
- New layers of distribution were established to provide competition and, over time, these layers have been transformed into solutions providers capable of providing more customized and intimate service than are the vendors they once supported.
- The customer has greater choice of solutions providers than ever.

IMPLICATIONS FOR MARKETERS

Fight for the end customer

The model describes a situation where all the levels of distribution are now positioning themselves as total solutions providers to the end customer. Ownership of the end customer is hotly contested territory and not every company can credibly support this position. Whilst striving for prime partner status with the customer where competencies justify this role, companies will have to be effective sub-contractors for others where customer needs so mandate. It is imperative in such a world that all companies make themselves known for a competitive set of competencies, both with end customers and distribution players. Corporate branding and finding a unique and defensible position based on the competencies are top priorities for all information industry marketers.

Computer vendors and telcos are increasingly marketing driven and focused on end customers. Substantial investments are being made by companies like Intel, Compaq, Microsoft, Vodafone,

Mercury and IBM in not only the information systems departments of large corporations, but senior executives and sophisticated users who influence those departments.

Distributors and VARs, despite being significant comperes, are largely unknown outside the IS and purchasing departments. Traditionally they added value through logistics and service and there was no need for greater awareness or corporate branding. As they expand their role in the industries, they will need a different set of conversations with a different level and type of management.

Retailers will play an increasing role with small offices and home users.

Flexing

In reality, no single level of the chain can be prime partner for all customer problems, so the subset of customers for whom any competitor can be prime partner is limited. Few firms can commercially sustain a policy of not participating with customers who choose other prime partners. Therefore most companies must accept that they will operate in a variety of modes from strategic business partner to commodity supplier. Companies, and their customer-facing people, will need to operate across these modes simultaneously, a term called 'style flexing' within the human resources establishment.

Flexing allows a company to be credible as a partner with senior managers on some projects, whilst being seen as a willing supplier on low value-added work to junior managers at the same time. Getting it wrong risks alienating a group of buyers and limiting the scope of business the market judges you suitable for.

Preferred partner status

Channels become channels for other channels, and vendors can become channels for their channels; the market is this confused. If a company cannot always be the prime partner, and thus directly control its destiny, the next best position is to be the preferred partner (supplier) to a company that is often the prime partner to customers.

If outsourcing becomes as popular with customers as many predict, vendors and telcos will need to build relationships with firms specializing in outsourcing. Conversely, as some vendors become very influential, then other vendors and distributors will want to be recommended by them.

There is activity in this area already, for example:

- Major software vendors have partnership programmes with smaller software vendors and VARs using their programme as input into the final product.
- Sophisticated vendors and telcos provide sales support for IT consultants through product literature, education seminars and special help lines.
- Local telcos sell and service other larger international telcos world-wide, outsourcing products or data networks. They would rather have the traffic even if they don't own the customer.

The role of marketing

In most of the companies ForeFront researched, channel decisions are made by sales establishments who are expert at qualifying distributors and the tough price/volume negotiations in which few marketers get involved. Given that channel policy is of paramount importance to an organization's corporate positioning and marketing strategy, ForeFront suggests marketers must get involved in channel management. There is a strong case for the marketing department to be prominent in defining who is the customer, at which level of the channel the company will compete and how services will be branded through the chain and planning effective joint marketing activities with channel partners. Channel marketing cannot be a small footnote amongst the four Ps in the information industries.

Cost structures, focus, specialization and outsourcing

In a world where partnering is the norm, companies will focus their resources on core competencies where they add value and outsource high overhead areas to those who operate more cost-effectively. These areas include selling, supply, installation, service and marketing communications. If no one company can supply a total solution to end customers, then no one company can afford building the capabilities to do so and remain cost competitive.

Whilst this restructuring is not unique to the information industry, arguably it is most advanced in computing where the study found all of the market leading vendors outsourcing substantial and strategic parts of their product. Examples included software vendors looking to outsource customer help lines and parts of their sales function, a large hardware manufacturer contracting out the role of marketing director and most vendors outsourcing their inventory management and collection functions to distributors.

The 'new' telecommunications companies interviewed are very much in the computing model. However, the author of this study suggests that the largest telcos seem to prefer building total solutions in-house, and partner more through acquisition than true sharing arrangements. This study questions that policy and suggests that they will find themselves with structures that are too costly and complex compared with their new competitors, particularly as telecommunications becomes more a part of the information world than a public utility.

CONCLUSIONS

Marketing in the information industries will not escape the discipline imposed on the rest of the economy. Companies must identify where they want to be positioned on the value/distribution chain vis-à-vis the customer and the industry. This positioning must be clearly communicated and marketers must avoid catch-all positioning statements of 'total solution' and 'customer driven'. Few companies have been focused enough in their thinking to achieve this, and few marketing departments have forced the issue in their companies.

Telecommunications companies will confront a shakeout akin to that in computing. The large international carriers, international data network suppliers and vertical targeted services are all on a confrontation course over ownership of the multinational customer. The traditional telco is disadvantaged in this contest; telecommunications represents a small share of the total information budget, telcos are not traditionally good at account management or developing integrated information systems for individual customers and their cost structures are probably not as lean as those of successful computing companies. The experience of the computer world suggests that they avoid the temptation to develop all the skills they lack in-house in favour of partnering with others in the value chain; namely systems integrators and VARs.

Companies closest to the customer, VARs, retailers, direct manufacturers in computing and specialist suppliers of telecommunications services must market themselves as well as the known vendors they are looking to compete with for share of customers' attention. Proximity to the customer and involvement in the implementation of technology change gives them much greater ability to develop powerful client relationships than those further up the chain. To date, few have taken the opportunity to position themselves as strategic partners with large corporations and to do so would require an investment in awareness-building amongst a new target group and sophisticated selling skills.

Stan Maklan is an independent marketer and founder of ForeFront, which promotes brand marketing disciplines within business-to-business companies. He has an MBA from the University of Western Ontario and has worked at a senior level for Unilever (as marketing director of Elida Gibbs), Cable & Wireless and Burson-Marsteller.

PART FOUR

AT THE TOP

Careers

INTRODUCTION

IT marketing is seldom regarded as a career. If you are a top salesperson or accountant, there may be a seat on the board. You can tell your grandchildren with some pride what you did during the dying years of the twentieth century.

But marketing? Marketing is a job that people either drift into, get pushed into or take on because a life selling on the road has finally got to them and they are in flight from it. Some people who get the marketing director or planning job simply feel they have been 'stitched up'. Chances are that you will never be in it long enough to ever feel that it defined your career.

That's a gloomy assessment considering that there is now another story to tell that is equally true.

Most companies will now say that marketing's importance is growing. Others want to be regarded as marketing- or market-led. The Marketing Group at the CSSA and the Institute of Marketing see a bright future for both marketing and the marketing professional. At the CSA's October 1994 marketing conference, there were 170 delegates. At least three recruitment consultancies owe their business to IT marketing alone.

And ask the few successful marketing directors who made the job their first choice what they think and they will generally say that no other job is so involved in every aspect of the organization's business and so critical to its success. They may even tell you how much they earn and you may start to see your own future in a more optimistic light.

For those of you contemplating putting an end to it all and changing careers, take heart from Leach and Sanders.

New Strategies for Marketing Information Technology.
Edited by Christopher Field
Published in 1996 by Chapman & Hall, London. ISBN 0 412 61520 7

Eric Leach asks, 'What makes a good marketer?' and shows that the successful marketing director needs an intimidatingly broad range of skills as well as large amounts of natural ability, not least common sense.

Dr Jerry Sanders traces the history of marketing and finds that empires were founded on its most basic principles.

13

WHAT MAKES A GOOD
IT MARKETER?

Eric Leach

What is a good IT marketer? Have you met one recently? Would you
know one if you met one? I haven't met many good ones – and I've
been in IT since 1967, in fact since long before the term 'IT' was even
invented.

It should be no surprise to anyone that there are few good IT
marketers. Who would have trained them? What books would they
have read? What chance do they have of becoming Managing
Directors? Would they be paid as much as (or more than) good IT
salespeople?

In this chapter I'll give you my personal opinions on what makes a
good IT marketer.

THE UK IT MARKETING CONTEXT

Many UK IT vendors are predominantly remote sales outlets for
foreign (mainly US) based manufacturers. These foreign manufacturers may have a marketing strategy – unfortunately quite a few of
them have only a sales strategy. And, of the few who do have a
marketing strategy, their strategy may not translate successfully to
the UK market.

New Strategies for Marketing Information Technology.
Edited by Christopher Field
Published in 1996 by Chapman & Hall, London. ISBN 0 412 61520 7

The people running these remote UK sales operations are normally successful salespeople. This is easy to understand as, when you set up a remote sales operation, you need a technical person and a salesperson to get it going. The salesperson is the one who is seen to be bringing in the money and so he or she is normally made the boss. Also, typically, salespeople 'sell' themselves better than technical people.

Indigenous IT companies are often a bunch of technical people who have got together and built something and then gone out on the road to sell it. So, in these companies, a technical person will be the boss.

In both the remote IT sales operations and indigenous IT manufacturing scenarios it is unlikely that an IT marketer will be involved in the birth of the UK company. There are very few UK IT Managing Directors who have come up the marketing route and, consequently, there are very few who have a marketing-centred view of the world.

SKILLS AND EXPERIENCE REQUIREMENTS

Here are some of the requirements for a good IT marketer:

- knowledge of the IT marketplace and IT customer needs;
- good grounding in the concepts of marketing;
- knowledge of, and experience of using, marketing communications (marcom) techniques (direct mail, PR, advertising, seminars, direct marketing, research, sales and presentation material);
- knowledge and experience of channel and partnership marketing;
- experience in product pricing;
- ability to create and acquire an adequate budget;
- ability to prioritize;
- ability to 'get on' with many different kinds of people;
- creativity;
- skill with words;
- technical background;
- not a sales background;
- skill at selling ideas at all levels;
- being a member of the marketing infrastructure pertaining to his/her market sector;
- inspirational leadership;
- common sense.

KNOWLEDGE OF THE IT MARKET, THE CUSTOMER AND IT MARCOM

It's difficult to get this knowledge from a book. Knowledge can only be gained by working in the IT marketplace, finding and listening to mentors and by reading newsletters, newspapers and magazines.

Whether your customer is an end user, an IT Director or a reseller, it's obviously important that you should continuously monitor what their needs are. Having once been a customer certainly helps. It also helps to be able to talk to customers in a language that they understand.

Generic marketing communications experience is useful, but IT marketing communications experience is vital.

PUBLIC RELATIONS

Whether you use a PR agency or not, you have to understand how the press operates. The UK IT trade press is large – second only in size to the healthcare press – and it's also aggressive, well-informed and hates 'bullshit' and lies (lie to one journalist and you've lied to them all). In addition, the UK press is not completely parochial. For example, APT's 'Unigram.X', whose origins lie in London's Soho, is very well read in the USA.

The ability to handle the press is a skill that can be learned – certain personal traits, however, make one better (or worse) equipped to do it well (Table 13.1).

We live in a very connected world and the public relations process involves the whole of the infrastructure of your particular sector (more on this later).

Table 13.1 Ability to handle the press

Good traits	Bad traits
Gregarious	Unsociable
You like journalists	You dislike journalists
Articulate	Shy
Enthusiastic	'Sales' persona
Honest	Dishonest/inconsistent
Like smoky pubs	Dislike smoky pubs
Know what you are talking about	Try to bluff

ADVERTISING

Regis McKenna, the high priest of IT marketing, described and analysed the obsolescence of advertising in his famous 'Marketing is Everything' paper in the January/February 1991 issue of the *Harvard Business Review*. In this piece, McKenna exposes ' . . . advertising's dirty little secret: it serves no useful purpose'.

Good IT marketers are, and should be, profoundly suspicious of advertising. It's expensive, inflexible, difficult to adapt and unresponsive.

I do have some sympathy with some IT marketers who are brave enough to admit that they spend money on advertising primarily because it stops salespeople complaining that marketing is doing nothing to help them.

SEMINARS

Direct mail based seminar marketing has been the tried and tested method for generating leads for high value hardware and software products in the UK for over 10 years. Good lists, regularly refreshed with new lists, are one of the keys to successful seminar attendance.

RESEARCH

All good IT marketers are keen on research – on two levels. Firstly, they will buy the best research available on their target market. They will also meet end users (and resellers, if relevant) on a regular basis. They will continually test their market assumptions against reality. They know that what customers think and need today will not necessarily hold true in six months' time.

ORGANIZATIONAL CONTEXT

The Marketing Director needs to be a Board Member. And there also needs to be a Sales Director on the Board. What you don't want is a Sales and Marketing Director – and here, courtesy of Bob Rockwell, Chief Technology Officer of Softlab GmbH, is why:

> Putting one person in charge of marketing and sales is not a wise move. Marketing is long term, sales is short term. The

person appointed will be good at only one of the disciplines (probably sales). So very often where you have a Sales and Marketing Director, there is no one (at Board level) running marketing. If marketing must be teamed with another function, make it research and development maybe, but never sales.

The UK recession has brought about the downsizing of many UK subsidiaries of foreign based IT companies, and they have become just sales offices. The marketing component has been removed, or reduced to the 'Tracey/Justin' level, i.e. the girl or boy who used to be the MD's Personal Assistant who has been promoted into running the marketing/marcom/PR/ad 'thing'. (It's interesting that they are never given the R&D or Finance 'thing' to run.)

A successful IT marketer in the UK office of a foreign high tech vendor will have to be skilled at dealing with foreign HQ management. He or she needs to have the knowledge and people handling skills to persuade foreign management to allocate sufficient budget and allow local implementation flexibility. They must be strong enough to resist the pressures imposed by the foreign HQ to implement marketing programmes and messages which are inappropriate to the local geography.

INFRASTRUCTURE

Every market sector has its own marketing infrastructure. Members of this infrastructure normally include:

- trade associations
- press
- consultants
- conference and exhibition organizers
- research companies
- publishers
- recruitment agencies
- user groups
- partners
- suppliers
- competitors
- users
- resellers
- PR agencies.

You need to be part of the infrastructure for your market sector. If it is a new sector, then you need to be instrumental in creating the infrastructure.

I have been lucky enough to have had the opportunity to contribute to the creation of the object technology infrastructure in the UK. Other individuals (e.g. Samit Khosla of Andersen Consulting), suppliers (e.g. Object Designers), publishers (e.g. SIGS Publications) and trade associations (e.g. The British Computer Society) have also been instrumental in the creation and development of this infrastructure. My company established The Object Management Group (OMG) in the UK and also launched and runs the Object World UK trade show. OMG is now the world's largest software development consortium with over 420 members – 26 of them in the UK. Over a five-year period, we also 'exposed' over 30 UK journalists to the nature and importance of object technology. Over this time the infrastructure has grown not just nationally, but globally. The availability and use of the Internet has been a major enabling component of this infrastructure.

Last year, in association with two other people, I helped form a cross-platform user group called VISUAL, and have run the object technology user forum within VISUAL. As part of Object World UK we have produced, (in 1993 and again in 1994), a major, unique research study on the state of Object Technology in the UK. Selling these studies at a low price has led to wide dissemination of information throughout the object technology infrastructure. We have worked with recruitment agencies, publishers, suppliers, PR agencies (competitors!), users and trade associations. And, whether they know it or not, all these organizations are part of the object technology infrastructure in the UK.

I tell this story, not to blow my own trumpet, but as a living, breathing example of UK IT marketing infrastructure creation and development.

Infrastructures should not be cartels or exclusive groups, they should be open and organic. The smart IT marketers know that these infrastructures support multiple, multi-faceted relationships. For example, one day you are competing with an individual from another company for a sale and the next day you are sitting next to them at a trade association meeting. And then, the following month, you find out that your two companies are partners in a big systems integration deal. The next month you share a stage with them in a debate at a conference, in which you are both on the same side, and so on.

One thing we have all learned in IT in the last few years is that no one company can satisfy all an organization's IT needs. The IT industry is still very new, very immature and very dynamic.

Above all the other key attributes of an IT marketer, he or she must be adept at forming and nurturing partnerships with other IT suppliers. To make these partnerships work takes a range of skills and experience. These include a blend of deal making, technical, people, creative and flexibility skills. An IT marketer must be able to form peer relationships with partners.

The 1990s will be the era of business peer relationships – one day selling to a peer, the next day buying from the same peer. The good IT marketer of the 1990s will have to be a master at – to borrow some IT jargon – peer to peer networking.

Eric Leach owns Eric Leach Marketing (ELM). He started as a software developer for Plessey and Sperry Univac. Since 1979, he has worked as a marketing and PR consultant specializing in IT. His clients have included BT, Data General, DEC, Hoskyns, Information Builders, Ingres, Pacific Telesis, Unisys and Wang. ELM, founded in 1983, is a well-established high-tech PR agency which also represents the interests of OMG and Object World Expositions in the UK.

14

THE NEW COLONIALS MEET SANDERS' PARADOX

Jerry Sanders

These few words are an attempt to outline the macroeconomic, political and social links which bind marketing activity and information technology into a tight feedback loop. Use it as a swift refresher romp through economic history, and amaze your friends and clients with your grasp of past, present and future affairs.

But also use it to remind yourself of this: that amongst all the professions in which a marketing expert could choose to practice, the IT marketer enjoys one of the most critical – and thus influential – roles in the development of not just their company's future but also that of the world economic model. If you ever feel in danger of losing sight of your job satisfaction, this chapter might just help to get you back into top gear.

Let's establish a first principle. For marketing to succeed, one particular condition emerges above all others. There must be one or more colonies of willing consumers, not merely receptive to your message, but able to consume.

Information technology has replaced the ocean-going ship as the tool for acquiring colonies of consumers. But there have been signs

New Strategies for Marketing Information Technology.
Edited by Christopher Field
Published in 1996 by Chapman & Hall, London. ISBN 0 412 61520 7

that, by reducing the working population, it is reducing the availability of disposable income with which to consume.

This is the paradox which marketers and information technology suppliers, in the long term, ignore at their peril.

EVANGELISM AND COLONIALISM

In the 1990s, just as in 90 AD, the influence of a man of thirty-something dominates the development of the Western World.

In the 1990s though, this 30-year-old is different. He isn't teaching that the meek will inherit the earth. In fact the gospel according to Saint William says that the strong, the forward-looking and the bold can, should and will elbow anyone without a PC on their desk out of the way.

Where his predecessor threw the businessmen out through the temple door, Saint William is holding the temple gates wide open and calling them all back in.

As professionals in the information technology business, you are all apostles of the information age. You know from experience that there's no better job security for you today than to partner with the corporate IT specialist who backs the right technology and delivers competitive advantage to the board.

Often, that means technology that increases efficiency and reduces cost, including the greatest cost of all: the work force.

A CAUTIONARY TALE

The father of the modern factory production line, Henry Ford, was born of native Irish stock. Henry, on a visit to Cork, was greeted by a group of men who welcomed him to his parents' birthplace and asked him to make a donation in their memory for a new hospital. Ford graciously made out a cheque for $5,000 and they thanked him.

The next day the Cork newspaper announced incorrectly that Ford had made a $50,000 donation. The men returned to Ford's hotel room with the editor of the daily to apologize for the mistake and promised the newspaper would publish a correction.

Instead, Ford asked the men to return the cheque. He wrote them a new cheque for $50,000 which he handed over with only one request. 'Over the portals of this hospital', Ford said, 'I want an inscription I have in mind.'

To this day, the inscription carved in stone reads: 'I came amongst you and you took me in.'[1]

Working people, both blue and white collar, are beginning to believe IT has now been doing just that for a generation. Today every IT professional you deal with is probably aware that they are likely to make, in their own lifetime, a contribution to the unemployment statistics. If they're very good, and are well-advised, the jobs that go won't be their own. Today's cruel aphorism is: 'Measure the success of your customer by the number of other people's jobs he wastes.'

If that sounds nasty and brutish, cast your minds back a generation. There were no PCs in the swinging sixties, but the magazines, newspapers, economists and politicians were all full of a crazy, science fiction notion: 'automation is coming, computers will empty the factories of human workers, prepare for the leisure society' they said.

Factory automation was a great creator of employment, and fuelled economic growth in the school textbook way: it took land (to build factories), added capital (to fill them with machine tools), hired labour (to produce value-added output).

National, and now corporate, wealth depended on the coexistence of two conditions: adding value to raw materials and components, thus permitting them to be resold at a profit; and consumers with disposable incomes able to buy the very things they had made – something the first industrial revolution, which replaced rural poverty with urban poverty, did not achieve.

Today, PCs are commodities. With rare exceptions, the economic and producing power of a modern corporation lies more in its intellectual and service capabilities than in its hard assets – land, plant and equipment.[2] Increasingly we have the leisure, but not the leisure society.[3]

It's one of the great ironies of the nineties that, thanks to official foresight, the ten-year DSS operational strategy rightly anticipated an enormous increase in the colony of people claiming benefits today, and created a national computer system powerful enough to dispense those benefits to all who needed them. What they didn't foresee was that the nation would be too poor to pay them. Why not?

MARKETING – THE NEW COLONIALS

We've all heard the cliché that today's technologies make the world a smaller place. It's true. And in that small world, some major economic drivers that have worked for almost two thousand years are going up in the historical equivalent of a puff of smoke – access to new markets and acting on inside information.

Real-time datafeeds handled by commodity microprocessors let more and more brokers trade less and less profitably in real businesses. Capital has less and less of substance to mate with, and as the avalanche of derivatives shows, we now bet at three, four or five removes from investments of substance.

Today's investment possibilities begin to look increasingly sterile when compared with the fabulous promise of return – and enormous risk – offered by Christopher Columbus to Queen Isabella of Castille.

It seems that capital has less and less opportunity to reproduce; which is why developed nations are dismantling their family silver, selling public concerns for cash to reduce budget deficits. Capital stops being able to reproduce itself when there are no workers to exploit, when there's no demand for land, and when opportunities for insider trading are closed out.

The rise to prominence, power and business authority of the marketing professions can be logged alongside the elimination from the world's economic model of the territories known as 'the colonies'.

The great invention of 1492 was colonialism: and the Catholic soldiers and priests were the marketers of the renaissance. Centuries later, the Industrial Revolution added physical goods to the spiritual and natural exports of the colonial powers and the colonies themselves gave us large markets for our greatly increased production capacity.

By 1776 Adam Smith was in a position to see exactly how the commercial world market was evolving. 'To found a great empire for the sole purpose of raising up a people of customers, may at first sight appear a project fit only for a nation of shopkeepers. It is however, a project altogether unfit for a nation of shopkeepers . . . but extremely fit for a nation whose government is influenced by shopkeepers.'[4]

The colonies required two business enablers, ships and their captains, to transport the goods and repatriate the wealth; and administrators to keep the natives subdued and give the plantation owners legal back-up when they revolted or protested.

Of course, colonialism started getting a bad press long before information technology became a major business development tool. In 1954 segregation in US schools was ruled to be unconstitutional. And in 1960 Harold MacMillan's Wind of Change speech in Cape

Town shocked his listeners by acknowledging the inevitability of independence throughout Africa.

Soon, far from providing UK businesses with markets, the former colonies and commonwealths were exporting their goods to Europe, often undercutting home-grown produce. By the 1950s a system of government subsidies was already at work trying to protect UK farmers from going out of business, and by the 1970s the former European colonial powers attempted to create an artificial Common Market for protection, complete with 350 million captive consumers.

As the prospect of untapped, virgin colonial markets began to fade, as the real need to protect existing markets was felt, a curious change overcame the business process. The persistence of manufactured goods unaccountably began to decline, and television advertising gave marketers a direct and regular line into the domestic budget negotiations. In the post-war 1950s, the consumer society restored market scope – provided goods didn't last too long. Hence the experiences with which we are all familiar: purchases that fall to pieces or need servicing literally days after the warranty expires. Hence the invention of paper underwear, washing machines, walkmans and, quintessentially, information, that most hyper-perishable of products.

No sooner is information acquired, it becomes obsolete. Fuelled by electronics we have finally begun to kick off the new waves of consumerism and service industries based around the electronic devices we need to handle information. And to restore the colonies of consumers, enter the mighty database, the modern-day equivalent of Columbus' Peru, of Victoria's India.

WHAT'S AHEAD

If the current socio-political upheavals tell us one thing, it's that there is no going back. Though the old colonial powers continue to fantasize, out of the tragedies of Bosnia, Rwanda, Sudan, Somalia and countless others, colonial opportunities of the old style will not emerge.

But we can expect that, by the year 2000, politically incorrect old colonialism will have successfully been substituted, courtesy of information technology, by ultra-correct new colonialism. The connection between old colonialism and ultra-modern technology can be summed up in one word – markets.

The social and ideological evils of colonialism are likely dead and buried, and most will say good riddance. But what of the economic good – the large new markets that fuel economic growth? Now that the manipulation of entire native populations is adjudged intolerable, how are business to sustain not only large communities of existing customers, but new colonies of virgin consumers?

Business today knows that the products and services you can provide are the answer. Instead of sending the fleet out to uncharted lands and unknown populations, prospects and leads can now be collected from amongst all known peoples, and held, sustained, analysed and prospected as pure data.

Tomorrow's successful businesses will define themselves by the number of customers and transactions they can afford to service. Today only the largest organizations have the capability to manage millions of customers' records. Yet such is the rate of change in IT products that by the year 2000 every ambitious business in the UK, large or small, will have a dataset containing fine-grain details of every member of every UK, or perhaps even European, household.

Information about their incomes, likes and dislikes, hobbies and interests will be constantly updated from all manner of data sources.

Each year on their birthdays, salary review dates or other key lifetime moments, automatic routines could trigger relationships with campaigns for different product types. When a teenager in a household with a professional, golf-playing mother turns 16 and a half, they could start receiving direct mail from car, car insurance and related businesses aiming to influence their motoring preferences, and increase the pressure on Mum and Dad to release the funds.

The database holds the key to identifying, subjugating and exploiting new colonies of consumers. A new swathe of companies will thus be able to practice service-driven prospecting on ever-larger colonies of consumers.

Or will they? We here make one important assumption, and in doing so arrive at Sanders' Paradox. We are assuming, at all times, that the consumers continue to be able to consume: but as we have already seen, in our survey of macroeconomic, social and political evolution, the very computers that hold and manipulate the new colonies have the unfortunate habit of eating jobs and bankrupting administrations. Fewer jobs equals less disposable income, equals less consumption.

As Sanders' Paradox states: the number of consumers available to the marketplace varies in inverse proportion to the aggregate number of citizen's records manipulated in the totality of vendor databases.

This may seem an exaggeration of what will happen in the real world, but it serves to describe a clearly tight feedback loop that links information technology marketing and business success so intimately, and explains why, if you think competition for the hearts and minds of your own customers is already fierce, 'you ain't seen nothing yet'.

Jerry Sanders is the editor of *Computing*, the weekly magazine that last year won the UK Press Gazette award for Best Editorial Team (Weekly Title). He is a former news editor of *Microscope*, editor of *PC User* and launched *Parallelogram*, the international journal of parallel and super computing.

PART FIVE

STRETCHING THE SINEWS OF WAR

Budgeting

INTRODUCTION

Large budgets and large departments are still the official indicators of the relative success of the marketing director's career. The budget therefore is still regarded by most marketers as the foundation on which all marketing is built. Many directors owe their success to their budgeting and presentation skills.

Civil services appear to have taught businesses all they need to know about budgeting – ask for more than you want, get more than you need and make damn sure you spend it all before year end. Then ask for more because, you say, you didn't get enough last year. All this is well documented and IT marketers need look no further than any how-to book available at all mainline railway station news-agents.

These books will confirm that the machismo of a large budget goes a long way to convince the board that good things are going on in marketing, particularly if the department is engaged in other classic money-eating techniques such as the BIG EVENT. The big event used to be something like a product launch that had such a high profile in the company that no one got around to finding out what impact it had on the target market. However, big budgets and skilled budgeting may soon become redundant.

Every department in the organization now has to fight that much harder for money and come up with more convincing measurement indicators than ever before. Marketing must do the same but often has the added disadvantage of not being regarded as essential in the first place. Well-produced and well-argued budget proposals are unlikely to be enough.

Moreover, marketing itself may be changing such that there may be no budget to argue for in the first place. More and more elements

New Strategies for Marketing Information Technology.
Edited by Christopher Field
Published in 1996 by Chapman & Hall, London. ISBN 0 412 61520 7

in the marketing box of tricks are likely to be distributed to other departments until marketing as it is understood now will vanish. Business units now have the technology and the budgets to produce literature and other marketing collateral. Some are promoting their own salespeople into discrete, highly-focused marketing roles. Others are organizing small-scale customer sales events. Unless the marketing director is pulling all the strings in this budget-diminished scenario, their empire may vanish.

Some of the authors of this book are already talking about the post-marketing department organization, about the marketing-led organization where every employee is involved in marketing. They describe marketing as a spirit that drives the organization. Controlling, budgeting and measuring marketing in that environment are skills yet to be defined.

Concept 20:20's research gives a clue to some of the changes and looks at what IT companies spend their marketing budgets on, and the changes. We can already see that generally the IT industry is taking marketing more seriously and that traditional methods such as advertising and large trade shows are no longer popular.

Michael Spring of Oracle says that it is all to easy to divide marketing up into its component parts, PR, advertising, direct mail, publishing, below-the-line and so on, attach a sum of money to each, tack on some market research and take the whole budget to the board. Although it works, the budget is unlikely to be the sort of sum that will get the dramatic results that marketers dare not even dream of.

He offers advice to marketers seeking to justify their budget spend to the board and says that the big idea that works may just grow out of a threat: if it was your money, would you spend it?

15

PUTTING YOUR MONEY WHERE YOUR MOUTH IS – IT MARKETING TRENDS

Refocusing IT marketing

Rob Pankhurst

The steady move over the last 15 years from centralized IT bureaucracies towards distributed, desktop and portable computing has provided the ever more computer literate end user with burgeoning purchasing power. As a result, it has also presented IT companies with the constant headache of how to make contact, and create a consistent image, with a constantly increasing number of diverse vertical markets. Typical markets now range from architecture and civil engineering, through central and local government, healthcare, leisure and media, to retail, transport and distribution.

From our research, IT personnel are slowly losing control over purchasing decisions to divisional/departmental personnel. While the crucial evaluation and recommendation of IT products and services continues to be undertaken by both IT functions and divisional/departmental personnel, IT personnel now make up only 44% of the

New Strategies for Marketing Information Technology.
Edited by Christopher Field
Published in 1996 by Chapman & Hall, London. ISBN 0 412 61520 7

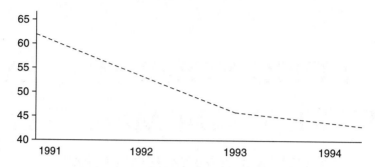

Figure 15.1 Percentage of IT personnel involved in evaluation and recommendation decisions.

decision-makers in this area, compared with well over 60% in 1991 (Figure 15.1).

The ever-growing power of the end-user departments, together with the recent recession, has forced IT companies to treat their use of available marketing tools with increasing levels of sophistication. In particular, it has forced a rethink over their use of old favourites such as advertising and exhibitions, which are often now used as image reinforcing elements of more fully integrated marketing campaigns, rather than as core activities in their own right.

THE RESEARCH

In June 1994, The Concept Company published the fourth annual *UK IT Marketing Survey* – the first and most authoritative guide to marketing activity in the industry today. It was researched and published by Concept 20:20, the research division of The Concept Company, in association with the CSA, and sponsored by VNU Business Publications. The results of the survey provide marketing executives with the information they need to plan, budget and implement highly effective marketing campaigns for their organizations.

As a marketing consultancy, we've always found that most IT companies set their marketing budgets on the basis of what they did last year and the year before. Typically, they add 10% to what they did last year, and see if they can get their new budget approved. Almost always, decisions are made, and priorities set, despite a complete lack of knowledge of what's happening in the industry overall and, in particular, how much comparable companies are spending on specific marketing activities. Because of this, we've always found it very surprising that no major research survey had ever been undertaken to give marketing decision-makers within the industry a means of correcting this problem.

As a result, in 1990, we undertook the first survey into this area, with a long-term view of making it an annual survey, offering IT companies an intelligent management tool that can be used to effectively compare, and therefore plan, their expenditure on marketing activities with comparable competitive companies.

An example of the possible benefits comes from our experience of PR pitches. Typically, the client will ask the agencies pitching for their account, 'What should I do and how much should I spend?' As a result, they receive proposals from different agencies that differ dramatically in cost and depth of service, with no means of knowing which level of spend would be appropriate to a company of their type or size. By comparison, if they were able to say, 'Typically, companies of our size and in our market are spending 8% of their budget, split 60:40 between corporate and product/service PR – so what can you do for £30,000 a year?' they would retain far greater control over the cost effectiveness of an agency's pitch, and be able to make real comparisons between the quality of service that they would expect to receive.

From another point of view, what do you do if you or your marketing department has to adjust its marketing budget, and yet maintain or increase the level of sales leads that it gains from its activities? Knowing whether advertising, PR or attendance at exhibitions is more effective in achieving various marketing goals then becomes exceptionally important. Especially when you have to decide how to redistribute your marketing budget.

In order to gain the marketing information required to answer these sorts of questions, in March of 1994, we distributed a detailed questionnaire to around 7,500 identified suppliers of IT-related products and services in the UK. We received a response of approximately 2.5% of completed questionnaires, which represents a good return given the highly sensitive nature of the information requested.

Each company size and industry sector was well represented, with even a relatively high number of the very largest companies providing responses. The sample also matched reasonably closely the distribution of companies for which we have turnover and industry sector figures on our database, and the distribution of companies that responded in previous years.

The sample was large enough to allow statistical comparisons to be made regarding two main areas – changes over the next 12 months in overall industry expenditure on particular marketing activities; and the perceived relative effectiveness of each activity. Comparisons or variations across major product and market types, where applicable, have also been highlighted.

THE RESULTS

Over 65% of all IT companies now possess a formal marketing strategy – an increase from last year's (1994) 60%. By a formal marketing strategy, we mean one where a budget is allocated to a variety of marketing activities such as advertising, press relations, product/service and corporate literature, and so on, over at least the next 12 months. This increase is largely due to a decrease in the number of small companies, with turnovers of less than £500k, that have no formal marketing plan. This number has decreased from 69% to 60% of these companies.

IT companies are clearly beginning to place greater emphasis on planning and implementing marketing strategies that not only reflect their financial objectives, but also the levels of marketing expenditure by the industry overall.

UK IT companies are projecting to spend 4.9% of their annual turnover on marketing activities this year (1995) – an increase of 14% when compared with the 4.3% actually spent during the previous 12 months, which is in turn a 10% increase on actual expenditure reported in the results in last year's survey. These increases follow three years of relatively static expenditure, probably due to the recession, with levels at just below 4% of turnover.

Not all areas of the industry, however, have experienced static actual marketing expenditure. The VAR sector has displayed substantial and consistent growth over the last four years to bring their expenditure up to the industry average. These companies are expected to spend approximately 4.8% of their turnover on marketing over the next 12 months, a relative increase on the 4.2% expenditure of the last 12 months. When compared with the results from the last two years' surveys, where VARs predicted 29% and 27% increases in marketing expenditure – from 2.5% to 3.2% to 4.2% of turnover – it can be seen that this grouping of companies is expected to increase relative marketing expenditure by approximately 92% over its level in 1991.

The results

Overall marketing spend by activity

This year's survey indicates that direct marketing has very nearly removed advertising from its number one slot in attracting marketing budgets, as predicted in last year's survey. Both advertising and direct mail are expected to represent 20% of a typical company's marketing budget. However, the number of companies that spend on direct mail has been steadily increasing over the last four years, to the stage that, for the last two years, more companies have spent on direct mail than advertising.

This shift away from advertising to direct mail represents a reassessment of the relative cost-effectiveness of various marketing activities and is a reaction to a paradox that has been highlighted in our surveys over the last four years. This was that IT companies continued to spend very large proportions of their marketing budgets on high-cost media such as advertising and exhibitions, even though they perceive lower cost tools such as direct mail and PR to be much more effective in achieving their marketing goals.

This point is further reinforced by the perceived relative effectiveness of marketing activities in achieving overall marketing goals. Product/service literature, presentation material and direct mail have consistently been perceived as the most effective means by which companies can achieve their overall marketing goals, whereas advertising and exhibitions have languished in the bottom half of the rankings in this area throughout the last four years. Indeed, during the last two years, they have dropped right to the bottom of the rankings in effectiveness, with corresponding falls in relative expenditure.

General trends

The shifts in expenditure can be demonstrated when we look at the general trends in expenditure on these activities over the last four years. For example, projected spend on advertising from one year to the next has dropped significantly from 1992's high of 27% of a typical marketing budget to around 20% in 1994 (Figure 15.2).

Similarly, projected spend on exhibitions has fallen from a high of around 15% of marketing budgets in 1990 to just 10% of budgets in 1994 (Figure 15.3).

A converse increase in expenditure on telemarketing is almost certainly also taking place, with an increase from around 1% of marketing budgets being devoted to this area in 1991 to approximately 8% in 1994 (Figure 15.4). However, the relative increase may

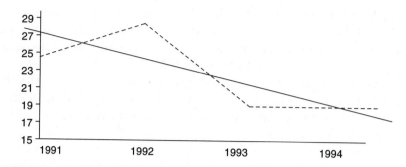

Figure 15.2   Change in expenditure on advertising.

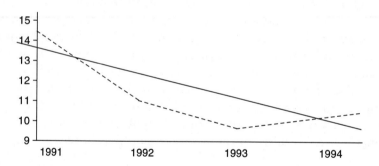

Figure 15.3   Change in expenditure on exhibitions.

be somewhat lower, because this year was the first time that a category for telemarketing was specifically included on the question-naire.

Given the cost-cutting effect of the recession, the reason for the shifts becomes clear when you look at what advertising and direct mail are actually used for within the marketing mix. Advertising is used primarily as an awareness-building tool for a relatively wide target audience, not all of whom are necessarily interested in the company or product or service in question, whereas direct market-ing, when used properly, not only builds awareness of a company and its products within a very specific target audience, but offers a more immediate response mechanism, which as a result generates a

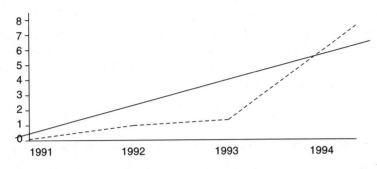

Figure 15.4 Change in expenditure on telemarketing.

higher level of sales leads per cost unit. This also explains the increasing use of telemarketing within the product/service marketing area, as a tool that cost-effectively allows companies to establish contact with and qualify their potential customer base.

It also goes a long way to explaining the declining popularity of general IT exhibitions over the last few years. The demise of the *Which Computer?* Show in 1992 is a good example of this phenomenon. A few years ago, it would have been unthinkable for the top computer companies not to attend the show in order to reinforce their corporate standing within the industry. These days, because their VARs and dealers attend the majority of the relevant exhibitions anyway, it is no longer considered as cost-effective to attend large general exhibitions that are often irrelevant to specific areas of their product/service range, when they can spend their money on attending a wide range of very targeted shows and seminar-style conference events.

Other trends that do not necessarily follow from the changing marketplace are dependent on company size, and almost certainly on their access to both appropriate budgets and marketing experience. For example, comparing this year's results with those of previous years' surveys confirms that it is the smaller companies of less than £1m p.a. turnover that spend the largest proportions of their marketing budgets on advertising, and that relative expenditure on this activity declines as a company grows. Advertising is traditionally the first marketing activity that companies undertake and, as a result, tends to remain a core activity for a large proportion of a company's growth cycle. Conversely, expenditure on activities such as seminars and sponsorship generally increases with turnover, as companies become more sophisticated in integrating their use of marketing activities. There is also a clear threshold at which IT companies typically want to reinforce their corporate standing by spending significantly more on corporate literature than all other size groupings. This has consistently been around the £3–5m turnover mark, when a company has typically built up market share in the marketplace against severe competition, and wants to use its new found corporate standing as a further differentiator.

Corporate and product/service marketing spend by activity

Marketing expenditure has consistently been split 75:25 between product/service marketing and corporate image marketing. Within these splits there is a clear differentiation between the use of different marketing activities for different goals. Direct mail and advertising dominate the marketing activities used for achieving product/service marketing goals, with direct marketing remaining the primary activity in this area, after it replaced advertising in the number one slot in last year's survey. Telemarketing is also confirmed as a recognized product/service marketing tool for IT companies, following its inclusion in the questionnaire.

By contrast, achieving corporate marketing goals requires massive investment in corporate literature, and substantially higher investment in PR campaigns, when compared with product/service marketing. This is again reflected to a large extent in the perceived effectiveness of these activities in achieving corporate identity goals, where PR and corporate literature are ranked first and third, and direct mail is ranked seventh.

WHAT IT ALL MEANS

What all these results and observations mean is that IT companies are finally putting their money where their mouths are and rethinking the scope and objectives of their marketing campaigns and the tools they use within them. Rather than just saying that activities such as advertising and exhibitions are not as effective as others in achieving various marketing goals, but continuing to spend heavily on them as core activities, IT companies are placing more emphasis on the cost-effectiveness of all activities as part of individual integrated marketing campaigns, and adjusting their budgets appropriately.

Rob Pankhurst is co-founder and joint Managing Director of The Concept Company Limited, a specialist high-tech marketing consultancy. Rob has worked for ten years in the marketing industry, seven of which have been involved with the IT industry. He has a B.A. (Hons) in Business Studies, specializing in marketing and French. He is a member of both the Chartered Institute of Marketing and the Institute of Directors; and is also an associate member of the Market Research Society, of which he holds the Society's diploma.

THE REPORT

The *UK IT Marketing Survey 1994* is available from Concept 20:20, priced at £250.00 per copy (excluding VAT).

16

MARKETING AS AN EXCHANGE OF VALUE

Michael Spring

Obviously the title didn't put you off. It's just there to show that I can use the jargon with the best of them. Actually, I'm a simple soul when it comes to marketing; for me, a good definition might be 'the application of common sense'. So maybe the title is a little too academic for what is really a brief exposition of some homespun philosophy.

First, let me start with a warning that I think is overdue. I believe (with David Ogilvy, who founded Ogilvy and Mather) that what you do may be counter-productive. Let me say that again. Your marketing efforts may actually get in the way of making sales. In Ogilvy's book, *Ogilvy on Advertising*, he quotes an occasion where Ford placed ads in alternate copies of *Reader's Digest*. At the end of the year, those exposed to the advertising bought fewer Fords than those who had not had the opportunity to see it.

Now, if that sends marketing people scurrying away to think again about how their budgets are being spent, that might, in the short term at least, be no bad thing.

Because marketing people love spending money – I know I do – budgets have to be large, because that's a measure of success and importance, just as government departments have to have huge numbers of people to justify the honours list graced by those who

New Strategies for Marketing Information Technology.
Edited by Christopher Field
Published in 1996 by Chapman & Hall, London. ISBN 0 412 61520 7

run them. In marketing, every agency, consultancy or practice you'll ever work with is saying (or at least, implying), 'Spend!'

I don't have a way to apply common sense to the particular issue of what to spend and where, but I can offer you the words of my old boss in the car business, who, when I went to him with a proposal, used to ask, 'If it was your money, would you spend it this way?'

('No, I'd hide it under the mattress.')

What I do know is that you should focus, not so much on how much your budget is, but on how you can get the best value for money in your particular sector of the business, and how your marketing campaigns should always offer something to the audiences to which they are directed.

Best value for money generally equates to asking that 'If it was your money . . .' question over and over again. It means not getting tired when someone is pursuing your budget with something you think may do no more for you than those Ford advertisements in *Reader's Digest*. It means resisting the temptation to offer sponsorship even though the person who runs the charity is persistent. It means avoiding the siren song of your agencies when they tell you how much your major competitor is spending.

The best place to start in all of this is to be as precise as you possibly can be about the issues you face and where you want your marketing to take you. ('You idiot!' – but I'll come back to that.)

Marketing has a single goal wherever it is practised. It is practised in its purest form in markets, and it is here that you see with most clarity its desired effect. This is simply to make salespeople into order-takers. The less trouble salespeople have in selling, the more they can sell.

That's why they make the Coxes apples look shiny, and put tissue paper round the cauliflowers. And that's why you are doing all that PR, placing those ads, running those seminars, sponsoring that race, or mailing chief executives. And it is the only reason, too, or ought to be.

But between you and your market is a lot of science ('segmentation', 'life cycle management', 'relationship marketing') as well as a lot of guesswork, intuition or experience, depending on your point of view. (Who can tell if people will buy more if they think better of you? Maybe they like buying from arrogant ex-double glazing sales reps?)

Well, here's where you earn your crust, because if you can find someone out there who can tell you with any certainty what qualities your marketing programme should be aiming at, buy him or her a mansion, and lock them in it. Because, while many people will be able to suggest some worthy objectives which you can hope to achieve, I've never found one who would guarantee success. If it comes to that, I've rarely found anyone willing to stay around long enough to see the effects of their advice, but maybe I've just been unlucky.

Meanwhile, it's up to you, and after all, you would want to earn your salary, wouldn't you?

It can be difficult though. I once worked for a chief executive who really believed that there was a marketing 'golden key,' something incredibly simple that you could just use to create the most astounding effect on the market, and hence guarantee the future of the company. He spent so much time searching for it that he forgot the basics (like actually working hard). And the roof gradually fell in (despite the efforts of underlings like myself to keep it propped up).

It was ironic really, since I am convinced to this day that if we had just been able to do the basic, normal, things that reading this book is stopping you from doing, we could have had a huge success on our hands.

What can I suggest as points of departure? (You'll know by now that my marketing training is as thin as my suit.)

Well, here's what I would do:

- Find out the dynamics of the market. (That's just me being flashy. In other words, what is making the market change? If it's not changing, why isn't it? When you can position yourself and your products at the centre of change, then you are a long way towards capitalizing on it.)
- Try to own the issues that matter. Sometimes you have to guess about these things, but who in the information technology business could ignore open systems, distributed computing, rightsizing, object technology or the information highway? Spring's First Law says, 'One who owns the concept, makes the sale'.
- Owning the issues means demonstrating concern for them, putting effort into shaping them and their effects, educating the market. So don't try and use them as veneer for a naff product.

On the other hand, if you really have got a good story to tell on an issue like this, tell it as widely as you can for as long as you can, or as long as it seems to you to make sense.

So what, you are probably asking yourselves, is all this 'exchange of value' stuff.

Well, what makes you read/listen to and act upon advertising? The first thing I'd put to you is humour. Even if I weren't a lager lout (actually I'm not, but only because I'm too old) I think I'd remember Carling Black Label, and confronted with a number of unknown brands, that's the one I'd pick.

But information technology isn't quite the same as packaged goods. For your customers, it can mean a long-term commitment. It can mean their job, if they take the wrong option. It can be a long and intricate process before any kind of purchasing decision gets made. (Apropos of nothing much, I remember meeting someone at a party who told me that his job was selling oil-rigs. 'How many have you sold?' I asked. He told me that he had good hopes of concluding his first sale in about three months. He'd been working on that order for five years.)

So what can you hope to achieve through marketing?

The first thing is positioning. In other words, getting a broad understanding of what it is you offer and who it is for. In some businesses, you don't have to work hard at this. A car can be for the family, for the upwardly mobile, for the outdoor lover. (On the other hand, it takes considerable insight to position your car as a 'car for winter', as Saab used to do, something they still revert back to every now and then.)

In IT, you do have to work hard at it, but it may not be obvious why.

I was on a seminar once where some people who worked in the airline business were asked what business they were in. Well, it's simple isn't it? Getting people from A to B. But one of the individuals wrote on his white board, 'Exotic locations'. When that happened, the lights went on.

For, just as airlines are about exotic locations, IT could be about getting new products off the ground (not yours, your customer's), excitement, an empowered workforce, a better relationship with your customer's customers, or whatever you are smart enough to come up with, which coincides with the broadest market appeal. (Or in other words, the issue that is taxing everyone's mind.)

So positioning is your first challenge. The second is finding ways to take up the position you want, and to do it in a way that gives your audience that 'exchange of value' that you've been waiting to hear more about.

To explain that, I'll start by talking about fish.

There's a management philosophy that divides people into three categories: carp, sharks and dolphins. (Yes, I know dolphins aren't fish, but let's not be picky.)

In this philosophy, carp are content to swim around at the bottom of the pond, hoping they can hide in a vast shoal, but knowing that some of them are going to get eaten. Sharks are concerned with getting their retaliation in first. They know that if they are going to get the food, they have to do it by fighting for it. Their gain is someone else's loss, so they have to be aggressive or die.

And then there are dolphins. Dolphins co-operate. They help each other. They communicate together. They look for solutions to problems (like getting food) which will help them all.

Despite the slightly 'brown rice' tone of all that, the search for the win/win agenda (sharks have a win/lose view, just for comparison) is what makes smart marketing.

Some years ago, I was involved in a project for Lotus, who could see that their 1–2–3 product was being used by accountants and money people, but the idea of spreadsheets wasn't really catching on with the average businessperson (in marketing, for example).

In response to this, an idea called the Lotus Business Challenge was born. It was a management competition which was run in conjunction with the Institute of Directors (lots of credibility there) and in which cross-disciplinary 'teams' from individual companies ran a fictitious company.

They did it, of course, with Lotus 1–2–3, looking at all kinds of effects of possible scenarios. They had to work together, and they all in the process found out what Lotus could do for them and their particular piece of the business.

Not only was this a huge success in terms of publicity (not least with the people who took part), but Lotus found that they could actually charge for the privilege of participating, because it was such an educational, team-building exercise.

So there they were with an income-generating positioning device ('Lotus is for business teams making decisions') which also made money. It ran for years (it may still do). I wish I could find a few more of those.

But the key was the value inherent in the exercise, which made everyone feel like they got something back.

Now, I would argue that the actual value can be small or large. It doesn't so much matter. What matters is the perceived value to the people who might actually respond to the marketing programme you have in mind. And what is central is the idea of creating a dialogue with your market.

Another example. When Sun wanted to dramatize the concept of 'rightsizing' (getting things in proportion, rather than a euphemism for firing everyone who hasn't made a sale this week) it offered a copy of an essay written over 50 years ago by a relatively unknown British scientist. It so happened that 'On Being the Right Size' was not only immediately intriguing, it was delicious in its content, even though it contained no technology whatever. The fact that the essay had appeared originally in the more-than-slightly leftish *Morning Star* added to its appeal.

So, in response to the slightly quirky advertising which featured 'Our Hero', J.B.S. Haldane, came a flood of mail. It came from the scientific community, from managing directors, even from the author of *2001: A Space Odyssey*, Arthur C. Clarke, writing from Malaysia, to say that J.B.S. Haldane was his hero too.

And they were writing in for a copy of an essay which covered just four sides of paper.

Finally, and I promise this is finally, unless you are fatally convinced to the contrary, avoid what I can only call snottiness.

The head of the US agency Andersen and Lembke has a useful rule here. If you can add the words 'You Idiot', to your headline and it still makes sense, you are being snotty. So headlines like, 'When Did You Last Really Evaluate Your Software?' or 'Why Buy the Most Expensive When You Could Buy Ours?' really have a high problem quotient on the A+L scoring system.

And that's what you wanted to hear all along isn't it?

Michael Spring is Head of Communications for Oracle Corporation. He has worked in the technology industry for more years than he cares to remember (but if pushed he can tell you how to assemble a 16K Apple II). Even before that he worked in marketing, starting in marketing consultancy working on building products, then in the car industry with Peugeot. After Apple, he worked as a consultant with PA, with the X/Open Company, and before Oracle with Sun Microsystems. He still believes in UNIX and thinks the Triumph Vitesse (convertible) was the best car he ever owned.

PART SIX

PLAYING WITH THE TEAM YOU DIDN'T PICK

Corporate culture

INTRODUCTION

When marketing, or indeed any business function, meets the people that have to perform it, and when those people meet the organization they are undertaking it on behalf of, you have a problem. It's called human beings, the scourge of theorists who want to believe that marketing practice is simply a series of logical steps on the road to a goal.

Any number of business functions can only be as successful as the organization, or lack of it, will allow. Marketing, however, has a bigger problem. There is still very little consensus on the value of marketing outside the department and often there is downright enmity; the sales force denies that marketing is of any benefit to them and the rest of the company feels that it is no part of their job and therefore can be safely ignored. How often has the chairman's secretary briskly told a journalist that the chairman simply doesn't talk to journalists? How often has the receptionist denied to a caller the existence of a marketing department? How often has the MD rejected virtually the whole marketing strategy in favour of an advertising campaign? And how often has the accounts department been downright rude to a caller?

This book and most of the contributors to it are biased. They believe that marketing should imbue the entire organization and in some cases define it. And unless marketing professionals are in control of the marketing function and actively promoting it both internally and externally, its fate will continue to lie in the hands of people who have no interest in or understanding of it.

Michael Juer says that more and more departments can be involved in marketing if they are given democratic access to data.

New Strategies for Marketing Information Technology.
Edited by Christopher Field
Published in 1996 by Chapman & Hall, London. ISBN 0 412 61520 7

But he says that senior managers must lead the cultural changes if they are to succeed.

Laurie Young talks politics and says, 'Unless the political dynamic of the workplace, particularly at the top level, is understood and managed by marketing professionals very few of their plans and actions will actually take root in the marketplace, and they will not do the job they are employed to do.'

Ian Ryder argues that marketing has changed so much that many people no longer recognize it for what it once was and it has spread throughout many organizations to become part of the culture.

17

THE NEW CULTURE

Michael Juer

The last three decades have seen a business climate where 'the need to buy was greater then the need to sell'. This has engendered our classic view of salesmen and to a great extent they have deserved their image as mavericks and mercenaries, although this is rapidly changing. What they are, however, is largely due to the job they have had to do, how they have been asked to do it and the training and resources we have provided them with, i.e. what we have made them.

The culture of a company is primarily governed by the Directors and Senior Management of that company. In many organizations much of the key business is generated and maintained by those same Directors and Management. Those contacts and customers are usually jealously guarded by these individuals, and it is interesting that part of the salesperson's culture is the privacy of their contacts and information. This issue is at the very heart of cultural change, as the organization needs to understand the requirement for this type of information to be available to, and be used by, everybody. Only in this way can the company best organize itself to service the customer at the least cost and highest return. In all cases where companies have successfully changed the culture of their organization in this way, it has been led from the very top.

As we move into a world where 'the need to sell is greater then the need to buy', so we need to change and create a new culture for selling and marketing.

New Strategies for Marketing Information Technology.
Edited by Christopher Field
Published in 1996 by Chapman & Hall, London. ISBN 0 412 61520 7

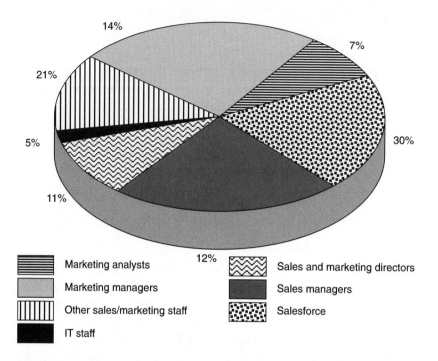

Figure 17.1 Breakdown of users by job role (source: *The Price Waterhouse Sales & Marketing Software Handbook 1994*).

TECHNOLOGY FOR CHANGE

Communications technology is a very important ingredient within this change. The last five years have seen the introduction of technology to all aspects of the sales and marketing mix and field sales are at the forefront of this.

The salesforce forms the largest group of users (Figure 17.1).

The introduction of technology to field sales is a major catalyst for change and enables the proper integration of selling into all other processes within the organization.

Notebook computers and communication links support greater teamwork and provide accountability. They also enable the recognition of the role of field sales in qualitative terms and properly includes them as part of the team.

Distributed databases (more accurately database replication), for field and regional office sales operations, with full data integrity and automatic data routing are becoming commonplace. Information can now be delivered to and from field sales with ease, providing opportunities for more professional selling practices.

The ability of these systems to provide shared information across the team is a powerful tool in the business of gaining and retaining customers. Through shared information, sales teams can work in a co-ordinated fashion with national or international customers and across geographic boundaries. Sales staff can communicate new-found information to each other and can instruct colleagues in their customer management roles. Technology not only makes this very easily achievable, but also provides a 'follow through' because that activity is visible to all.

Senior sales management, above all, must embrace this technology as it will deliver to them the information they require to understand market opportunities and future direction. However, often it is management that resist the change.

> Research suggests that the stereotyped image of the salesman as a computerphobe is misleading. It appears that people barriers to the use of systems come not from salespeople but from their managers. Some sales managers are reluctant to use the system, reluctant to share information and are inclined to view the systems existence as a threat – whether this is justified or not.
>
> *The Impact of Computerised Sales & Marketing Systems*, HCG Publications, Barclay House, 13 High Street, Olney, Bucks.

MARKET CHANGE

Companies today are coming under intense pressure from all quarters. Shrinking and fragmenting markets, increased competition, smaller margins and the need to reduce costs all demand change.

A reaction to these issues based on familiar business criteria such as lead or enquiry levels is no longer valid. Nor can we assume that the orders will keep 'coming in the door'. Marketing spend and sales strategy must be closely correlated to the cost of business and the margin earned.

Sales and marketing activity must be based on qualitative information – information about competitors, market trends, sales activity and marketing performance. Moreover, the strategic plans that are devised as a result of this information must be measurable and controllable, and the salespeople who carry out the tactical elements of the strategy must be accountable.

THE CUSTOMER AND RELATIONSHIP MANAGEMENT

Allied with market change, customers are becoming more discerning and no longer wish to deal with 'suppliers' but 'partners'. Partnerships are expected to be long-term and, in a few cases, customers actively seek profitable business for their suppliers.

Partnerships with customers means understanding the principles of Relationship Management. We need to create highly organized teams of marketing, support and sales staff who work as a single co-ordinated unit and understand the management of the many relationships a company has with its customers.

The effect that production, distribution, service and finance have on the customer is understood only too well by a salesperson, but to date the salesperson has had little influence on these functions and even less information.

Yet the relationship with customers at all these interfaces is crucial to the salesperson's success and profitability. Managing these relationships, and understanding the pivotal role of the salesperson, is crucial. Creating the people and technology links to support this team approach demands changing the way we work and think.

The question of whether sales or marketing is pre-eminent becomes secondary to the issue of binding the two together. Focus on product marketing as a result of lack of customers; sales performance and competitor information will change to a focus on client marketing as a result of better information and use of communications technology.

As John Hadlow of Silicon Graphics commented on the re-engineering of the company's processes and attitudes through a sales system implementation:

> The one man business that was each salesman is now part of a team with information sharing and strategy part of the day to day process.
>
> *The Impact of Computerised Sales & Marketing Systems*, HCG Publications, Barclay House, 13 High Street, Olney, Bucks.

Selling can then be seen as 'relationship management' with the salesperson as the prime mover in the relationship between a company and its customers and therefore in its future profitability.

If we accept that the future is less and less about creating new business and more and more about retaining current business, then forming long-term binding relationships with customers is a key to the future. Existing customers cost less to retain than new customers cost to keep. Happy long-term customers provide free 'advertising' through word of mouth. Long-term customers provide cross selling opportunities. Retained customers make it harder for competitors to gain market share.

CULTURAL CHANGE

Companies implementing such systems have to achieve a cultural change to support the new way of working. Without a cultural change there will be little strategic or operational benefit.

Senior and middle management need to change the way they view and run the salesforce. The term 'empowering salespeople' is used extensively when companies discuss field sales automation. Companies use the term differently but what is clear is that there is more emphasis on 'self-management' and devolving responsibility. This goes hand in hand with providing the salesperson with more and better information and acknowledging the responsibility their role carries. In turn this demands a more professional salesperson with a greater responsibility than just creating new business.

The salesperson must understand the whole process that supports them and also understand the need to consider structured processes within their work and the need to be responsible and accountable to the sales and marketing operation as a whole.

> The main emphasis of companies implementing systems lies with linking sales activity to marketing knowledge controlling that activity in detail, 'empowering the salespeople' with information that would help them perform better and bringing critical field derived data to sales managers for analysis and action.'
>
> *The Impact of Computerised Sales & Marketing Systems*, HCG Publications, Barclay House, 13 High Street, Olney, Bucks.

For the field sales professional the commitment and support of the whole company to his or her role is vital to their future success as a 'relationship manager'. Extensive retraining and refocus is needed for the whole team.

As important as the support the salesperson needs is the feedback the company needs on their activity and information gathering. They need to learn that information is no longer personal but should be considered a corporate asset. Sharing it will also provide them with a return. They need to understand that they can no longer work in isolation but are a key and lead part of a team. The team must take the information and knowledge they gain, analyse it and provide feedback to make the salesperson more effective.

SUMMARY

To achieve a new culture for selling will demand investment. Investment in training, technology, resources and education.

It is a sad fact of life, however, that one can achieve an MBA in marketing but that no equivalent qualification exists for selling. The lack of recognized formal qualifications for selling is a powerful factor in the culture that exists today. Perhaps as we change the culture of selling and organizations' attitude towards it then we will see the emergence of nationally recognized qualifications for salespeople. This would not be before time.

Investments in technology, training and resources will need to be supported by a change in culture and attitude towards the role of selling. This needs to be led from the top and it is the responsibility of senior management to understand and implement this change. Without this we will simply prolong the image of the 'fast talking and hard selling' salesperson and not that of a highly trained and motivated professional member of the team who has a key role in the company's future success in its markets.

Michael Juer is the Managing Director of Workstations International, a leading developer and supplier of sales and marketing systems. It was the first UK company to develop a Computer Aided Sales and Marketing System in 1986 and Michael is the founder member of the Association for Information Systems in Sales & Marketing. He lectures extensively on the subject.

18

'ALL THE OTHER GAMES
ARE FOR CHILDREN'

Managing the politics of organizations
in order to sell marketing strategies
to the board

Laurie Young

UNDERSTANDING THE POLITICS OF ORGANIZATIONS

Introduction

The quotation in the title of this chapter is a response of the American president John F. Kennedy to the question 'Why go into politics?'. Many successful people understand how to negotiate and manipulate the power bases around them. They learn the various ways people handle and react to power. They develop the art of the possible – in short, how to get things done. Sadly, the majority of marketers do not.

So this section of the book is about a subject which everybody knows is a reality at work but very few talk about openly: 'politics', the way people handle and react to power. The chapter will outline the current power bases in the computer industry and how marketing people should interact with them. It exposes some common

New Strategies for Marketing Information Technology.
Edited by Christopher Field
Published in 1996 by Chapman & Hall, London. ISBN 0 412 61520 7

perceptions of marketing and sets out some very practical ways of making sure that marketing strategies are put into practice.

The importance of political skills to the success of marketing

Unless the political dynamic of the workplace, particularly at the top level, is understood and managed by marketing professionals very few of their plans and actions will actually take root in the marketplace, and they will not do the job they are employed to do.

In general, marketing people are awful at marketing themselves and their profession. Marketing is still poorly understood by the top management of many major companies in the UK and Europe. Most top managers seem to regard it as either an adjunct to sales or a superfluous, creative advertising department. In very few board-rooms are the professional techniques of strategic market analysis or the benefits of good quality marketing understood. The 'marketing concept' (whereby marketing is the responsibility of everybody in the organization) is barely a reality.

One manifestation of this is the fact that, during the recession, most companies cut back their communications budget and their marketing department. In many companies where there was a choice between the sales department or the marketing department, it was the latter that was cut hard (in some places altogether) when funds were short. This in an indication that marketing is one of the least valued of the professions.

In many boardrooms the voice of the accountant, or the technologist or the sales manager, is the most powerful in terms of winning resources and getting plans implemented. Marketing is often seen as a cost and an unnecessary staff overhead. And yet, the computer industry critically needs marketing. Why? Because of its place in the industry maturity curve.

In the 1970s and 1980s it went through the growth cycle of industry maturity as world-wide users of IT grew dramatically. Companies could make profits by presenting faster, more technically advanced products to customers who needed to buy more advanced computing in order to keep up with the perceived 'white heat of technology'. Salespeople merely had to identify opportunities and present the benefits of new products. Then, with many companies locked into a proprietary base, suppliers simply had to manage the process of upgrades.

Much of the senior management in the big computer companies therefore came from the most successful function of the time, sales.

These people tended to take a very deal-driven approach to business expecting the growth to continue. Like many other industries before them, they thought it would go on forever. However, the computer industry hit maturity. (It is unfortunate that this also coincided with world-wide economic recession and an increase in the price of borrowing!) Blue-chip names such as IBM, DEC, Unisys and Wang hit major troubles for the first time. Apart from downsizing they also thrashed around for new things to sell. (Interestingly, many of them, failing to get margin out of mainframes, are now trying to sell services. It bemuses many people to see these companies trying to get into consultancy-led sales when the big management consultancies are in trouble themselves because their own industry has hit maturity!)

It is in these circumstances that good quality marketing strategy and a market-led approach to business will really pay off. Now is the time for the technologists and sales people of the computer industry to give way and listen to the voice of marketing reason. However, doing so will mean that power will have to shift from formerly successful functions to newer types of managers. Where this doesn't happen companies will simply go out of business, progressively cutting staff and resources in a vicious downward cycle. In the meantime, long serving employees will be doing all they can to preserve their position.

So how can marketers get a hearing in this viciously political environment?

All marketing is about change. For instance, marketing strategy is about a change in the direction of a company and new product development means a change to manufacturing or service support. A change in marketing communications might mean a change in design of materials or sales approach. Even a straightforward new marketing campaign is trying to change the company's position in the market. All the functions and actions of marketing create change in a company with varying degrees of impact.

Change, however, is a threat. A threat to the status quo. And because companies are based on economic power, a threat to someone's power base!

All companies have some form of 'politics'. Politics is often derogatorily used to describe the way people manipulate power in an organization to their own ends. The phrase 'they are very political' normally refers to somebody who is rather crass or inept at managing the power base around them. But good 'political operators' achieve their aims by carefully crafting their actions and understanding the dynamics of power around them. They know that people can have a status given to them by their job which is not reality. Some people lower in the organization have more perceived power and influence than others with a greater span of control. Similarly, differences in culture mean that things get done inside companies in totally different ways. It is essential that, in order to effect change, marketers begin to understand the dynamics of power, how different people react to power and how they can manage the changes in power to their own ends. You can't be a professional marketer, you can't do the job properly, without being good at politics.

The perspective of other board functions

The first step in understanding the dynamic of power is to really appreciate how top management and the culture of the whole organization regards marketing. The board has its own views and, because they arise from years of successful experience, they are hard to shift. Naturally board level people think they understand marketing but this is often a very limited definition and different functions have different caricatures of how marketing works and what marketing is. For example a number of managing directors regard marketing as their personal PA or PR department. They rely on the marketer to produce well-crafted documents – asking them to 'come up with a glossy' which communicates the benefits of products and services to their target audience. This type of managing director often has their marketer at their beck and call, asking them to write speeches or ensure that external publications are well-produced. They do not rely on the marketer for substantial strategies which produce changes in direction and are often relying on either the production director or the accountant to be the real powerhouse of the company. Other senior figures rely on the marketer to be familiar with and report on every single deal that is in progress. Some regard marketing as sales, whereas others regard it as a creative function which is an add-on to the main functions of the business. Many still believe that marketing begins and ends with the marketing department.

Some accountants regard marketers as an overhead who merely want to spend money. They do not see many marketing campaigns (whether large-budget external advertising or targeted direct marketing programmes) as directly able to generate business. Also, as much marketing technique is so appallingly taught and executed, they regard the profession as shallow and imprecise. They question the professionalism of many marketing techniques and do not see marketers demonstrating a precise professional approach to the development of strategy in their organization. They often accuse marketers' work of not being measurable (it should be of course).

Sales directors and managers have a fascinating attitude to marketing! In an organization where marketing does not exist they often bemoan the fact that it doesn't. They will lobby for marketing people to be brought into the organization, looking for them to find target customers to attack, to produce sales support materials, exhibitions and other ways of generating business. They will be particularly vociferous if the company is going through difficult times, if they see their patches running dry of potential business or if they are not achieving their targets! However, the self same people will often attack marketers once they are in place. Ten years ago I joined the marketing department in an organization where the sales teams had been making exactly those protestations. The new marketers, on arrival, made a shopping list of their needs and, within six months, all the requests had been fulfilled. However, the salespeople were still complaining that marketing had 'not delivered' when it came to assessing their achievement of targets. Salespeople, even when they understand the marketing process, do not appreciate the full range of the marketing job or its role in the organization.

The final function that has an ambivalent attitude to marketing is that of the operations director or the service director. They tend to regard marketing as imprecise or disruptive to the smooth running of their operations.

So, a board can judge a marketing function on the things it does not deliver – according to their own preconceptions as much as what it actually does. If so, it will tend to make business plans first and consult marketing afterwards, asking the marketing director to take to market what is already planned. There are therefore many vested interests and prejudices against the marketing director as they face board colleagues from different functional backgrounds.

The real role of marketing at board level

In addition the marketing director might have problems defining the true role of top level marketing and its contribution to an organization. The role and function of marketing will be outlined in detail elsewhere in this book. My own view, however, is that marketing can best be compared to architecture.

An architect works to a clear brief from a client about their needs for a building. Often the architect will help the client to define their needs into a specification. They will then use years of professional training and learnt techniques to create a plan of how that building will be built to client expectations and budget. Once that has been agreed, the architect will then assemble a team of disparate functions and specialities in order to build the building. This might range from contractors and builders through to structural engineers and quantity surveyors. By managing this interdisciplinary team, alongside the client's expectations and changing budget requirements, the building is finally put up. At the end of the day the architect will then have their creation criticized as either being 'a carbuncle on society' or a masterpiece of modern architecture.

The marketing director is there to build the company of the future. They identify the true needs of the customers and then use good quality, professional techniques to create an appropriate plan and strategy. Poor quality marketers, with inadequate experience and training, do not know how to construct good quality market audits, market plans and marketing strategies based on decent market analysis. A well trained and experienced marketer will draw together various functional disciplines (e.g. advertising, direct marketing, public relations, database management, print and design) in order to achieve the plan. Professional training for a marketer ought to take years. A good marketing director ought to be qualified in marketing and have some ten years' experience of successful and unsuccessful campaigns. If people are tempted to take marketing staff from sales, accounts or any other function and put them straight into marketing management or directorship without training they should think about the analogy of the architect. If you took somebody out of your accounts department or your sales department and asked them to design, without training or experience, a building in which your company would operate, would you then work in that building?

Marketers are the commercial architects of an organization. The trouble is that people look at the end products of some very successful marketing strategies and try to copy just the form of the final creation. They don't see the years of experience that went into its creation nor the client management, strategy development and the interdisciplinary management that made the project successful.

The fact of the matter is that, in a mature market such as the computer industry today, if a marketing function is hindered by the perceptions of people in power, the performance of the company will also be hindered. (This, by the way, is a source of competitive advantage. The political environment of a company will affect its actions in the marketplace, whatever it proclaims in press releases. Marketers are not competing against amorphous 'companies', they are competing against individuals in a work environment. By mapping out the key individuals in a competitor, their career history, their track record in terms of decisions taken and their degree of influence, it is possible to predict the competitive actions of the company more accurately than some of the esoteric macroeconomic models suggested by academics.)

The marketing director's own perspective

There is one further hindrance to good quality board level marketing: the marketing director's own background.

One of the prime tasks of the marketing director is to sell the role to the board. If the marketing director is from a sales background and does not know how to make a case for marketing they need to first understand the full discipline and how it can affect the performance of the company. In this case the marketer should either hire somebody to work for them or work with a consultant who is skilled in this area. The ex-sales director should take personal training in order to understand how marketing can affect company strategy and how good quality marketing, plans and strategy can be developed. They also ought to understand how an audit of their current marketing capability and its effect on the firm can be undertaken.

In addition, the marketing directors might inherit an under-developed infrastructure of marketing and sales. There may not be robust processes or systems, or there may be some aspect of marketing which simply has not been done in the past. Other operational functions might have more reliable statistics and be much more ingrained in the culture of the organization. Alternatively, the marketer's boss might be asking them to spend too much time in the wrong places, doing the wrong things. In this instance, the marketer should spend extra time creating the right strategy and the right infrastructure. By meeting the requirements and expectations that exist, in addition to building the necessary resources to move in the right direction, the marketer will win the respect to change direction. Finally the marketing director may not be on the board and may not be powerful enough. In which case they have to develop a mentor or ally in order to make sure that their function contributes in the way it should.

How marketing can create the business differentiator in today's computer market

Many other industries have been through the same harsh lessons that the computer industry is currently going through. They have been through the fast growth in the sales cycle and then the rigours of market maturity. As a result many industry players have gone out of business and others have survived by changing their business model in order to cope with greatly reduced margins. In such industries the use of marketing and marketing techniques to drive the business has become an accepted practice. Companies have used product development and, in particular, brand management techniques in order to preserve the differentiation of their products and services. They have earned real profits over time. (Such long-term brand strategies are rarely seen in the sales led computer industry.) In addition they have managed sophisticated marketing communications programmes and deployed marketing information very effectively. An example of the latter is competitive information. Many mature industries have detailed competitive information which is provided, at the behest of competitors in the market, by independent organizations and supported by the players in that market because they have learned that it is to the mutual benefit of everyone concerned to set up such systems.

There are many ways in which the computer industry must learn to deal with new market dynamics. Good marketing directors can cut short much of the painful learning process.

'PLUS POLITICS' – THE ART OF SUCCESSFUL BOARD LEVEL MARKETING

'Plus politics' is the noble art of managing and influencing the way people react to power to a positive end. It is very practical and is a learnt skill.

There are a number of things that marketing directors can do to ensure that marketing is successfully presented at board level. These include the following.

Create a general strategy to educate the board

It is true that many senior managers in the computer industry have succeeded in an environment which was radically different from today's computer market. They also have perceptions created by their own functions and by the fact that previous actions and styles of management were successful. They need to come to the conclusion that, not only has the industry environment changed once and for all, but they need to find new techniques to be competitively successful. It is essential therefore that the marketing director sets a strategy to educate their colleagues in the role of corporate strategy and marketing in a mature market.

One way of handling this is to bring in external authorities to communicate at board level the true nature of marketing. If functional colleagues feel that they are receiving messages from people other than the marketing director about the true role of marketing they will press him or her to move in the direction that they want to go. This is particularly crucial if the marketing director, as is often the case in the computer industry, is trying to bring marketing to an area where it has not existed before. They should try to find ways in which respected academics or industry leaders can educate people at top level on the true nature of marketing.

The marketing director should try to take responsibility for developing strategies and plans whereby they can facilitate the thinking of the board towards industry knowledge, market maturity and competitive action. In doing this the marketing director has two very powerful pieces of information at their disposal: the attitude of customers and the attitude of competition. By continually seeing customers, researching customers and tracking the competition, they can keep reminding the board of the external perspective. If the board is confident in the techniques by which the marketing director finds this information, they will then develop the power to influence the direction the company moves in, but it must be through facilitation and general education not dictat.

Specific presentations to the board

If the marketing director is presenting a specific programme or strategy they should do the following:

- Listen in advance to colleagues' attitudes on a one-to-one basis or in meetings (or to influential employees who work for them). By doing so the marketing director can understand, in advance of the meeting, the likely opposition and blockages to the presentation.
- Involve them in the preparation. As far as possible involve board level colleagues in a difficult subject before it comes to the board. That way they feel their views have already been taken into

account and will take some ownership of the presentation arguing alongside the marketing function.

- Gain allies. It is important in a contentious or even a straight-forward presentation to the board to ensure that there are people who back the proposal. If these are people who have perceived power in the organization then the plan will be agreed.

All of the above are methods of pre-selling the presentation. It is essential that, with any board level presentation, the marketing director pre-sells the presentation by communicating the proposed content to colleagues and adjusting the message to take account of their objections or their contributions. That way they feel their attitudes have already been taken into account and a proposal will be agreed more easily.

Finally, of course, prepare the presentation in detail. It is worth-while being as serious in preparing a board presentation as any formal presentation to customers. This might seem self evident to newcomers but after some years of operating at senior level, there is a temptation to cut corners and not prepare properly. There are more good strategies and programmes lost through this than any other means. It is worthwhile spending nights preparing the presentation and rehearsing it with other colleagues. If of course people who work for the marketing director are making a presentation to the board they should be rehearsed and they should also be supported during the presentation.

Preparing a marketing plan

A marketing plan is a crucial document for the company and should be prepared very, very carefully. In my view the content of a marketing plan should be well debated and each marketing director should develop their own process of producing one. However, it is essential that market plans are produced at the speed at which changes in the market dictate and not to internal planning timetables. Some academic authors and strategists suggest that there should be an annual planning cycle which starts with the market audit and finishes with the fully prepared market plan ready for the new financial year. This of course contradicts the marketing perspective which says that companies should take action in the marketplace as the market changes. It is therefore essential that the marketing plan is produced in time with changes in the marketplace. The marketing director must therefore have a clear market information process which produces timely information as the market changes.

Having said that, it is necessary to educate the board in the need for up to date marketing information and for a marketing plan. Then the following should be done to achieve a successful board level market plan.

Balance

A market plan should not be too theoretical and it should not be too practical. It should start with a clear link to corporate strategy working through marketing objectives, market analysis and the programmes necessary to achieve changes in the marketplace on towards internal changes that should result. Any implications to organization structure, pay, bonuses, staff levels or budgets should be clearly identified. Each of these should be pre-sold well in advance of presentation to the board and all the budgets linked together.

It is essential also that an action plan be produced which shows what action is to be taken, who is going to take it, what the cost will be and what the benefit will be. By doing this, the marketing director is clearly showing that the actions in the market plan will be managed. They should suggest that colleagues involved report on a monthly basis on each of those actions. This ensures that the marketing plan becomes more than a theoretical document. My own experience is that, after two years of such an approach, colleagues begin to realize that marketing is more than just a theoretical exercise and begin to argue more vociferously for (or against) different programmes because they know that action will be taken.

Pre-sell

The marketing plan needs to be pre-sold to all colleagues with the implications clearly drawn out before the board level presentation. One way of doing this is to prepare a schedule for production of the market plan and to get colleagues to buy into that so they know when to expect each particular part of it to be ready.

Keep to a formal programme

If a schedule is produced of how a market plan will be prepared this should be reported formally at the board so that it is taken as seriously as some of the other business performance figures. It is very powerful to have the managing director or chairman reviewing progress on the production of the market plan to a clear month by month schedule.

Involve, involve, involve!

All board colleagues and their functions, should in some way be involved in the production of the market plan (even if this is only a superficial excuse to get them to buy in) so that they feel it is their document.

Bidding for the budget

This really depends on the maturity of the organization, how it views marketing and what provisions have been made for marketing in the past. The first principle to establish is that marketing is not a cost or an overhead. Marketing directors would be wise to use the word 'investment' in all presentations on marketing programmes. They should try to do break-even analysis and demonstrate the payback on programmes. That way colleagues begin to expect them to present programmes in a way that will demonstrate their effect on the business.

In making budget bids the marketing director should demonstrate that they understand the priorities of the business and the changes other colleagues are making. For instance, in one senior job, we had the choice between funding marketing programmes and people's salaries. It was very clear that, if I substantially increased marketing programmes in order to generate business, we would have to sacrifice people through redundancy schemes in order to create the budget to do so. Most colleagues accepted the need to grow and generate the business but I had to be sensitive to very carefully control budget bids and had to rigorously examine agency estimates and projected payback.

Having said all this, the budget is power. And budget control ensures the ability to get things done. The marketing director should ensure that they have tight control on last year's expenditure, on estimates of spend this year and spend of projects that have been approved. Tight control of budgets gives the freedom to act and hence the ability to demonstrate the effectiveness of marketing work.

Selling specific campaigns

The best way to fund specific campaigns is to get approval for an overall marketing budget once a year and to get the freedom to act. However, if an individual campaign needs specific board level approval it should be treated as a major project which should be sold at board level as outlined earlier. In this instance, it is normally easier to get substantial backing from a number of colleagues because mock-ups of the campaign can be made and people will see the more tangible end product of the marketing campaign. Some people find it easier to support a plan where they can see a tangible representation of it.

Strategy and tactics

Do both! If you just design and run tactical plans, you are not doing the full job. If you just create strategy when you first start, people will wonder when you are going to deliver. Create both thrusts in an interdependent timetable.

Selling the idea of marketing in general

There are several ways of doing this; the first is internal marketing programmes which communicate to all staff the value of an external orientation and, by default, marketing. Also a marketing element should be introduced to all management training courses and key marketing speakers introduced to internal meetings. In addition, wherever possible, people should be taken out of line functions and drafted into the marketing department to do marketing jobs. They will then take the marketing message back into the organization. For example, there is normally not a necessity to have a dedicated product development function in a small organization. Taking people out of the line to develop new product ideas into product plans is an excellent idea. The person responsible becomes the champion of that product and then takes that back into the line function with them.

Communicate progress

Quite a lot of marketing work is not visible. Whilst plans are being laid, for instance, people wonder what is going on. Communicate what you are doing without being seen to be advertising your skills. For example, a monthly market report (comprising state of the market, programme results and progress in strategic plans) is a straightforward way to keep the internal audience informed.

Study politics

Management texts are not the best place to learn the political art. Apart from political biographies, the people who are best at understanding how people handle power are artists and creative writers. They are excellent observers. For instance, the Shakespearean king plays have lessons to teach about the political workplace because they are excellent observations of the way people used and reacted to the power of the times. For instance, I recently saw the chairman of a company reacting like Richard II. He thought he was there as a result of a divine right to govern. In fact, through his own inadequacy, he was causing the decay of the organization. I have also seen people behave like Hamlet, Lear and Macbeth.

In addition there are obvious roles to observe. For instance, I have seen the 'bully' become manifest. A bully is someone who reacts to having power in a particular way and, by understanding their motives and fears, it is possible to achieve the objectives that the marketing director desires. The bully is somebody who is emotionally insecure and tends to empire build and defend strongly their own empire. A bully in sales or operations would attack the marketing director's function vigorously because it is a challenge to their authority. The way to react to such a person is either to stand up to them or to get their own people on your side so the latter can put forward your ideas as though they were their own. The bully will then inevitably endorse them. There are other obvious ways that people with power behave and it will be easier to achieve goals if they are understood and managed.

Charles Handy wrote an excellent book which contains some of the political dynamics of organizations called *Understanding Organizations*. Finally, read the ultimate book on politics: Machiavelli's *The Prince*. Machiavelli has an undeservedly bad press. He saw his role as maintaining a stable environment for his people whilst the political powers above him kept changing. Some of his techniques work out excellently at work. Machiavelli ought to be standard reading on all marketing strategy courses.

Get a mentor

At the age of 27 I was given a remarkable opportunity by being offered a job as assistant to the new Deputy Chairman of BT, recruited to manage the company side of privatization. He was a very senior businessman, having been Deputy Chairman of Barclays Bank before joining the company. So, I was close to the top of the business, city and Government during the privatization process. I learnt more from him in those frenetic two years than any other business experience before or since – including my MBA. One of the lessons I learnt was that professionalism is not only about working hard and doing the work thoroughly; it is also about understanding human interactions sufficiently to get things done. And some of these observations are only learnt through the experience of someone who has been there before.

In the film *Color of Money* the experienced 'hustler' Fast Eddie comes across a phenomenon I've seen many time in marketing: someone really talented, with exceptional skill, working hard but not progressing quickly. He decided to take the new talent under his tutelage. Early on in their conversation he says: 'Pool excellence is not about excellent pool. It's about becoming someone. You've got to become a student of the human move'. This is also true of marketing. Get a mentor.

Maintain your integrity

Politics gets a bad name if people detect that the objective of the people involved in primarily self-interest. This is a delicate balance. There is nothing wrong with talented people being ambitious but the interests of the job, and the contribution of the job to the company, must come first. Marketers must maintain a professional integrity. The marketing strategy that best suits a computer company in today's mature market will continually clash with a technology or sales led culture. The marketing professional is employed to change that culture because that is in the best interests of shareholders, customers and employees. It may take time and there will be many compromises but this end objective should not be compromised. For instance, in recession and through the dark days of downsizing it is tempting to keep low and not rock the boat in order to preserve your job. This is stupid. By doing so, the company will miss out on vital input. And, if the worse comes to the worse, talented marketers can make as much money for themselves as they can for any corporate company. Maintain the integrity of the role and the profession. If you don't, people will sense it; you will then lose respect and the voice of influence.

In short then, marketing directors can only really do their job properly and serve their organization well if they understand the dynamics of power inside the organization and manage those dynamics with as much care and attention as they manage any other professional marketing task. This is the ultimate difference between marketing managers and marketing directors. It is a challenging, powerful and responsible role. Organizational politics are a serious game and an important game. All the other games are for children!

Laurie Young is a specialist in services marketing and customer care. He is an associate with the Avanti Consultancy and runs his own services marketing consultancy.

19

MARKETING
Fact or faction?

Ian Ryder

'Marketing at the Cross-roads' – a real headline relating to a Coopers & Lybrand survey done in early 1994. This widely-referred report contains some excellent pointers and research, however, there has been interpretation of some of its findings as casting doubt on the existence of marketing, which is certainly contentious. What it does highlight very successfully, though, is a development phase in the life of the function.

'Marketing IT' therefore needs to consider first what we actually mean by the term 'marketing' before looking at its application in the world of information technology. 'The brand is no longer king and

"The statistics on death are quite convincing . . . one out of one dies."

George Bernard Shaw

New Strategies for Marketing Information Technology.
Edited by Christopher Field
Published in 1996 by Chapman & Hall, London. ISBN 0 412 61520 7

the search for a new paradigm has begun' heralds an article in the March 1994 issue of *Management Today*, which also sees fit to quote from the previous national Coopers & Lybrand study. What is going on?

'I'm from marketing and I'm here to help you' was the phrase most guaranteed to either bring the house down with laughter or receive pitying murmurs anywhere within the IT industry and yet, in the world of 'consumer marketing', the mere mention of the title 'brand manager' caused an enormous sense of pride in the owner and carried with it huge power over product, distribution, pricing and promotion within organizations. Now, suddenly, we have experienced, very senior marketers, chairmen and eminent consulting organizations casting serious doubt on the validity of their (consumer-based) model of marketing – just as the IT industry has reached the point of its own life cycle when a very serious dose of real marketing, as we thought we knew it, is needed as never before.

All these companies, Abbey National, Bass, Electrolux, Elida Gibbs, Hertz, IBM, Microsoft, Philips, Lever Brothers have undergone major marketing reorganization in the last 12–24 months. One of the core precepts which has been followed moved the various 'local' brand management freedoms into more regional, even global, strategy responsibilities with the local operations reducing to one of sales support/business development. But wait a minute. Isn't this precisely what the IT industry has had in place, albeit unwittingly and unmanaged, for the last 20 years – and hasn't it been a royal battle within most of the larger companies between country, region and HQ?!

For example, Digital Equipment Corporation had no less than 17 quite major reorganizations between 1989 and 1994, during which time the marketing team in, for example, the UK was reduced from an almost unbelievable peak of 190 people to about 30. IBM, Hewlett-Packard, UNISYS and almost any other technology company, hardware, software or services related, all went through the same traumas. This was due, in large part, to inadequately trained and qualified marketing staff (Table 19.1) and, it must be said, boards of directors and chief executives who, unlike their consumer counterparts, were not knowledgeable or experienced enough in marketing.

Success came almost without trying to those of us in IT during the last 25 years, as we were privileged to live through a major technology revolution whose impact has gone far beyond that of the last industrial revolution. As we've reached the end of the first epoch,

Table 19.1 FMCG versus business-to-business

	FMCG	Business-to-business
Formal training/qualifications	80%	20%
Usage of outside consultants	94%	55%
Usage of brand research:		
Quite often	50%	10%
Never	0%	50%

Source: Primary Contact research conducted in March 1994 of 'brand custodians'.

we now need to understand how we can all survive and prosper in a highly competitive global market.

'Market', and 'Customer', are the key words. Whatever anybody says, at the end of the day, company A is competing with company B (C, D . . .) to provide products (tangible or intangible) to a purchaser (individual or group/corporate body). Equally, the purchasers need to select what to buy and from whom, with that huge array of evaluation criteria which comprise the dimensions along which the suppliers plan their strategies – in short, the science/art of marketing.

But those who are, lemming-like, following the contemporary debate and questioning the very existence of marketing are overlooking, or failing to recognize, what is actually happening. Finance departments no longer have rows of ledger clerks with quill pens, factory production lines no longer (in many cases at least) have serried ranks of women and men routinely and monotonously adding the same component to other components day after day. These functions have changed, evolved and adapted to new circumstances and advances in – yes, TECHNOLOGY! We in IT have had a huge impact on the way tasks can now be performed. The concept of the responsible 'work group' in a manufacturing environment, together with IT, has enriched the lives of many previously under-utilized factory staff.

Marketing is going through its own puberty. The brand isn't dead, but the way in which companies organize to manage it may be. Marketing isn't something only one department does – it is an entire culture, an ethos, a way of behaving and there is not one single area within any commercial organization which does not have a 'marketing' dimension to its activity.

(Those of us who are marketing practitioners have a responsibility for the development of the function for sure; evidence the expansion of the four Ps concept to 6 or even 7! However, this development,

197

covered in more depth under 'relationship marketing', actually enhances and increases the importance of a 'marketing' focus in organizations. Read about 'relationship marketing', for further evidence.)

Successfully 'marketing IT' then will come from a number of actions:

1. Ensure that those 'driving' the company are qualified and experienced, and really understand what marketing truly means – no more of the pitiful 'We don't do that here', which is usually synonymous for 'I don't understand it so I'll stop it'.

2. Clear articulation of who the customer is, what they require and how that requirement can be serviced (e.g. are your distribution channels really sorted out?) – ensure this is understood by everyone in the company.

3. As part of (2), equally clear articulation of brand strategy and values, again fully understood and, critically, LIVED by the whole organization.

4. No more internal marketing 'wars'. Each component part of the organization must understand its role and 'freedoms' and not go off at a tangent to, for example, implement independent and conflicting communications programmes simply because it has a budget.

5. Leading on from point (4), engineer your organization to have clear processes for essential activities which may include the outsourcing of non-core support, and will almost certainly include extensive use of agencies.

6. Respond to the customer. Don't just listen (or, worse, pretend to listen). For evidence, please consider how strong Digital Equipment (and IBM for that matter) was in 1989 when loyal customers were saying how poor they were at customer service, organizational clarity, ease to deal with and how they had an arrogant sales force. Despite the words of intent from management, nothing changed (except the organization, of course!) and it is now a matter of history how the customer and competition have spoken.

7. Reject the notion of the internal customer for marketing. This does not support the critical understanding that we are all in marketing. Equally, however, excellent internal communications are of paramount importance.

8. Brand or be branded! Customer cognizance of those symbolic and functional components attributed to your brand will drive decision-making. Don't leave it unmanaged.

9. Understand YOUR business. Too many IT companies try to be all things to all people. If you are confused, imagine how your market feels!

10. Use professionals. If you hire them – use them. It is no good asking, for example, a solicitor for advice, ignoring it and then complaining if things don't work out. The expertise is available and you only have yourself to blame if you don't make use of it.

IT and marketing are both functions which are going through something of a mid-life crisis. Put together and implemented professionally, they form the basis for a long and happy relationship.

Ian Ryder runs his own outsourced marketing services company and has held senior marketing roles at Hewlett-Packard, WYSE Technology, Digital Equipment Systems and Computer Sciences where he was Marketing Director. He has been responsible for several major sponsorship, TV and press campaigns and is a graduate of the International Institute for Management Development in Lausanne.

PART SEVEN

PLAYING COWBOYS AND INDIANS

Supplier management

INTRODUCTION

A marketing director who can successfully manage a network of suppliers can go a long way to overcoming their own lack of skills and experience. How often in IT does the best salesperson get 'rewarded' with the job of marketing director. And how often do they simply start to act as sales manager. There are, however, ways to learn on the job and get the job done at the same time.

One such director who used to work for a large hardware manufacturer was able to commission work of the highest quality from her suppliers. Her secret was to give them a great deal of freedom, but pull them up sharply if they strayed from the guidelines; show them enormous loyalty, but get rid of them if they showed anything less than the same back; and pay over the going rate for work, but query every single item on invoices. Her critics within the company called her unprofessional and resented the loyalty she showed to outsiders. Her fans rated her highly as a marketer and praised the creativity and market orientation of her work.

Her experience at other companies had proved to her once and for all that she was unlikely to get what she needed from her own department. The company employees tended to be first–class marketing administrators and strategists but lacked both creativity and objectivity in the work they actually produced. Their work tended to look the same, year in year out.

At the hardware company, she hired a marketing consultant to advise her, a PR co-ordinator to manage the PR network, an advertising consultant to advise on corporate design, a freelance journalist to oversee corporate literature copy, an exhibition consultant to advise on events and so on. Each of these individuals was

New Strategies for Marketing Information Technology.
Edited by Christopher Field
Published in 1996 by Chapman & Hall, London. ISBN 0 412 61520 7

an expert in their field but none of them was paid for their advice, only for the work that actually grew out of it. Their incentive was to pitch for work by proposing ideas based on the marketing strategy and consultation with the departmental business managers. They then had to justify those ideas to their peers at a monthly suppliers review meeting.

The trend that this marketing director had clearly identified was that more and more marketing professionals are choosing to work for themselves. She generally avoided using consultants from large organizations, claiming that individuals would always give better service. She effectively operated a virtual company within a company, one that got close enough to collectively develop a fierce loyalty on behalf of its employer but one that remained distant enough to tell the blunt truth employees often balk at.

Much of the dynamic between her and her team would be of as much interest to a psychologist as other marketers. She found working with other women difficult and restricted them to administrative roles. She gave appalling briefs, something that Horley and West insist are absolutely critical. She made everything personal rather than professional. Oddly enough she was criticized for all the things that tend to pass without comment when the manager is a man, and in fact she had plenty of the qualities that make women perfectly cut out to be top marketers.

In the end, corporate resentment got the better of her and, as the only woman of any calibre at middle-management level, she was vulnerable. But not before the company had won awards for its work and the universal acclaim of the salespeople and customers, the very groups at which most of the marketing was aimed.

She had another secret. She loved marketing and she loved being in IT. It is still rare to find both in one person so I am not putting her up as an ideal of supplier-led marketing. However, she did distinguish the company in marketing at a time when its product and market orientation were way off beam. She built up a brand that helped the company survive while its product and service portfolio was all but being dumped. And she created the beginnings of a marketing culture within the company at a time when the salespeople were regarded as the only business drivers.

Nick Horley looks at how to service an agency in order to get the best out of them.

Andy West advises on how to choose a PR agency.

David Mankin shows how to brief a design consultancy.

20

HOW TO SERVICE
AN AGENCY

Nick Horley

'How to service an agency? What a daft thing to worry about. I thought the agency was supposed to service me!' It's an understandable attitude, but one that wastes a good deal of clients' money.

You might be forgiven for thinking that outsourcing your PR to consultants absolves you from a certain amount of responsibility. This is debatable. The truth is that you take on a share of the management and motivation of a whole team of people. However well your agency is run, you can extract much better service from the executives on your account if you can make them feel that they work for you, not just the person who signs the salary cheques. They will bend every rule in the agency's book to give you a premium service if they feel that you are 'part of the team', rather than a distant, forbidding figure.

Your relationship with the agency starts, not when you hire it, but when you first brief it to pitch for your account. You may be briefing three, four or more agencies, but take care. Ask searching questions, but treat them as if they were your own employees. Firstly, they will put more work into their proposals. Secondly, one of the teams will be working for you in a few weeks. And just as you are trying to sense whether the chemistry is right, they are already classifying you, comparing you with the scores of in-house types they have met before.

New Strategies for Marketing Information Technology.
Edited by Christopher Field
Published in 1996 by Chapman & Hall, London. ISBN 0 412 61520 7

Do you intimidate, in the belief that getting value out of the agency is like squeezing an orange? Are you one of the insecure ones who worries that the agency is going to show them up? Perhaps you're simply inert, a paper pushing administrator who stares blankly when they proffer some creative thinking. Or do you inspire them to dream of the greatest, most award-winning client–agency partnership of their career?

Bear in mind that agencies are generally staffed by creative types. Unlike your sales force they don't respond well to endless stick and carrot; but if you can create an enthusiastic atmosphere and show appreciation of good work, which costs nothing, your team will walk over hot coals for you. Even more useful (and less painful) they will strive to give you one of those brilliant opportunist ideas which results in a publicity coup for very little investment. If you encourage them to be adventurous, a creative team will reward you with one of these sooner or later. But if you encourage them, like salespeople, to fear failure, they will stick to tried and tested techniques, and the results, although worthy and professional, will lack sparkle.

The judgements the agency forms about you at the briefing stage can set the tone for your entire relationship with it, and mistakes made now can be costly. For example, you may at first be understandably reluctant to give the agency sensitive information, but honesty and openness are absolutely vital. In the hype-ridden IT industry, marketing departments can all too easily be infected by the salesperson's compulsion to treat every outsider, even the PR consultant, as a potential customer. But if the agency is given nothing but sales messages to regurgitate to the press, it will lose 75% of its value to you. If you want to devise a strategy to convince everyone that you are number one, you must first explain why you are not. Occasionally you will also have bad news for it to handle, and if you give your agency the full picture it will be much better equipped to defend you.

Having hired your agency, it's important to establish the correct chain of command. The agency will be able to achieve far more if it is reporting to someone who is not afraid to provide access to your top management when necessary. This generally requires an individual who has respect and authority within your organization, and who understands PR. On the whole, marketing managers, marketing directors and experienced PR managers fit the bill; but junior marketing communications executives generally don't. Neither do office managers or PAs who have been given the job title of PR manager as a reward for long service. Such people become a barrier to the agency and quickly reduce it to the role of press release factory.

One easy way to wreck a good agency relationship is to allow the agency to get close to your chief executive when your company is young and then, as your organization grows, make it report to a new recruit who feels threatened by its familiarity with the boss.

Sadly, this is a regular occurrence in the computer industry, where high growth start-ups and UK subsidiaries are launched every week. The agency throws everything into the launch, spends days closeted away conducting interviews with the inspiring, charismatic chief executive, and becomes devoted to him or her. Thereafter, the agency will stop at nothing to give the client the best reputation in its market.

But soon enough, the company grows (thanks partly to the agency's efforts) and a marketing manager is hired. Unless the new recruit is a mature, confident individual, you can be sure that the political games will start, and PR will immediately suffer. Agencies make useful pawns in power struggles because their output gets the attention of the board. But if your agency has to spend all its time treading on eggshells it will never be able to give you any robust advice, and you will lose the benefit of its objective viewpoint. Wasn't that one of the reasons you hired an external consultant in the first place?

Of course, the agency's reporting point is only part of the equation. You need to integrate it closely into the rest of your organization, so that it can function in the same way as an internal PR department. Put it on your e-mail system. This not only makes communication physically easier, it is an important symbol of your trust in the agency, and will encourage your staff to be open, helpful and responsive. Arrange for your divisional managers to brief the agency; let the agency discover the grass roots opinions on your company's PR requirements and you can be sure it will approach its task with extra conviction.

Don't assume that all your staff know exactly what a PR consultant does; some of them will be under the impression that a 'press agent' is some sort of surrogate journalist who feeds company secrets straight to the papers while others will assume that, like an advertising agency, the PR consultant can simply 'book' coverage and, conversely, stop journalists from writing negative stories.

Perhaps most importantly, introduce the agency to your sales force. In many IT companies neither side will relish this occasion, and nor will you. In the computer industry's sales-driven culture we all know what the sales staff tend to think of the marketing department, and the fat cat PR consultant will be viewed with equal suspicion. How can they charge £100 an hour just for arranging the champagne and strawberries and the Wimbledon tickets?

You must tackle this head on; your customers are one of your strongest PR weapons, but without the co-operation of the sales force your agency will never be able to exploit them. If your agency can prove that it is in the interest of sales to co-operate with PR, the benefits will be substantial. This was proved abundantly at Sequent, where the sales staff perceived that a prominent contract story in *Computing* would help their careers and that the PR agency could deliver it for them. Thereafter the aspiring sales directors were always on the phone to the agency with all the juicy details of the latest war stories. The results were clear to everyone in the industry: Sequent's contract wins almost always generated full scale news stories, while everyone else's tended to languish in the orders column.

Assuming that you haven't alienated everyone in your organization by now, turn your attention to some of the basics. Agencies thrive on information, so give them everything you can; send round a van with last year's press clippings, press releases, brochures, videos, technical articles, anything. Invite them to your customer seminars and your kick-off meetings. Let them attend meetings about product directions, competitive strategies and corporate issues. Encourage them to ask questions, and not to be afraid of showing ignorance on occasion. Make sure that they have ready access to trained spokespeople and that their requests are dealt with promptly. The press will often give the agency no notice when requesting information or comment, so be sensitive to its demands for your attention. If your account team resort to sending you a fax which starts 'I couldn't get hold of you yesterday . . . ', take notice. They are doing their best to be diplomatic as usual, but if you read between the lines it probably says 'We've missed five opportunities for coverage this week because you never return our bloody calls'. Many organizations are guilty of this and they waste a high proportion of their opportunities for coverage, but take ICL as an example. You might expect such a large company with so many divisions to be particularly slow to respond, but the PR manager, who is herself a former PR consultant, uses all her clout to ensure that her agencies get instant responses from spokespeople; when opportunities for coverage are missed, the agencies can hardly ever blame the client. If ICL can do it, so can you.

As soon as your PR machine is running smoothly, it is time to take stock and review the PR programme. You are probably three months down the line from the pitch by now, and if you and your account team stand back and look at their original proposal, you may both concede that in the light of what they have since found out about you it needs considerable modification. This is normal. After all, it was never going to be possible to give the team the full brief until after you had hired them. It is vital that you now encourage them to propose an updated programme. It is amazing how many clients and agencies omit this simple step. The result is that the big ideas in the original proposal are left on the shelf, but nothing is put forward to replace them. The programme then plods on, bereft of proactive projects, for months or even years, until the client one day notices that the agency has 'failed' to revitalize the company's image. At this point mutual frustrations inhibit further progress and the relationship may be sundered completely.

Having passed these initial hurdles, the next challenge for you and your agency is to keep the relationship productive in the long term. Many clients think it is good practice to switch agencies every couple of years in order to 'inject some new blood'. Apart from being a waste of an investment of hundreds of work hours, this is frequently an admission that the client–agency relationship broke down.

The best way to avoid this is to manage and motivate the agency staff as if they were your own employees. Set the targets every year and hold formal progress reviews. Keep them enthused about the company's direction by ensuring regular exposure to top management. Show how you value their input by asking them to update the PR strategy and present it to the board every year. Of course you must upbraid them when they are at fault, but don't forget to praise them when they succeed – in writing. You can be sure that a letter of congratulation will be seen by everyone in the agency, and if you combine this with an invitation to your company's excursions to the races or the rugby you can ensure that the agency's best people will be clamouring to work on your account.

If you want your team to lie awake at night devising new ways to make you famous and give you hours of extra service at no charge, agree to help them enter a campaign for one of the PR industry's several award schemes. This may require you to fund some research to measure the effect of their work; but you should be doing that anyway. It will do wonders for your own reputation, as well as the agency's.

If these techniques don't give you the relationship you're looking for, it's time you sat down with the agency for a frank exchange of views; you probably do need to sack them after all.

The final ingredient in the mix should be the courage to invest in the commodity which the press value most highly: controversy. For all their aggression and determination in the marketplace, it is astonishing how many computer companies cannot muster a spokesperson to talk about any subject less boring than his or her products. The rewards for being controversial are enormous and if the client is honest about the risks beforehand, they can be neutralized with careful preparation.

Look at Data Sciences; when it became the umpteenth vendor to launch a point of sale package for life and pension salespeople, it hardly mentioned the product. It talked about the 500,000 people who, according to the Securities and Investment Board, had been wrongly advised to contract out of the state pension scheme and the suspension of the Norwich Union sales force and the role of the computer as a replacement for the salesperson. Instead of a couple of paragraphs in the trade press, Data Sciences was rewarded with substantial articles in the broadsheets, a radio spot and a call from *The Money Programme*. But it had to come very close to publicly criticizing its own future customers. It was every PR consultant's dream!

Nick Horley is Managing Director of Buffalo Communications, providers of PR and marketing services to the computer industry and winners of a commendation for Best Business Campaign at the 1994 PR Week Awards. Buffalo's clients include ICL, Dun & Bradstreet Software and PhoneLink. Nick, formerly with Firefly Communications and IBM, has represented Ambra, Data Sciences, Dell, Oracle and Sequent.

21

CHOOSING A PR COMPANY

Andy West

'Why the heck am I doing this?' 'How do I know if they have succeeded?' If people asked these two simple questions before they embark on choosing a PR company then the chances of implementing a successful programme would increase dramatically. If, on the other hand, people embark on the exercise without taking stock, then failure, or at least disappointment, is not far away. There are of course many other questions and steps you should take and in this article we hope to cover these. However, if you only take one thing away from this – please remember to ask yourself the famous 'why?' question. It will save you a great deal of time and trouble later on if you can answer it honestly.

So why do you need PR? Perhaps it is because you see your competition's name in the media or perhaps it is because you want to generate sales leads. In its simplest form, good PR will generate press coverage and sales leads for your company and its products. However you should not view PR solely as a lead generating exercise. It is much more. Good PR working as part of an overall marketing campaign can build brand image for products, build a strong corporate profile, educate the marketplace and influence both specifiers and approvers. In short, PR should be viewed as creating a positive environment for your company and, ultimately, for your products.

New Strategies for Marketing Information Technology.
Edited by Christopher Field
Published in 1996 by Chapman & Hall, London. ISBN 0 412 61520 7

To be successful, PR must be viewed as a core marketing discipline. It must also receive the buy-in of top management. If it is not at the heart of your thinking it will not make a real impact on your business. It is like a person replacing a typewriter with a word processor — all it does is automate the task, whereas installing a computer may have given the opportunity to provide not just word processing capabilities but a range of information services not previously available — in short it would revolutionize the business. In the same way, if you ensure that your marketing structure is designed to work with PR then you can look forward to a real return on your investment.

Having established that PR is an essential part of the marketing mix, the next decision is normally whether to appoint an agency or to take the PR function in-house. There are arguments for both. It very much depends on the resources available, the precise nature of the job being created and the commitment to good PR. If you are committed to implementing a high level, creative PR campaign, then unless you have the facilities to develop a sophisticated in-house department the agency route is likely to be the best one. This is simply because the agency team you choose should provide the objectivity and creativity needed at a price which is more cost-effective than recruiting a team of in-house experts.

You have made the decision to appoint an agency; what steps should you now take internally and what should you look for in the agencies invited to pitch? The first step is for you to absolutely understand what you want from PR. If it is simply to generate sales leads and nothing more, then you may be better off looking at other marketing activities. However if you wish to develop an image, build a strong brand for your products or services, perhaps enter a new market, or provide support to a demand creation programme, then PR is the right discipline. All too often, however, client companies view PR simply as a means of generating press coverage. The trend, however, is towards more focused, more direct PR campaigns. In other words, the agency you select should be able to deliver a broad range of services which are tailored to communicate your business message to your entire audience — not just to the media. Consider the IT manager, the consumer, the reseller channel, the market analysts, your employees. Each can be reached in a variety of ways, not all of which rely upon the media.

Appointing an agency should be done through a combination of qualitative and quantitative processes. It is recommended by PR's professional bodies that every client company prepares a thorough brief and that it evaluates at least five agencies before drawing up a shortlist of perhaps three. It is not necessary to send the brief to all agencies at the outset. It is better to invite them all in to deliver a credentials presentation from which you should be able to make the shortlist. Draw up the shortlist from predetermined criteria. Look at the agencies' specific experience in your market sector, look closely at their client lists and talk to third parties such as existing clients and journalists. From this and from the quality of the credentials presentation, it should become immediately obvious who has the experience and capability to handle your PR. A few words of warning here: beware of men (and women) in dark suits! Do not be beguiled by senior management from the agency. They will be present at the credentials stage but insist on seeing the actual account team at the pitch.

In an ideal situation, every agency would like at least two weeks from receiving the brief to actually presenting its proposal. During this period, give each agency the opportunity to ask questions of the brief and, if appropriate, to meet with you. One of the most common questions asked at this stage is 'What is the budget?'. The decision on whether to reveal the available budget is a very individual one, however, from the agency perspective it is always better for the client to say what they have to spend. That way, the subsequent proposal is tailored to available resources.

The pitch process itself is a time consuming event for both the client and the agency. Aim to hear all pitches in one day as this is the only way you can really make an assessment on different agencies. There are many different ways of evaluating the quality of an agency's presentation. Some companies prefer to score each agency according to set criteria. Others just rely on 'gut feel'. Obviously the agency should present a proposal which meets the brief, which is realistic without being bland and which is cost effective. Depending on the brief, you should also score each agency on its creativity, its approach to the basic requirements, its understanding of your marketplace and the audience, its breadth of services and on the overall strategy of the campaign. Finally the other key element you should be looking for is how the agency measures its effectiveness.

Measuring PR is not a black art. At its crudest level it may simply be presenting a sheaf of press cuttings on a monthly or quarterly basis. Also, beware of agencies who place emphasis on activity levels such as 'we will write six press releases' as their measurement of success. Any agency can write six press releases a month – ask yourself what results those releases generated. On a more sophistic-ated level, agencies should be suggesting message checks, attitudinal surveys and a variety of other more 'personalized' measurement services. The bottom line is that, during the pitch, you should insist on establishing the measurement criteria.

The other vital element in the subsequent client–agency relationship is chemistry and there is no better time to evaluate whether you could work with an agency than at the pitch. Remember that PR requires time commitment and if the working relationship is successful it is likely that you will be working very closely with the account team.

Appointing a PR company is not an exercise you should undertake lightly. It is time consuming, it exposes the heart of your organization to outside scrutiny and it is thought provoking. It is also the start of a long-term commitment. Do not chop and change agencies as, unlike other forms of marketing, it takes time for the effects of good PR to become apparent. Over time both client and agency build up an understanding of the cultures involved, of the marketplace and of the long-term business strategy of the client organization. Without this synergy many PR campaigns are doomed to fail. However, by working as a team, by integrating PR into the overall marketing department and by appointing a creative, dynamic and experienced consultancy, PR will have an extremely positive effect on your company's image.

A 10-POINT GUIDE TO SELECTING THE RIGHT PR AGENCY

1. **Evaluation of needs**: you define your business objectives and from that you define what it is you want to achieve from PR. You should also spend time asking yourself why you are taking this step. Simply because your competitor has a PR consultancy is not good enough.
2. **Internal assessment**: you assess whether you have the resources and the skills to run an effective PR campaign. This means allocating not only your time but that of the proposed spokespeople.
3. **Define the brief**: set down on paper what you are trying to achieve as a company and what you want to achieve with PR. Set out your future plans as a company and the importance of each of your markets.
4. **Research consultancies**: talk to the media you want to be in, talk to other companies who you feel have a good profile and draw up a suitable list of potential consultancies.

5. **Credentials**: allow each of the potential consultancies to present their credentials so that you may shortlist three to four companies for the final pitch. Get them to show you work from clients with similar challenges.

6. **Brief the consultancies**: supply a written brief to each of the consultancies which will pitch for the work. If appropriate arrange a meeting with them so that they can ask the ensuing questions and clarify all elements of the brief.

7. **Pitch**: each consultancy responds to your initial brief with a set of proposals which outline what they would do, what it would cost and how they will be measured. Allow plenty of time for this – two hours per consultancy should be fine. Also aim to have all consultancies present on the same day so that you can easily compare the proposals.

8. **References**: seek references on the agency and the staff who will be working on your account. Any well-qualified consultancy should be able to supply these.

9. **Inform**: inform the agencies of your choice. Remember consultancies will have invested a great deal of their own time and money in the process so don't keep them hanging on any longer than is necessary. Also if you can provide feedback to those chosen it will be much appreciated.

10. **Commit**: now you've made your choice you must ensure the consultancy gets everything they need to do a good job. The most important of which is your commitment to the task.

Andy West is an Associate Director of Text 100, Europe's leading PR consultancy specializing in the high technology sector.

22

BRIEFING A DESIGN CONSULTANCY

David Mankin

Design for print is a fundamental element of IT marketing whether it is being utilized for a direct mail campaign, a corporate magazine, a press invitation or the implementation of a new corporate image across a broad range of media. Design can help you generate response, increase customer loyalty, sell more products and services, change perceptions and attitudes, improve communications and above all boost the bottom line.

Getting design to work effectively for you and your company is often a tortuous process with many design consultancies just not delivering the design concepts and ideas which you asked for!

The prime cause of this situation is the brief and the briefing meeting. Constructing a brief and communicating it accurately is often the most demanding part of any design exercise. It may be difficult pulling together all the necessary inputs from your company and explaining the total picture to design consultants unfamiliar with its culture. But putting together the brief is worth taking trouble over: a good brief saves money, time and disappointment.

Most briefs will be developed verbally between client and designer and it may be the design company who finally sets the agreed version in writing. Nonetheless it should be helpful to you and will protect your interests should anything go wrong, to think through and write your own agenda in advance.

New Strategies for Marketing Information Technology.
Edited by Christopher Field
Published in 1996 by Chapman & Hall, London. ISBN 0 412 61520 7

The briefs typically given to design consultancies tend to fall into one of two categories, the 'back of the envelope' type or the weighty document full of detailed specifications. Each has its limitations: the back of the envelope variety rarely gives enough information, while a weighty document may labour the details but omit the overall concept of what a company is trying to achieve.

As a way of covering all bases, you could offer a ten-point brief, consisting of the following.

Company background

Putting the company and product or service in context. Inform the designer of the main activities, organizational culture and market position, actual and perceived. With all design projects it is important to set the scene giving the design company a snapshot of who you are, what business you are in and what the aims and ethos of the organization are. Also an idea of other marketing activities that you are involved in can help complete the picture.

The competition

Explaining where you sit in relation to the competition allows the designer to start building up a mental picture of your marketing needs, the market position and the required image.

Marketing objectives

This should be clear cut in terms of market share, position relative to the competition, value of business and projected turnover.

Communications objectives

What core messages do you want to put across and what do you want to achieve through the design project – direct response, increased loyalty, increased awareness, change of perceptions and attitudes, a purchase?

The target audience

Who are they, what are they like and what part do they play in the acquisition of products and services you have on offer? What existing literature are they receiving from you and the competition?

Product features and benefits

This is the nitty-gritty of the product or service. What are the USPs of your product/service over the competition? The designer will not need lengthy, detailed technical notes on how a product works, rather a succinct overview of the character of the product and its attributes.

Communications requirements and tone of voice

Is it a direct mail campaign, a quarterly newsletter or magazine, graphics for an exhibition, a complete overhaul of the corporate image, a brochure, an information pack or a simple invitation to a seminar on networking? Furthermore what tone of voice do you see the literature having? Serious? Playful? Cool? Austere? Corporate? Open? Assertive?

Schedule

When do you need it and are there any critical dates within the schedule, presentation of the visual concepts to senior management or the need to distribute the leaflet at a particular exhibition, for example?

Budget

Often people commission design on the basis of: I want to achieve this, how much is it going to cost me? This is a difficult situation for a design consultancy to work within. There are always a multitude of variables which can increase and decrease the costs. It is important that there are sufficient guidelines for the design company to work within to produce design concepts which meet the brief and can then be produced within the budget.

Likes and dislikes and existing literature

Design is a highly subjective topic fraught with differences of opinion. If you have strong opinions on the style you require it is important that you inform the designers of your likes and dislikes. At the very least it helps the designer determine the right tone and after all you are more immersed in the relevant part of the market. However, be prepared to listen to the designers' suggestions, even if you do not immediately agree. A good designer will design appropriately for the brief and the market achieving the set objectives, but without necessarily designing to suit your personal tastes.

THE DOs AND DON'Ts OF BRIEFING DESIGN

- Do set a written brief and stick to it.
- Don't change your mind halfway through the project without expecting to be charged for work already completed.
- Do try to have text supplied by yourself as complete as possible. Amendments made once artwork is underway will be charged as extra.
- Do be realistic about the time required to complete the various stages of the project. Unrealistic deadlines can cause mistakes and loss of quality, apart from possible rush charges.
- Don't say: 'How much will it cost?', say 'What can you achieve within a budget of X'. Or provide a maximum/minimum range in which the project must be completed.
- Do tell the designer if there are any indirect items to be deducted from their budget, e.g. postage.
- Do warn the designer of any industry clichés you wish to avoid.
- Don't get bogged down in technical detail or product attributes.
- Do keep technical details, and indeed the entire brief, as simple as possible.
- Do allow a large enough proportion of your budget for the design concept stage of a project. A project is always more successful when it is planned and thought through.
- Don't assume that, because the design concepts and planning are less tangible than production, they are less important.
- Do encourage your designer to report back to you at frequent intervals.
- Do check that the designer understands the brief and encourage questions.
- Do allocate enough time for the briefing meeting. A rushed brief is almost guaranteed to cause misunderstanding.
- Do provide as much background literature and information as possible, both from your own company and the market in general. It provides the designer with a visual focus of the area in which they will be working.
- Don't expect the designer to come up with an immediate solution. He will want time to assimilate the brief and immerse himself in the background information.

- Do tell the designer who will be responsible for the approval of the design.
- Do tell the designer who will be the point of contact for queries and administration.
- Do inform the designer of any constraints or sensitivities – colour, typographic styles, language, etc.
- Do consider the need to resize film for international use.

CHECKLIST

- company background
- the competition
- marketing objectives
- communications objectives
- the target audience
- product features and benefits
- communications requirements and tone of voice
- schedule
- budget
- likes and dislikes and existing literature.

Remember to consider and discuss:

- visual matter – charts, diagrams, photographs, illustrations
- format – landscape, portrait, concertina fold
- size – A4, A5, non-standard dimensions
- quality – overall production standards, paper quality, number of colours
- quantity – print run
- paper – white, tinted, recycled
- finishing – lamination, spiral binding, etc.

David Mankin is a partner at SPY Design, a graphic design and marketing company dedicated to producing outstanding and articulate visual solutions to marketing communications problems. Technology companies are strongly represented in the company's portfolio.

PART EIGHT
LET'S GO FLY A KITE
Public relations

INTRODUCTION

Many companies choose a PR company on the same emotional criteria they use to buy a sports car. Rust and reliability come a poor second to speed and appeal. If they are first-time users, they will have no experience of what to expect other than anecdotal. Although the industry's professional body, the Public Relations Consultants Association (PRCA), can take some of the pain out of the process, it still appears to be true that companies' first taste of PR is not a happy one.

Everyone has an opinion about PR; it all depends on who you ask and on what day you ask it. If you ask a journalist, chances are they will say that it is a waste of time, particularly theirs. Ask a marketing manager and they will often say that PR is not a strategic marketing tool and that the results are impossible to measure. Ask the audience at which PR is directed and they will say it is the art of the half-truth. Perhaps PR is always destined to be given a hard time, considering the small percentage of turnover that companies commit to it. It does seem odd just how much negative reaction it inspires.

This negative view obscures what is also true about public relations – that more and more companies are doing it and spending more and more money on it. Ask the same journalist tomorrow and they will say that they depend on PR agencies to get access to stories, the same marketing manager will admit that it is the most flexible of marketing disciplines and that they can control the cost like no other marketing discipline; the audience will say that editorial that is largely fed by PR is accepted as the facts, facts that advertising cannot deliver.

PR agencies are thriving on this success and at last count there were over 100 companies in the UK deriving their income solely from IT PR, not counting those that set up divisions and saved their

New Strategies for Marketing Information Technology.
Edited by Christopher Field
Published in 1996 by Chapman & Hall, London. ISBN 0 412 61520 7

recessionary bacons. These same agencies have also pioneered full service marketing consultancy in a way that other specialist agencies have not. Many PR consultancies can now provide direct marketing, contract publishing, events management and graphic design at a level to compete with the specialists. Where they do not have the skills in-house, they will subcontract claiming that it will always be cheaper for their customers to use networked resources rather than pay for the overheads of keeping the resources in-house, full time.

Gordon Knight confronts PR's greatest challenge, to measure and demonstrate results.

Mike Park, with first-hand experience at Apple, shows how the injection of some non-IT brand management can make all the difference to your public relations.

23

OUTPUT OR RESULTS?
Measuring PR effectiveness

Gordon Knight

In any business, investment requires justification. If a company is about to embark upon the expense of an investment in PR, not only does it want to be able to measure the output of the campaign, but it also needs to see the results. More importantly, it needs to be able to measure those results and, if possible, translate them into value for money.

Public relations is traditionally considered a difficult discipline to measure. PR programmes often constitute just one agreed element of a marketing strategy for a company and, as such, it is sometimes difficult to separate the achievements of PR from the other components of the marketing mix.

Unhelpfully, the objectives set for PR programmes often revolve around nebulous notions such as an 'improvement in image' or 'greater share of voice', which are hard to measure accurately.

Also, it has to be conceded, such effort as has been put into developing new measurement techniques by the PR industry itself has focused largely on media coverage – or output – measurement, rather than true results measurement.

Public relations in industry is essentially about changing people's perceptions and, ultimately, influencing the way they behave, in ways that help a business achieve its objectives. Accurate measurement, therefore, must start with a clear understanding of the required role of PR in contributing to the company's success.

New Strategies for Marketing Information Technology.
Edited by Christopher Field
Published in 1996 by Chapman & Hall, London. ISBN 0 412 61520 7

Once business objectives are clearly defined, then it should be possible to identify PR aims that will have a meaningful impact in helping to achieve them.

An obvious example of a business objective in the IT sector might be to build or retain market share in a highly competitive niche area. A corresponding PR aim could therefore be to position a company as the authority in those issues that most affect customers in the sector, thereby creating the optimum environment for a sales dialogue.

Equally, PR might have an important role in dealing with serious corporate issues – such as to counter planned regulations that could have a negative impact on a company's business prospects, for example.

The PR aim against this particular business objective could be to convince legislators and the opinion formers that influence them that self-regulation is a better approach and more appropriate to an open competitive market.

Essentially, the common factor between an organization's business objectives and its corresponding PR aims is that attitudinal change should result in behaviour or decisions by the target audiences that impact positively on the organization's business.

Attitudinal monitoring thus needs to play a key role in the measurement of the effectiveness of most PR programmes. A really professionally planned programme should, ideally, start with the benefit of some initial research to identify the issues that most affect the various target groups.

The research will also help isolate the perceptions that the PR programme needs to address and make some evaluation of the benefits to the business of changing or enhancing them.

Naturally, existing company research into perceptions of the organization will often serve as the benchmark needed to set targets and monitor results. Indeed, it may be that the problems identified through existing company-commissioned research have dictated the need for a corrective PR programme in the first place. However, where existing research does not exist, there is little alternative in most cases but to commission it. Failure to undertake this preliminary step will mean 'flying blind'.

The cost of research is, of course, a point of resistance for many IT companies planning PR campaigns. That is why the PR industry is now examining ways of making such research – essential as it is to plan and measure PR effectively – affordable to companies operating on tight budgets.

So what sort of elements should be included in a research package specially designed for validating and measuring the results of PR campaigns?

Essentially it needs to be flexible enough to cover the wide range of alternative techniques often deployed in PR campaigns, also focused enough to allow meaningful measurement at relatively low costs.

Typical modules in the package might include the following.

Validation module

A structured qualitative group, representing the key target audience for the PR campaign, to validate the messages, principal media and techniques to be deployed in the programme.

For an IT campaign, this could involve 10–12 of the key decision makers and/or influencers involved in the buying process in a session to validate and refine the entire approach to a PR campaign before it kicks off.

Media module

A telephone research-based module, using a 10–15 minute question-naire, to assess the attitudes to the company and its key competitors of a sample of up to 25 influential media. This kind of survey can reveal important prejudices or misconceptions that will need to be addressed right at the outset of the campaign.

Opinion former module

A further telephone-based module, again using a 10–15 minute questionnaire, to measure perceptions of a sample of, say, up to 50 important opinion formers of the company and key competitors. Opinion formers could include user groups, influential industry bodies, consultants, analysts or academics, whose opinions are regularly sought by the media or potential customers.

Consumer module

For businesses where consumers are in themselves decision makers, e.g. the SoHo market, evaluation research could be conducted through a computer-based omnibus covering up to 2,000 UK households, which can accurately measure consumer perceptions of a company and its products or services, either nationally or, where relevant, in local communities. The latter could be especially important where expansion is intended and planning applications and appeals could be involved.

Employee module

A special employee module, perhaps using postal questionnaires mailed to employees' home addresses, would be an invaluable way to measure employees' and, if appropriate, families' attitudes to a company, its culture and policies.

Such a module might come into play at the start of a major cultural change process, when measuring employees' perceptions and attitudes during the communications programme accompanying the change could be critical to its successful accomplishment.

Special events module

A module, using telephone research among attendees and non-attendees at company-organized special events, is one of the best ways to assess the impact of and responses to major seminars, roadshows, corporate hospitality, factory openings or similar events carried out as part of PR campaigns. Specifically, such research measures not only the effect of the activity on those people who take part, but explores the perceptions of those who decline.

Sponsorship module

Businesses making heavy use of publicity sponsorship really need a continuous research module, interviewing several thousand consumers per annum, to track awareness of, and attitudes to, the kind of large-scale sponsorship that is aimed at mass consumer audiences.

Each of the modules above needs, of course, to be open to adaptation and tailoring to meet specific requirements and, most importantly, needs to be able to establish and track target audience attitudes even for smaller campaigns, without a disproportionate share of costs being diverted to research.

The particular value of this type of approach is that it can be used to measure the great majority of PR campaigns – even those which are not designed to achieve media coverage.

For example, often a PR campaign's key objective can be to manage the communication of an issue in such a way that it doesn't 'hit the press': a major redundancy exercise or board-level restructuring is not necessarily something a business wants to see openly aired in the media.

Equally, there may simply be much more effective ways of reaching a small number of key decision makers than broadcasting to them through the media, and therefore media coverage measurement has little, if any, role to play.

However, media coverage measurement, it must be said, is widely used as a measure of PR success and, in many cases, is the only measure undertaken.

Certainly, it can make a useful contribution to PR evaluation – as long as it is recognized that it is really no more than output, not results, measurement.

Commercially available techniques used for measuring media coverage range from the largely discredited measurement of advertising equivalence (i.e. using a multiple of the cost of the equivalent advertising space) to advanced, computer-based systems for tracking key word mentions, bias and tone in news and feature items covering virtually the entire output of the British, European or world media.

Costs can equally vary from a few tens of pounds per month for a basic impact and content analysis up to several thousand for a full-scale monitoring of a company's and its competitors' coverage throughout the entire UK and even international media.

Many of the better PR agencies – recognizing the importance of demonstrating value for money to their clients – offer media coverage analysis free as part of their fee arrangements.

So what sort of characteristics should be looked for in a well-designed media coverage analysis system?

Firstly, of course, the system should begin with the elimination of any incidental coverage not generated by the programme and/or any coverage not delivering the agreed campaign messages.

The remaining coverage should then be evaluated using criteria such as the following, which includes all the key measures relevant to determine the effect on the target audiences:

- **Total audience reach**: the combined reach or 'cumulative opportunities to see' (COTS) of all the items of coverage generated by the programme, calculated in terms of the readership of printed media and total audience of live media programmes.
- **Target audience reach**: the 'audience factor' of each item of media coverage in terms of the reach among the target audiences (if data is available) of the journal or programme in which it appears.
- **Impact**: the rating of each item in terms of its likely impact on the target groups by virtue of its length, content and exclusivity.

- **Frequency**: the number of items achieved in nominated key target media during the period of the programme.
- **Message delivery**: the success of each item in delivering the agreed messages (often it is important to differentiate between the various messages to determine which are being delivered most successfully).
- **Cost per 1000 COTS**: the cost-effectiveness of the coverage in achieving the total audience reach, usually expressed in cost per thousand 'COTS'.

No PR evaluation system can, of course, ever be definitive. As markets change and new media develop, PR effectiveness measurement must deploy new techniques to maintain its relevance.

Ultimately, however, every company using public relations will in one way or another set its own criteria for a successful programme: assistance with sales leads generation, growing industry authority, more frequent invitations to tender, success with planning permissions, easier local recruitment, etc.

Measurement of media coverage or the changes in target audience attitudes and perceptions that result from PR activity – important though their contribution may be – need to be ultimately related to clearly defined business goals such as the above.

Once the public relations industry can meet that challenge effectively and consistently then it really will make a quantum leap forward in the respect – and budgets – it commands in the IT and other business sectors.

Gordon Knight started in public relations in 1970 and was a founder director of Paragon Communications. Still a director there, he was one of the management team that floated the company on the Stock Exchange in 1987 and led the agency's corporate and business to business team to over a dozen major awards.

24

IT PUBLIC RELATIONS

Brands and benefits

Mike Park

In 1984 I was public relations consultant to Apple Computer. In one briefing session, my client talked about the new dimension in user friendly computing that was about to change the way the world would do business.

The paradox was that this man, who was charged with explaining just why the Macintosh revolution was possible, was himself rooted in the past world of computer-speak for computer professionals. His style of communication should have been killed off at Apple during their previous years of experience when the personal computer had already reached mass markets – where the use of data processing jargon blunted sales to the masses.

But our client was an earnest, loyal and professional servant of his company. He was anxious that his public relations consultants should receive every detail of the wonder machine's technical specification. But, of course, he could have simply handed over a printed sheet and bade us goodbye. We could not get him to explain why this new computer would change the business world. So, to my colleague and I, so far, the Macintosh revolution remained stillborn in our minds.

Yet the operating system described to us was later to be imitated by Microsoft founder, Bill Gates, making the creator of Windows one of the richest men on Earth. As this book goes to press, nearly 50 million users of Macintosh and Windows exist around the world.

New Strategies for Marketing Information Technology.
Edited by Christopher Field
Published in 1996 by Chapman & Hall, London. ISBN 0 412 61520 7

However, the significance of my advance insight into the future of computing was not obvious to me after that first briefing. It became clear through talking to people outside the computer world – architects, project managers or accountants.

These were the footsoldiers of the armies of independent, free thinking personal computer users who, Apple hoped, were about to throw off the shackles of domination by the likes of IBM and Digital. These megacorporations we, in 1984, regarded as the forces of darkness, in cahoots with the old order of data processing managers whom, it was widely believed, they controlled.

But it didn't take long, after we launched Macintosh to over 120 eager journalists, for Apple to follow the appointment of Pepsi's John Sculley as its Chief Executive with a radically new style of boss for the UK too. He came from the marketing department of Gillette and transformed the way in which Macintosh was sold. The expression 'computer literate' was banned. Brand management was introduced. Apple Centres of channel distribution were established to reach audiences who were only interested in business-enhancement messages. A 'test-drive' programme of product reviews evoked massive publicity for the Mac.

IBM: FROM SELF-IMMOLATION TO RESTORATION

If the advent of the Mac was seminal to modern computing and its implications for IT public relations, then the history of IBM's communications must also provide unforgettable lessons for communicators.

That same year, 1984, the British management writer, Robert Heller, bet me that Apple would not succeed against IBM. The business guru's confidence in Big Blue was typical of the way IBM was regarded in the early eighties.

Subsequently, no IT company's troubles – no company's troubles anywhere – have been examined in greater detail and with such serious glee, bordering on malevolence, than the problems of IBM. The company's underlying decline, attributed by battalions of commentators to failed R&D, marketing and management strategies (with a thick leavening of missed opportunities and suicidal US Government relations) eventually led to the biggest corporate loss in history in 1993. The publishers of the book *Computer Wars* called this process 'self-immolation'.

The end of the end was predicted, starting with the death of IBM's mainframe business. Just as few commentators in 1984 would have given any rival a prayer in the face of IBM's marketing might, in early 1994, equally few pundits were giving IBM a prayer in the face of the unstoppable success of the likes of Microsoft, Intel and Compaq. These three firms had long since inherited Silicon Valley's free-spirit mantle from an Apple that had lost its shine.

Now see what happened. A new IBM chief executive was appointed. He realigned the mainframe division to meet modern markets. He reorganized the company according to vertical markets where its customers operate. And he told the world what he was doing – without overstatement and with considerable applause from those listening, including the media.

By mid-1994, Lou Gerstner of IBM was getting a better press than Bill Gates. Far better. Suddenly it was Microsoft who represented the forces of darkness while IBM could be seen as a beacon of hope – not just for its employees, but in continuing to protect the West from Japan.

This image U-turn is no accident. Influential third parties had been consulted. Customers, analysts and journalists liked what they heard – and said so. This was public relations that contributed to company resurgence. It started at the top, was bought throughout the company and teamwork made it happen. Media now praise IBM's shedding its former reputation for high prices and high-handed customer relations.

The lesson is simple. The old IBM was perceived to operate in such a way that public relations were simply not part of the culture. Today, IBM uses public relations as successfully as its rivals did in the past to make its brand rise above the noise level in the markets of the present.

BRAND VALUES AND THE COMMODITY GUTTER

Talk to public relations practitioners in the IT world today and you will be told that the name of the game is either brand values or selling benefits – or both, since branding is all about creating a better sales environment, one in which you can put a premium price on your product. For the Compaq-inspired price wars started in 1993 have placed great emphasis on the need to rise above the commodity gutter in which the price brawl rumbles.

Public relations is better-placed to keep a brand name out of the commodity gutter than any other form of corporate or marketing communication. This is because public relations differs from all other communications. How? Because it specifically employs the use of third parties to inform and persuade.

Public relations is word of mouth amplified and managed. And word of mouth recommendation, as all businesspeople from your local plumber to Richard Branson will tell you, is the most powerful sales tool known.

The most effective public relations programme will generate these recommendations through every or any channel of endorsement, whether implied through press publicity or explicitly through customer case histories. Mobilize dealer, consultant and academic commentator support for maximum credibility.

Credibility is a word that public relations people bandy about all the time. That's because, at the end of the practitioner's working day, he or she enjoys great professional satisfaction if they know they have delivered plenty of it on behalf of their clients or company bosses. Credibility is the cement that holds the brand values together to make them acceptable to the market. Without credibility, these values just don't stack up.

CREDIBILITY AND THE MEDIA CUSTOMER

The way marketers can ensure a better level of credible editorial publicity is to understand and exploit the business of journalism. This is not really hard to do, because all you have to remember is that the world of the journalist is about news, information and opinions – and deadlines. Treat journalists as if they were customers. They need genuine news, their own angles on a story, access to authoritative comment and product users, as well as time to write an article that does justice to the subject, supporting and promoting your brand values.

Big budget advertising, direct mail or exhibitions may promote a brand louder, but compared to user-led media relations, the missing credibility factor means these are expensive ways to communicate messages that have a relatively low level of acceptance. This is because the audience knows that these forms of marketing communications merely amount to a company talking about itself.

So add it all up. Talk benefits, not jargon. Let your customers and industry partners do your talking for you. Treat journalists as customers and they will repay you with supportive coverage. Use public relations to get your brand hovering above the profane noise level of the street market. Get the public to believe that it is worth paying extra to buy your brand.

Fine talk in theory, but how is this all achieved? What are the stages that need to be passed to get on to this public relations high ground?

STRATEGIES THAT EXPLOIT IT'S NEW WORLD ORDER

The most coherent public relations programme starts by recognizing the task. The fact that the IT world is constantly changing is the public relations world's big opportunity. Informing and persuading have become critical factors in selling products and services that meet the new priorities.

These are the objectives of public relations programmes in a new IT world order that can so rapidly self-destruct to become tomorrow's old world ashes. Computing professionals need to know where they stand in all this. Vendors have to be able to position their products and their reputations as supporting their customers whatever the current architectural or environmental fad. This means deciding what a company's strengths are and exactly why no rival vendors have an equal proposition for the market.

That is what dictates public relations strategy: defining the task and the unique proposition, then single-mindedly communicating to support the brand. Setting such objectives also provides the criteria by which a public relations programme can be measured. But what do you measure? What positions are agreed against which progress can be judged? What are the measurement techniques?

There are probably as many sophisticated computerized analysis techniques for measuring public relations effectiveness as there are high-tech public relations consultancies. The questions to be asked about them are: do these techniques make you any the wiser than conventional press cuttings analysis – and how much do these research techniques cost? Any measurement activity has also to take into account factors like activity against plan, sales force participation and their satisfaction with the programme, dealer and opinion-former co-operation and, vitally, the role of customers.

I started by talking about Apple and then IBM. Both companies have ridden the swings and roundabouts of those twin impostors, triumph and disaster. What all companies need is consistent public relations promoting consistent brand values, majoring on the benefits of dealing with that company. Purchasing is as much about a company's reputation as it is about the product. The fortunes of any firm can change dramatically. The market can also become unrecognizable apparently overnight.

But consistency in communications should transcend temporary trading fluctuations. The brand doesn't have to yo-yo with them. Public relations can make the brand your most stable asset.

Mike Park is an independent public relations consultant. He was previously a Board Director at Lowe Hell Communications and the Rowland Company. He launched the Apple Macintosh and Cellnet in the UK and has worked as a consultant for ICL, Research Machines and Digital Europe.

PART NINE

PLAYING THE
PIED PIPER
OF FLEET STREET

The press

INTRODUCTION

It is common for IT companies to target only those newspapers and magazines that they read themselves or ones that they hold in high regard. The *Financial Times* and the *Economist* are in this league of respect. Companies often feel that they know these chosen publications well and are therefore able to give them the sort of information that will be used.

However, the likelihood that their customers read the same publications will be coincidental rather than planned. Moreover, although a column in the *Financial Times* may impress the messenger, it may never reach the customer. If it does it will not necessarily have the desired effect. For instance, a PC software buyer is more likely to be in the mood to buy when they are reading *Computer Shopper*, which is often not a magazine on companies' hit lists, but is nevertheless an influential and widely read magazine.

And when you do commit to talking to the press, does the prospect fill you with apprehension because last time they printed something you feel you didn't say or because you made an appalling 'gaffe' that you felt unable to undo? The apprehension is often born of the fact that the press is enormously influential and can make and break both careers and companies.

However, at the level we are considering, the press is but one of the many channels that exist for you to communicate with your audiences. You need it perhaps slightly more than it needs you, but with planning, a professional approach, experience and training, you can reach those audiences in ways that persuade like no direct endorsement ever can.

Here are two articles from David Tebbutt and Peter Bartram which give advice on finding out how to make the press work for

New Strategies for Marketing Information Technology.
Edited by Christopher Field
Published in 1996 by Chapman & Hall, London. ISBN 0 412 61520 7

you. Find out how to speak to communicate with them so that they will come back again and again for a quote.

Bearing in mind that 'no comment' is no longer an option, the very least you can expect to achieve is positive and accurate information about your company in influential publications. At best, you can work with the press to position yourself as an industry spokesperson, above your competitors.

25

HANDLING THE PRESS

David Tebbutt

Isn't it odd that some people always manage to get good press coverage and others don't? It doesn't seem fair, yet there are very good reasons for the discrepancy. Success with the press is based on a clear understanding of how it works and on your ability to forge a decent relationship with the journalist.

When told this, a product manager of a large software publisher said 'but they're all scruffy, left-wing vegetarians.' His attitude revealed a huge culture gap. He wasn't comfortable working with people who marched to a different drummer, people whose values and attitudes were clearly different to his own. Although a cultural gulf may divide the interviewer and the interviewee, you simply cannot allow your own prejudices to create a barrier between your messages and their publication. The journalist is your only conduit to editorial coverage.

Of course, the press itself is accused of prejudice. Yet this shouldn't come as a great surprise. No newspaper makes a secret of its point of view. Nor does the computer press. Apple magazines and PC magazines are interested in different things. Even apparently competing magazines such as *Computer Weekly* and *Computing* each have a distinct angle. *Computing* has much more of a user focus than *Computer Weekly*. The first step to success with the press is to understand each title's point of view. You need to know who its readers are and why they read it. If you don't know, telephone the editorial office and ask. Or, if you're caught by surprise, simply ask

New Strategies for Marketing Information Technology.
Edited by Christopher Field
Published in 1996 by Chapman & Hall, London. ISBN 0 412 61520 7

the journalist who they see as their typical readers. They will be only too pleased to tell you and this will buy you valuable thinking time as well as helping you target your messages more accurately. The *Guardian* computer pages, for example, have to be written for 'the person on the Clapham omnibus'. In other words, its readers expect an interesting but neutral and jargon-free read. *Microscope*'s readers are value added resellers who want to keep up with personal computer industry news, opinions, products, companies and gossip.

Once you know who the readers are then, regardless of the knowledge, ability and personal habits of the journalist, you can 'angle' your story to their needs. This will hook the journalist's attention, providing the story itself is worth writing about. It has to be interesting and different from all the other stories that clamour for the journalist's attention. 'We are launching a lower-priced personal computer', simply won't work these days. Send a press release instead.

Bear in mind the six questions which live permanently in a journalist's mind. They are what, who, when, where, why and how. The answer to 'what?' determines whether the journalist is interested in the story. 'Man bites dog' would work. 'Small fire on the Isle of Wight, no one hurt' wouldn't. Then the journalist wants to know who's behind the story. You only have to read the papers to realize that a big name can get in the news with a small story, whereas an unknown name has to have a substantial story to achieve the same coverage.

Timing is important too. Something which will happen soon or which happened recently is far more valuable to a journalist than something less timely. Remember that journalists are rightly suspicious of companies which boast that they will do something at some point in the future. This trick is often adopted by large companies to derail competitors who are ahead of them.

Geographic location or industry sector may be important, depending on the publication. An interested journalist is one who is still talking to you after you have delivered the what, who, when and where of your message. You will have hooked their interest and you will be able to expand on the why and how more or less at your leisure. Telling journalists a story is a bit like telling a joke backwards. You start with the punchline, the 'what?' and gradually work backwards into the detail.

Be ready to meet journalists at all times by preparing four or five key messages. Two might be about your company and three about the part for which you are responsible. 'We have been profitable for nine consecutive quarters' sounds good coming from a company that was once close to bankruptcy. It's probably not the main message, but it's worth jamming into the conversation. Think of the messages as arrows in a quiver or bullets in a bandolier. They are your only weapons when the journalist starts putting you under pressure. Make each message pithy and easy to remember. Practice being a journalist by asking yourself cynical questions such as 'who cares', 'so what' and 'prove it'. If your message survives this then you have a good one.

Look for stories in product, company, customer and industry developments. It doesn't always have to be a new product, it could be an interesting installation or a comment on a major industry issue. Regrettably, journalists and readers find bad news far more interesting than good news. Readers will pick up the publication with the most arresting headline. The same story can generate two headlines: 'Company X wins major order' or 'Company Y ditched in favour of company X'. The second story implies drama, excitement and interest. The reader is far more interested in why company Y was ditched. You can use this fundamental quirk of human nature to your advantage.

You certainly don't want to push out bad news about your own company. But if you do have some particularly good news, it is bound to be bad for someone else. You have to be careful not to criticize your competitors, but there's nothing wrong with stating the facts in a way that helps the journalist see their headline value. 'We won against stiff competition' or 'our system completely replaced the one they had' would be quite enough to get the journalist's antennae twitching. All you have to do is wait for the questions and answer them honestly, without gloating.

Whatever you do, don't go 'off the record' to say something damaging about another company. In fact, avoid going off the record altogether. You really have to know and trust your journalist to use this technique. Most of the time, 'off the record' is used by someone to show off. Now and again, it is genuinely helpful in order to put something in context – 'We can't talk about this because we're about to be sued'. The trouble is that this information is now in the journalist's mind and, unless you've clearly agreed the terms of your disclosure, they may try to get the story from another source.

Avoid, too, the use of the expression 'no comment'. It means you're guilty. 'Is it true that you are about to sue company X?' asks the journalist. If you reply 'no comment' then this makes it sound as if you are about to sue. Mellow the term by saying 'I'm sure you realize that, even if it were true, we would not be able to comment.' Or, 'surely you don't expect me to answer silly questions like that.'

Or use the politician's trick of, 'perhaps the question you should be asking me is . . . ' and use this to get the journalist onto a subject with which you feel more comfortable. It's worth a try anyway.

Journalists fall into two broad categories – news and features. Feature writers are generally the more relaxing for you. Unless they are the crusading type, they're generally after factual information and your opinions in order to write well-balanced articles. The news hound, on the other hand is almost always frantic, tries to create stories with bite and rarely has enough space to do them full justice. Although feature writers usually appear quite laid back, they still have an armoury of tricks at the ready in case you start becoming evasive or unhelpful. When pushed, they can give you just as hard a time as a news writer. You should aim to be interesting, truthful, stick to what you're allowed to say and slip in messages if you get the opportunity. If journalists find you a useful source of information, they're less likely to give you a rough ride.

The main tricks used by journalists are all designed with one purpose, to make you blurt something you didn't mean to say. This guarantees the journalist exclusivity and possibly gives them a new story which they weren't expecting. They will induce the blurt in one of three ways. The first is to make you lose control of your thoughts. You'll know when this happens because, instead of talking about what you'd planned, you find yourself answering their increasingly rapid questions. Your answers are coming from what you know rather from what you're allowed to discuss. You have to slow the pace and stick with your own agenda.

Journalists may try to undermine your credibility by getting you to say something you didn't mean or to comment on a subject you know nothing about. They will then count on your personal embarrassment to drive you into a blurt to restore credibility. 'Well I can't tell you any more about that, but we are in the process of buying company X.' Blurt one of your messages, for goodness' sake.

Another trick is to lull you into a false sense of camaraderie. A sympathetic ear is very seductive and you can easily forget you are talking to a journalist. Indiscretions will slip out and the journalist will not even let on that this has happened. 'My boss couldn't manage their way out of a paper bag' doesn't look so funny in print.

Journalists will also vary hugely in their knowledge and experience. If you feel you're not making contact, ask the journalist what they already know about your subject. You have to do this sensitively. However frustrated you might feel – the editor may have sent a substitute – you can't afford to be confrontational. If the journalist's knowledge is slight, you have the perfect opportunity to help them see your story in a wider context. It will make them look good, and you will end up with decent coverage.

If you understand the life cycle of papers and magazines, you will be able to judge whether pressure is genuine or contrived. Most weekly computer industry papers 'go to bed' on Monday night. If a news journalist calls you on Wednesday saying they are 'going to run with this, unless you have anything to add', then you can be fairly sure that the pressure is simulated to get you to make an ill-considered comment. Offer to call back if you're not sure what to say, and then stick to your promise. Most journalists will be astonished. You will have not only given yourself a few minutes to think, you will also strengthen your relationship with that journalist.

Finally, make yourself available to the publications you value. If journalists know they can check facts with you or call you for a quote, you'll be amazed how your coverage improves.

David Tebbutt is a journalist. With Martin Banks, both winners of multiple 'technology columnist of the year' awards, he runs regular media skills training courses for leading computing companies. Their partnership, called Press Here, may be contacted on 0181 866 4400 or at Canada House, 272 Field End Road, Eastcote, Middlesex HA4 9NA.

26

TALKING TO THE PRESS

Peter Bartram

When a major UK software company organized a press trip to its US subsidiary, press officers failed to brief a key Stateside manager carefully enough about the dangers of talking about confidential client projects. During the visit, this errant manager revealed to delighted journalists that IBM's key 'data repository' project, on which the software company had been working, was starting again from scratch. The story made a front-page lead in most of the British computer newspapers and caused IBM considerable embarrassment. *Computer Weekly* headlined its story: 'IBM struggles to salvage data repository'. Other press comments: 'IBM has fallen on its sword'; 'They've taken two below the water line'; 'The repository is in the drunk tank'; 'It's all over the floor'. The story also diverted attention away from the main purpose of the visit.

The story underlines the dangers of speaking to the press. But does that mean managers should never speak to the press? In fact, talking to journalists is something many senior managers in IT companies no longer have an option about. The IT business is big news. And speaking to journalists can generate positive publicity when done effectively.

Before you face a journalist, there are a few important things that you should know. It pays to take the time to find out about them – if necessary with the help of your public relations advisers.

The things you need to know about fall into three main categories:

New Strategies for Marketing Information Technology.
Edited by Christopher Field
Published in 1996 by Chapman & Hall, London. ISBN 0 412 61520 7

1. What you should know about your interviewer

As with any business meeting, it pays to know something about the person or people you'll be meeting before you do so. It makes breaking the ice a little less painful when you do meet. It helps you to tune on to their wavelength more quickly. And, if we are honest, it gives you a psychological boost to know you've got 'something' on them.

Of course, it is not always practicable to find out much – or indeed anything – about the journalists you'll be meeting. At a press conference with 50 newshounds, you can't know all their names, let alone their life histories.

But there are certain circumstances when you really must take the time to brief yourself. These are:

- when you're facing a one-to-one interview;
- when you're holding a small briefing for a handful (say not more than four or five) of journalists;
- when you're going on a facility trip (an organized visit for journalists) with a similarly small group of journalists;
- when there is a handful of journalists who cover your industry or company and you're likely to meet them regularly at industry events or receive out-of-the-blue telephone calls from them for comments and quotes.

2. What you should know about the purpose of the interview

In some cases, you will have initiated the interview but in others the request for the interview may come from the journalist. In these cases, it is essential to find out from the journalist what the purpose and focus of the interview will be.

There could be a number of different reasons why a journalist wants to interview you:

- To pursue a specific hard news story or feature article. The focus is clear. It is about a specific product or project with which your company is involved, or about some corporate development in the company itself.
- To increase general understanding. The focus is fuzzy. It is about building background knowledge of your company or business area.
- To obtain an example for a planned feature. The focus is specific. It is about finding relevant examples for a specific article.

- To seek information for a specific topic article. The focus is clear but broad. The journalist may want 'educating' on a topic about which they know little.
- To seek evidence to support a point of view. The focus is clear, but may be unhelpful if you do not subscribe to the point of view the journalist will pursue in their article.
- To obtain information on customers or clients. The true focus of the interview may be hidden. The journalist may not be primarily seeking information about your company, but about a customer in which they are particularly interested.

In practically all cases, a journalist will be prepared to reveal the purpose of the interview in advance. Indeed you should beware if they are not prepared to do so.

3. What you should know about your company and its messages

To start with, you should be certain you have all the background information about your company – the kind of information that is too often overlooked – at your fingertips. Then you need to make sure you know the major proactive messages that your company is seeking to get across.

Next, you need to bear both of these in mind as you focus on the purpose of the interview in hand. You need to be certain you are completely up to date on your company's activities in whatever areas will be discussed. And you should try to anticipate the main areas that the interviewer is likely to want to know about and possible questions that may be asked. Remember that an interviewer will often want to probe behind the information you provide. When you volunteer information in an interview, have you thought about the likely supplementary questions it may provoke? Don't try and prepare answers to all the questions that could be asked. That would probably be impossible, and in any event would lead to a stilted and possibly unproductive interview for both parties. Some journalists requesting interviews with executives may be asked to submit a list of questions in advance. Generally, journalists are reluctant to do this. And, in any event, it gives an impression to the journalist that you're nervous about them finding out things about your company that you might wish to hide. But you should arrange to be well briefed on all the main areas that are likely to be discussed.

It is probably helpful to prepare a form of words to use in answer to questions about any especially sensitive areas, but you should avoid giving the appearance of parroting some kind of company line. You will also create a better impression by not reading from a prepared statement on a particular subject.

Finally, you need to make certain you have assembled everything you are likely to need during the interview before it starts. It gives an unprepared and unprofessional appearance not to have material to hand that an interviewer might reasonably expect you to have. It also wastes time and interrupts the flow of the interview if you have to search around for papers in the middle of it. Material you may need in an interview includes:

- company backgrounder
- product backgrounders
- annual report and accounts
- product/company literature
- case studies
- statistics about the company
- photographs
- diagrams/charts
- manager/interviewee biographies
- relevant quotes
- names of product users/dealers, etc. for further contact.

EIGHT RULES THAT WILL HELP YOU MAKE A GOOD IMPRESSION ON JOURNALISTS

As we have seen, you will be meeting journalists under a number of different circumstances. There will be special points to bear in mind for some of them, but there are also a number of general rules for creating a good impression with journalists.

Some of these rules may just seem like common sense. But they are mentioned here because they have all been broken at some time – in certain instances, many times – by managers meeting journalists.

1. If you have arranged a meeting with a journalist, keep it. Turn up yourself. Don't send along a deputy.
2. If you have arranged a meeting with a journalist don't keep them waiting. You may think you give an impression of an executive grappling with management problems while the journalist waits in reception, but you don't. You just create an image of bad-mannered boorishness. And you almost certainly get the interview off to a poor start. If punctuality is the politeness of princes, it should also be the politeness of managers.

3. A friendly greeting works wonders. It creates immediate empathy. It marks you out as one of nature's warm-hearted carers. It shows you're looking forward to the meeting and expect it to be useful. So cross the room to greet your interviewer. Get up from behind your desk with a smile on your face and your hand outstretched for a firm shake.

4. Adopt a positive, helpful attitude. The journalist wants to meet you and find out about your company. Act as though you want to meet them, not as if the interview is an unwelcome intrusion in a busy day (even if it is).

5. Give all your time to your interviewer. Put calls on hold. Tell your secretary to keep personal visitors in the outer office. Don't sit scanning letters or telexes while answering questions. Don't seem bored, or rushed, or look as though there are more important things you could be doing.

6. Make sure you meet in a setting that will do you credit. If your office is small and untidy reserve a meeting room. Remember, the journalist can write about what they see as well as about what you tell them. (If you don't want it mentioned, take the pictures of your five previous spouses off your desk!)

7. Behave in a way that portrays the style you want to convey: in the way you treat other members of staff the journalist meets while he or she is with you; in your approach to drivers, doormen and waiters (journalists are like receptionists in that they can usually tell who the 'nice' people are).

8. Moderation pays dividends. Don't use language that would make a sailor blush – especially with female journalists (although there are one or two who could themselves redden the cheeks of most of the Royal Navy). If entertainment is involved, drink moderately. Even if the journalist doesn't.

THE ESSENTIAL ELEMENTS OF GOOD INTERVIEW TECHNIQUE

Being a good interviewee is not a God-given gift. It is something that can be learned and developed. Nor is there anything mysterious about it. In a world in which business has to put its point of view, ability as an interviewee is another important management skill.

It is important to stress that there are very few 'natural' interviewees. And there is, after all, no reason why being a skilled interviewee should come any more naturally than being a skilled accountant or any other specialist. With knowledge, technique and training you can become an effective interviewee.

In being a good interviewee, you need to give attention to three main areas. These are:

1. What to do during an interview in order to be more effective

- Tell the truth. Never be caught in a lie – and if you try one, you surely will be. The journalist will never completely believe you again.
- Keep to the point. If you have done your preparation you will know what your point is. Keep to it. Don't wander off or be distracted. If you establish a clear focus, an interviewer will often respond with further questions in that area.
- Be sure of your facts. Only provide information that you're certain about. Having to back-track to correct yourself only undermines your authority as an interviewee.
- Be positive and direct. Use positive angles for your story. Even if there is a negative aspect to the story, accentuate the positive elements. But avoid unrealistic hype. Or claims you cannot substantiate.
- Keep your message simple. Simple messages make the most impact. Few people have the time or inclination to digest the minutiae of a finely developed case.
- Be informed and spontaneous. You will be well-briefed, but don't sound as though you are parroting a company line. Sound as though you actually believe what you're saying. And clearly understand the parameters of the information you want to give – and of the information you don't.
- Light up your message. Use examples, anecdotes or stories to bring your message to life. Try to find some well-turned phrases to bring your message home powerfully.
- Let your voice sell your message. Don't speak in a monotone. Adopt the right tone of voice for the message you're giving in the way you do in ordinary life.
- Be brief and clear. When you've made your point, stop. Don't ramble. And don't be ambiguous in your answers. Eschew jargon. Make it clear what you mean.
- Use the questions as pegs for your answers. You know what you want to say. Use the questions to steer towards what you want to say. That means you must listen carefully to the questions. But

don't tell the interviewer what questions to ask. And don't start cross-questioning the interviewer.

- Look at your interviewer. Talk to them. Listen carefully to nuances behind your interviewer's questions. Eye contact increases rapport between you. And it makes you appear open and honest. (Which, of course, you are!)

- Tackle distortions or untruths at once. Don't allow the interviewer to summarize your answers in a way that is not completely accurate or give your answer an emphasis you didn't intend. Make clear what you mean and what the truth is.

- Finally, be aware of the dangers of speaking 'off the record' unless you know the journalist well and trust them. Even then, be cautious. Off the record means that what you say is to guide the reporter but should not be written down. But off the record information is known to find its way into stories. Above all, never tell a journalist something and then add as an afterthought that it was 'off the record'. As a general rule of thumb:

  - If you don't know the journalist or only know them slightly, it is probably wisest only to give off the record information when the alternative is worse. For instance, when off the record information can defuse a potentially damaging story by providing the journalist with an understanding of background facts that will change their perception of it.

  - If you know the journalist well and have developed mutual trust, you can use off the record comments to steer them towards a story that may aid your company's business objectives, but with which you would not want to be directly connected.

  - It is worth remembering that some journalists prefer not to have off the record information. They might find out the information elsewhere and they want to be completely free to use it.

2. What not to do during an interview

Interviews can, and do, go wrong. In particular, there are a number of common mistakes that managers can make when interviewed by journalists.

- Don't give a journalist information 'not for attribution'. Except when you are confident the journalist will use it in a way that cannot be traced back to you. The information might not be attributed to you by name. But it could be attributed to a 'company spokesperson' or simply to the 'company', or a 'well-placed source'.

- Don't 'shoot from the hip'. You don't have to say the first thing that comes into your mind. If you're asked a tricky question, consider your answer before giving it. If it's a particularly sensitive area, make it clear to the journalist that you want to consider your answer before giving it.
- Don't get drawn into areas you don't want to talk about. If the journalist raises subjects you're not happy discussing – for instance, about the business prospects of competitors – don't be drawn. The journalist may be persistent. (They may try to second-guess you – what will your profit be next year? Will it be more than £10m? More than £20m?) But you must be politely firm.
- Don't be arrogant or pompous. You may be an important captain of industry used to commanding legions of minions, but don't show it. In an interview, a touch of humility serves you well. Don't interrupt when you're being asked questions. And on no account tell the journalist what questions to ask you.
- Never say: 'No comment'. In most cases, it is tantamount to admitting guilt. Choose a form of words that explains why you can't comment. For example: 'We haven't decided that yet' or 'We're not making a comment on that until next week'.

And, finally . . .

Many managers find their first interviews with journalists worrying. Provided you keep calm, there is no need for worry, though a little caution never does any harm. Being interviewed by a journalist need not be a torment.

Some managers even get to like it.

Peter Bartram is a business writer and journalist, the author of 16 books and more than 2,500 newspaper and magazine articles. With management consultant Colin Coulson-Thomas, he runs half-day and one-day training courses for managers meeting the media. Bartram and Coulson-Thomas are joint authors of *The Complete Spokesperson: a workbook for managers who meet the media* on which the courses are based. For further details telephone 01273 565505 or write to Peter Bartram at 29 Tivoli Road, Brighton, East Sussex BN1 5BG.

PART TEN

THE LEADER OF
THE BRAND
Advertising

INTRODUCTION

Compared to public relations, direct mail, telemarketing and database marketing, advertising hasn't done that well out of IT. Take Hutchison Telecom, Microsoft and IBM's spend away, and the total market will look rather small. For many companies, the cost is prohibitive and they will say that advertising simply cannot deliver customers quickly. Some companies have identified that as much as 80% of their revenue comes from 20% of their customers; advertising simply cannot do what more personal forms of marketing can.

But more importantly, the advertising industry has not shown itself willing or able to find ways to communicate the key messages. IT must take some of the blame – for promoting technology over benefits, putting the sausage before the sizzle. And so advertising has followed suit.

This approach or lack of one seems now to have backfired. Beyond the few notable campaigns for Microsoft, Orange and Compaq is a vast gap before the consumer arrives at sell-off-the-page advertising that makes up the bulk of so many personal computer magazines.

IT will say that advertising cannot deliver complex messages, ignoring the fact that selling messages should be simple. IT will also ignore that advertising is unbeatable for a number of things, chiefly its ability to introduce and reinforce brand names. Put simply, a brand is a well-known name that has values and qualities which are attractive to the consumer. Coca-Cola suggests unique taste, excitement, achievement and so on.

Brand creation and management are black arts to IT companies. So the irony is that they have a lot to learn from advertisers whilst generally believing it to be ineffective for the price.

Susan Goldsworthy dissects the Alpha AXP campaign and, despite the obviously large resources available to Digital, shows that fundamental marketing principles apply in good advertising as in any form of promotion.

New Strategies for Marketing Information Technology.
Edited by Christopher Field
Published in 1996 by Chapman & Hall, London. ISBN 0 412 61520 7

27

IMAGINE BEING THE ONE WITHOUT AN ADVERTISING STRATEGY

The golden rules of campaign advertising – targeting, impact, consistency, integration

Susan Goldsworthy

As more and more companies move away from mass marketing techniques, they are implementing the direct marketing concept of 'Acquisition and Retention', also known as 'Get Them and Keep Them'.

Whilst attracting new customers is essential, it is equally important to keep existing ones – bearing in mind that the cost of securing a new customer is anywhere between 3–30 times the cost of keeping a current one. The key to keeping customers is communication, and the key to good communication is clarity.

In advertising, it is important to focus on these areas:

● Targeting: define your primary, secondary and tertiary target audiences – who is it that you want to address? Only then can you begin to look at what messages and media are appropriate.

New Strategies for Marketing Information Technology.
Edited by Christopher Field
Published in 1996 by Chapman & Hall, London. ISBN 0 412 61520 7

- Impact: the IT marketplace is overcrowded with 'me too' messages. You need to make a strong initial impact with your target audience in order to stand out from the crowd.
- Consistency: once your campaign has captured the attention of your target audience, you must be consistent in delivering the same message over and over again. Changing your image and/or message regularly is counter-productive and confusing for the customer, so you need to stay with your approach over a period of time. Good examples of consistency are the popular consumer campaigns such as for Heineken and Guinness.
- Integration: integrate the campaign messages throughout the communications mix starting with the advertising, and apply your image and the key messages to all elements of the communications mix – from PR to direct mail to merchandising.

THE VALUE OF A COMMUNICATIONS AUDIT

Before developing your campaign strategy, it is vital that you assess your past and present communications activity. The best way to do this is by carrying out a comprehensive communications audit that evaluates all aspects of your current mix. This will provide you with an invaluable opportunity to step back and view your current strategy objectively before embarking on a new campaign.

This proved to be a crucial first move for us and the results clarified that we, too, were suffering from the effects of 'low differentiation' advertising, which, while creating a lot of 'noise' and communicating a diversity of messages to the marketplace, has no focus or consistency.

What we wanted to achieve with our new campaign was to provide an individual message reflecting the four rules of targeting, impact, consistency and integration.

We decided to invest a large proportion of our communications budget on promoting one key product with one focused message and, by association, raising our corporate profile. The product we selected was Alpha AXP – the world's fastest 64-bit microprocessor.

PREPARING THE MARKETING BRIEF

Your campaign objectives must be clearly thought out. Our campaign focused on two objectives – 'to put Alpha AXP on the shopping list of products to consider' and 'to promote Digital by association with Alpha AXP'.

In-depth knowledge of your target audience is vital. You need to know who they are, what their common business goals are, what actions you want them to take so that you achieve your business goals, what their key beliefs are and what sales messages will make them most responsive.

Finding out what your competitors think of you and your products will help you to counteract negative industry messages. Analysis revealed that our three primary competitors were attempting to exploit the fact that our product was new and therefore an untried and untested technology. We needed to raise its profile, emphasize its availability, and build credibility and confidence with our competitors' computer users.

So it is important from the outset to be clear about how you want your campaign positioned. Whether you create a completely new positioning or have to incorporate an existing one, it is crucial to know exactly how you want to be perceived by your target audience. We wanted to position Digital with a style that communicated leading edge technology in a way that would set us apart from our competitors. In addition, we had to consider and incorporate our current corporate advertising grid and the company positioning line 'Putting Imagination to Work'.

Your media strategy is crucial and can be one of the key elements in providing you with your 'uniqueness'. By researching our target audience, we found we could implement a media strategy that would consistently reach them at work, while they travelled and at home during their leisure time.

To fulfil the 'consistency' requirement and therefore achieve impact with your target audience, your branding device must be flexible enough to be integrated throughout the marketing mix.

And finally your marketing brief needs to clearly state your budget, broken down by campaign components such as creatives, execution, production, placement, research, public relations, direct mail, merchandising, etc. Digital had the advantage of a total budget of $4 million. However, it should be emphasized that a successful campaign is not merely a matter of money – innovation and creativity can be developed regardless of size of budget.

A CAMPAIGN IS BORN

Establishing a good working relationship with your advertising agency from the first briefing session is vital. Breaking down the traditional barriers of the client–supplier relationship is not always easy, but by fostering an environment of mutual trust it can be achieved. We maintained open lines of communication with our agency suppliers, dealing with ideas, queries and problems constructively and always enthusiastically. We joined brainstorming sessions and listened to any idea – however bizarre.

This relationship was vital in helping to build a strong commitment, from both sides – agency and us – to the eventual campaign, and was one of the major factors in gaining the full support and trust of our senior management. We were able to give them the confidence to take a risk with an approach that was completely different to any previous IT industry campaign.

When developing the campaign, remember to make sure you do not stray from your original marketing brief. Our campaign fitted our brief perfectly. Its theme and approach were exciting and flexible enough to be adapted to almost any scenario. It allowed us to be humorous, creative and a little bit controversial, but in a way which would not threaten our target audience. Most importantly for us, the campaign was unique in the IT world.

The new campaign's positioning line was 'Imagine being the one without the Alpha AXP'.

This targeted the individual by delivering a business message in a humorous way so that the person felt compelled – but not threatened – to put Alpha on his or her IT shopping list. The line also fitted in with our corporate branding, thereby reinforcing the Digital name.

Copy was short and non-technical. This was important because it ensured that all potential users, technical or non-technical, could easily and quickly relate to the message and understand the advantages of choosing our product.

The concepts were tested with in-depth one-to-one interviews with our primary audience, IT functional heads, to provide feedback on the ideas and the visual imagery included in the new campaign. All relevant comments were taken into account in modifying the conceptual approach.

The campaign was broken down in to the key elements of the communications mix: brand and product advertising, public relations, direct mail, media strategy and merchandising. Key audiences which are all too often neglected are the company's own employees and business partners, and it is important to inform these audiences about the details of your campaign before the launch.

RESEARCH

In any major campaign, research is advisable to ensure that you target accurately your audience and are able to evaluate campaign impact. Our campaign was aimed at changing the target audience's perception rather than generating responses which would act as a measurement, so it was important for us to determine a pre-campaign benchmark of current awareness and positive perception of both Alpha AXP and Digital. We also conducted a mid-campaign survey which allowed us to introduce changes to our media strategy, and post-campaign research to provide an overall assessment of campaign effectiveness.

The research involved telephone interviews with 300 IT functional heads and 40 value added resellers. The sample was split equally between respondents from companies with less than 500 employees, 501–1000 employees and those with more than 1000 employees.

EXTENDING THE ADVERTISING CAMPAIGN

The ideal campaign is one which can be extended into all types of advertising. When planning your advertising, always consider its 'campaignability' and potential life. If you are looking for a long-term campaign, the idea must be workable across several advertising media, not just one.

Our advertising was divided into four styles, all of which incorporated the new campaign positioning line. The styles considered were:

- **Image advertising**: aiming for image/brand awareness promoting Alpha AXP and by association, Digital, and placed across all target media, thereby reaching all target audiences.
- **Testimonial advertising**: combining creative treatment with customer testimonials for strategic placement within IT and vertical media.
- **Technical advertising**: tailored to a specific technical message, for example, workstations/servers.
- **Vertical advertising**: tailored to a specific vertical industry, for example, finance.

MEDIA STRATEGY

A creative and innovative media strategy is a crucial part in extending the 'uniqueness' of a campaign. Throughout unexpected advertising placements, you achieve impact.

Using full double page spreads, fireplace double page spreads, whole pages, shared pages and strips in our target media, we sought to secure high reach and recall among our target audience. Our placement media encompassed national press, computer and business press, general interest and frequent traveller titles.

To add further impact, momentum, and to liven up the campaign, we proactively sought out 'unique' opportunities for short-term tactical placement to take our target audience by surprise, often tailoring and/or personalizing the ads to suit the occasion. Examples follow.

- One of the creatives featuring horses was placed in three of the quality national broadsheets on the 'silks and colours' pages on Grand National Day. The placement of this ad was picked by the advertising trade publication *Campaign* who voted it 'Media Choice – Placement of the Week'.
- We developed a Christmas ad depicting 'Rudolph the red-nosed reindeer'. This was placed in national and trade press and developed into a corporate Christmas card.
- A Valentine's Day card was produced using the creative theme from one of our technical ads. This was tactically developed to target specifically a competitor's computer users who otherwise could not be reached. Again we achieved a spin-off with this ad when *Computing* decided to reproduce the card visuals on its back cover on the issue that coincided with Valentine's Day.

To coincide with the launch of the campaign, we included poster site advertising at 500 lit supersites throughout the UK for a two-week period. Later in this campaign, we used a creative execution of 'trains' and ran this at several London railway stations.

The consistency of the campaign's image and style was also reflected in our direct mail activity for the workstations sector, which was designed to focus more specifically on generating a response from the target audiences.

PUBLIC RELATIONS

Public relations is an effective method of addressing the questions and qualifying the perceptions that advertising raises in the minds of key audiences.

Secondary and supporting messages around applications, affordability and availability can be relayed to the audiences through the use of an integrated PR campaign.

Our advertising for Alpha AXP is supported by public relations techniques to emphasize claims for the brand and show them working in practice. PR techniques deployed include case studies, one-to-one interviews with journalists and issuing news about new product developments.

The public relations programme for Alpha AXP has been successful in reassuring target audiences that the features and benefits promoted in the advertising campaign are currently being enjoyed by customers in the marketplace to benefit the business computing operations of a wide range of organizations.

MERCHANDISING AND PROMOTION

Another aspect of a creative campaign is its ability to integrate into merchandising. Merchandising can extend the creativity of the campaign with employees and business partners to build enthusiasm and boost corporate loyalty, as well as helping to position the campaign in their minds.

Poster copies of all the ads were distributed to employees and business partners. The strategy behind the campaign was also explained in an introductory document, so that people felt ownership and understanding of the campaign as it began to roll out.

We also used a combination of promotional items such as posters, umbrellas, calendars, pens, post-it notes, car stickers and rules, which all received widespread distribution.

The campaign message was also put on the company franking stamp, and on all our delivery trucks.

FINAL OBSERVATIONS

- Remember, **targeting**, **impact**, **consistency** and **integration** are central to any effective communications campaign.
- Stand back, and look at what your company is currently achieving with its communications.
- Deal with opposition positively and enthusiastically to gain widespread support. Once the decision has been made, stick to it.
- Brief all your communications agencies at the same time using the same brief, and encourage agencies to communicate with each other and work together throughout the campaign.
- Be creative with media implementation. Look for opportunities to reach your target audience through unexpected placements and one-off executions.

Susan Goldsworthy majored in Public Relations at San Diego State University. She joined Digital in 1992 and previously worked at Hitachi Europe Ltd, where she rose to become Marketing Communications Manager – General Corporate Affairs. Susan holds a Diploma in Marketing from the Chartered Institute of Marketing and a Diploma in Direct Marketing from the Institute of Direct Marketing.

PART ELEVEN
SENDING OUT THE INVITATIONS
Databases

INTRODUCTION

THE CUSTOMER DATABASE – IT COMPANIES' MOST VALUABLE ASSET

Oddly enough, the very industry that invented the technology to enable database marketing is not a great user of it. Although most companies do have a database of some kind, the extent to which they use it for marketing is limited. The excuses given are that there is no one with the necessary skills to use it, or it is only available to a few users, or the costs are too great.

Part of the problem is that most companies already possess all the information needed to create a database, but the information is disseminated so widely across the organization that bringing it together can be a major undertaking. And buying a mailing contact list is no replacement for embarking on this rounding up exercise.

The greatest motivator to companies to start is the knowledge, or at least the belief, that their competitors probably have one. The database is the foundation for all communications with customers and prospects. Using detailed information about them, it is possible to ensure that all written, verbal and personal contact is initiated, executed and monitored.

Edwina Dunn, co-founder of database marketing consultancy Dunnhumby Associates, says companies often spend plenty of time setting up the technology for databases but not so much on actually getting good information on to the system. Here she provides a comprehensive guide to understanding database marketing, the benefits, building lists and assessing results.

Paul Stewart of Information Research Services puts the marketing database into the market context and discusses some of the issues.

New Strategies for Marketing Information Technology.
Edited by Christopher Field
Published in 1996 by Chapman & Hall, London. ISBN 0 412 61520 7

28

THE TROUBLE WITH DATABASE MARKETING

Edwina Dunn

If you want to get into database marketing, you have to invest in a marketing database. The marketing database is much more tangible than the activity (database marketing) based on the information held within it. The database encapsulates all the investment in data and the software system required to manipulate and hold such data.

Five years ago, companies were investing millions of pounds in databases. Many of these were abandoned before going live, falling foul of 'promises too difficult to achieve' or 'development programmes so lengthy and expensive that management changed business objectives before the systems went live'. Today, most organizations are more likely to put a toe in the water.

A recent survey shows just how little most of the major UK advertisers are spending (Figure 28.1). A sorry state of affairs considering how much these companies are pouring into advertising expenditure (on average £5 million a year) with little or poor return-on-investment measures!

And yet most of these same companies agree that technology to support marketing is without doubt the way of the future (Figure 28.2).

Most companies, especially those who are involved in computer technology, spend significant time and effort on the software and the functionality. Populating the database is usually seen as a secondary

New Strategies for Marketing Information Technology.
Edited by Christopher Field
Published in 1996 by Chapman & Hall, London. ISBN 0 412 61520 7

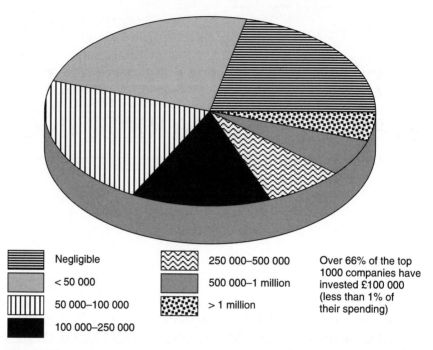

▬ Negligible	〰 250 000–500 000	Over 66% of the top 1000 companies have invested £100 000 (less than 1% of their spending)
▨ < 50 000	▨ 500 000–1 million	
‖ 50 000–100 000	⦙ > 1 million	
■ 100 000–250 000		

Figure 28.1 How much are companies spending on database marketing?

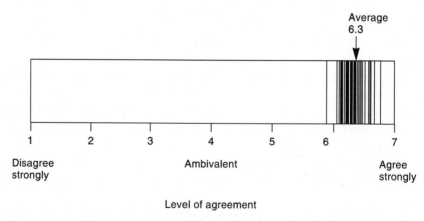

Figure 28.2 Attitudes – technology will grow.

process. Too often, the most perfect of systems is populated with the most imperfect of data. And what a disappointment it turns out to be!

274

The proof of the pudding is in the eating. A marketing database will only be used if the data held within it is deemed by its users to be accurate and (here's the rub) sufficiently complete to represent reality.

When a transaction processing or billing system is populated with its daily postings, there is little room for doubt about its accuracy. Hence most billing systems are implemented without too much conflict or fuss. However, when a marketing database is populated with data, there is rarely consensus on its reliability. Acceptance is not easily won.

Why is this? Well, most data needed to provide marketing with customer understanding is imperfect. Facts are incomplete or missing. Much of the data is sourced from outside the company where it is difficult to control quality and coverage.

For example, most companies selling to businesses need to build a database which contains a summary of all the companies falling within their market sector – even if they are not currently customers. This data is often acquired (rented or leased) from list owners, say Companies House data or major subscription lists (e.g. *Computer Weekly* or *PC User*).

Most of all, combining data from inside or from outside the organization, using matching techniques (or scoring algorithms), is far from a black and white science. For example, you may acquire a database of all companies within your target market. These companies may be holding companies, e.g. Barclays Bank PLC. There may be as many as 3,000–4,000 other companies with Barclays in their name (from a simple bank branch to Barclays Financial Services to Barclays Bank Ltd).

When it comes to matching this dataset with your own customer file, you have to develop rules to determine where your customers fall in this complex company hierarchy. Do you sell to the parent company? Do you sell to its subsidiaries? And, to complicate matters further, to which contacts do you sell and where are they based?

Computer matching is based on probability and may be deemed 'wrong' by different users who may have different objectives. Once doubt is cast, it can be a downward spiral.

WHAT IS DATABASE MARKETING?

Database marketing is an activity based on the intimate knowledge you gain from investing in relevant software and data about your customers, products and, most of all, market. The way you plan your marketing becomes driven by your understanding of customers and your ability to predict how they will behave.

Perhaps it would be easier if database marketing was replaced with the term data-based marketing. This more clearly explains the main principle behind the activity: marketing decision-making based on all the available facts and figures held within the database.

And database marketing is an activity. It is what marketing people do with a marketing database. Some practitioners restrict themselves to the more basic and obvious activities such as direct communication with customers. Others advance towards more complex decision-making, for example, evaluating which sales or media channels best reach key customer segments.

In any case, organizations which adopt database marketing have to change the way their people think and practice marketing on a day-to-day basis. This is not an easy task, nor an achievement which comes without significant disruption and retraining costs.

For example, at least one high street bank created a one-hundred-strong team from existing staff in an effort to develop and implement a database marketing environment. Since then, it has begun a training programme where senior managers spend up to ten days, over a six month period, learning about the database and best practices.

ARE THERE MYTHS AND MISCONCEPTIONS?

Yes, too often database marketing is confused with direct mail. Furthermore, it is seen as direct sell as opposed to better sell.

Distributors (or the third party 'channel') often view a software or information provider's investments in a marketing database as a direct threat to their own customer/sales relationship. They view the move as overtly aggressive, perceiving the database as a vehicle for the software or information provider to get to know, build a relationship with and then steal their customers.

Too much money is spent on marketing databases and not enough on the data to populate the systems. Database marketing changes the way an organization works.

Embracing database marketing within an organization means adopting and welcoming these changes. In other words, senior management need to 'buy in' to database marketing as a 'viable alternative communication and sales channel' right from the very beginning.

WHAT IS THE PAYBACK?

The payback is what you determine. You should set and agree milestones and specific achievements which will help you to argue the value of the marketing database within your own organization. What are the hot issues? How can you bring a new perspective to the issue by measuring all the relevant facts?

The payback includes:

- a new and keen perspective on customers, what they buy and the market as a whole;
- real opportunities to develop niche or key markets which can be targeted in a special and appropriate way;
- an ability to focus resources on best opportunities, quantified and measured, and to maximize return on investment;
- an ability to quantify the size of a risk or opportunity before going to market;
- a tool for test marketing or even for measuring the size and probable scope of a market using all known and available data.

Nowadays, with more powerful hardware, modular software and better data processing techniques, it is much easier to phase development to meet reasonable return-on-investment objectives.

Marketing databases are much more likely to evolve. Most marketing applications can be amply served using midrange computers – minicomputers or PC networks. Investments in data can be restricted to only that data relevant to show the power of database marketing or to tackle a number of pre-determined and specific business issues.

This means that the payback period can be phased, like the investment, and geared accordingly. For example:

Phase 1: business review

A plan to determine the precise business objectives which may be addressed and subsequently satisfied by the introduction of a marketing database.

Phase 2: data audit

A review of all the data available to help management understand their customers, products and market. This will include data currently not held or owned by the organization.

Phase 3: test

A revenue generating exercise to 'prove' the worth of the data which will subsequently be held in a marketing database. This may be one of many activities, for example:

- An analysis of existing customers (customer profile) to determine their distinguishing characteristics. From this it is possible to create a targeted campaign to sell more to the same customers (based on this greater understanding) or to find more (new customers) who have similar characteristics.
- A profile of all customers or businesses in the UK which fall within your target market. From this, you can identify where your current sales activity is focused. You can use this understanding to identify markets where you are particularly strong. These may be vertical markets (within the energy sector) or horizontal markets (within medium-size businesses, i.e. those with more than 50 employees but less than 100) or geographic markets (in the north-west of England or Western Europe). You can use this knowledge to find similar markets where you do not currently sell.
- If you want to address markets where you are weak, you can consider developing a 'niche' marketing strategy aimed at a different type of customer or perhaps develop a different product focus which better suits these customers' budgets.

Phase 4

Based on a successful campaign where significant new income has been generated for the business, you can calculate the value of maintaining this and other relevant data within a marketing database. Each new data source can be added after a one-off campaign or programme (series of campaigns) has demonstrated the tangible business benefits.

Rules can be developed to provide automatic or trigger campaigns. For example, new customers may automatically be selected for a 'welcome' phone call. This campaign may collect vital information which can be used to identify the next product or offer that may be offered to this customer (by mail or by the salesperson).

Modular software will provide a flexible vehicle for maintaining and adding more and more marketing data.

Phase 5

Once you have justified the investment in data and software, you can assess the best way to maintain, support and access your marketing database – in-house or via an out-sourcing agency.

Once value has been established using campaigns, the marketing database becomes a tool for the following:

- Assessing the value of key distributors in terms of existing or potential 'contribution to profit'.
- Segmenting the companies, in their primary target market, into specific types of contact, e.g. buyers, users, influencers, authorizers and technical advisors. This means that you can identify different marketing or selling communications to influence purchase or loyalty.
- Evaluating the strengths and weaknesses of the distributors, to help them provide prospects or customers with the specialist information or support they lack in order to secure business. This may mean that you provide information or back-up services directly to the end users.
- Analysing the effect of single campaigns or multiple campaigns over a period of time in the response or purchase behaviour of prospects or customers.
- Evaluating return on investment to enable you to re-evaluate your allocation of media/marketing spend.
- Identifying key segments which may benefit from a different relationship. For example, you may identify certain companies too small to interest the distributor but that you could support, using direct communication techniques (telephone or direct mail).

DATABASE MARKETING – WHAT DOES IT CHANGE?

It changes your opportunities to sell – not just direct but in complete co-operation with your sales force or third party channel. It helps you to identify weaknesses and gaps in the way you communicate with your customers. It provides a way of assessing different opportunities for meeting different customer needs or utilizing different supplier skills and resources.

Too many software or information providers communicate 'features' rather than 'benefits'. Even those who have learnt to convey what the product does rather than how it does it (jargon or no jargon), rarely adapt the business benefits to reflect the needs of the market segments they serve.

For example, customers in medium sized energy companies may buy a certain kind of software because transaction processing is fast and safe. Customers in large service organizations may buy because the software is more efficient over a Wide Area Network (WAN).

The marketing database can also help you to evaluate over time the role of the third party channel, 'friend', 'foe' or a little bit of both. How can you best make that work in your favour?

For example, do certain distributors only serve particular market segments or do they favour a particular technology that isn't always appropriate to all customers?

It changes the way people work. The marketing database provides the user with the perfect scientific tool – 'hypothesis', 'apparatus', 'method' and 'result'. This means that if a particular issue is hot, the marketing database should provide a new perspective, using all the available data.

It may even change the way your staff are incentivized. If you start to use direct and indirect selling it is important that remuneration is adjusted to allow for successes in both!

DATABASE MARKETING – WHAT CONFLICTS EMERGE?

The marketing database should also drive the creative concept. This is especially hard to change in most traditional marketing departments. Too often, organizations come up with the product, the offer and then look for the list. The size, characteristics and 'needs' of the prospects selected within the target market should more than influence the style, content and tone of the communication.

For example, customers who are 'solicitors' may respond better to a particular tone and language. Their needs will be very focused on document management and processing. Customers who are 'accountants' on the other hand may require a different approach and are more interested in spreadsheets and money management software. Both will have common characteristics as 'professional' workers, often small, privately run businesses.

The marketing database becomes a valuable management information system, quite often bringing together data from many different billing or transaction systems and often cutting across many different departments and lines of responsibility. The new perspective means that acceptance of the data and what it means has to be argued and won if the database is to win internal approval and support.

Dividing the marketing spend between the channel and direct sales will mean constant, fair and careful monitoring in terms of ROI (return on investment). It will take senior management backing to ensure that the right decisions are made – based on financial and good business logic and not departmental bias or sales targets.

Database marketing becomes a meeting ground where the need to sell the product or service must be matched to the principal objective of satisfying customer needs. Many IT companies are still very driven by technology innovation. There is tremendous power and budget held by the Product User Groups.

Who then is the guardian and protector of the customer's interest? Does he or she have equal powers? If not, the marketing database becomes little more than a repository of names and addresses which may be used from time to time, in isolation, by each of the Product User Managers. Campaigns may even conflict with each other. Customers may receive a series of conflicting offers or messages.

This is particularly true when software or information providers attempt to organize pan-European or international campaigns. The image and offers which are created within each country maximize local preferences and style. These are lost when a single 'look' is created.

Most companies have not yet solved the problems of one campaign, one offer, one look across all countries without creating major conflicts between local and international marketing departments.

FINAL THOUGHTS

Many companies fear the new perspective that database marketing provides management. For those that are willing to face this challenge, database marketing offers competitive edge through fresh insight.

If your database provided you with this information, would you change the way in which you market your business?

- Only 5% of customers are either 'loyal' or 'major accounts' and these account for 45% of our sales.
- One of our distribution channels controls 60% of our sales.
- 90% of our customers buy only one of our products (or services).
- 70% of our growth is currently sustained by old licence fees as opposed to new sales.

GUIDE TO DATABASE MARKETING AT A GLANCE

In an ideal situation, what sort of data is relevant to marketing?

The obvious data

Customer names and addresses derived from:

- product purchase data
- guarantee or helpline agreements
- helpline or support enquiries
- promotional response
- exhibition attendees
- PR leads and enquirers.

The less obvious data

Customer names and addresses derived from:

- third party customer/enquiry lists
- third party data providers, e.g. IT subscriber lists
- other IT suppliers who sell non-competitive products.

All customer name and address management and processing relies on specialist software which is based on Royal Mail's PAF (Postal Address File) in the UK. Applying these commercial packages successfully requires a thorough understanding of address structures and the inherent weaknesses of the input data sets.

By developing special call routines to deal with the complexities of poor or complex addresses, particularly company addresses, it is possible to significantly enhance the match rates and structure of a high proportion of addresses.

The even less obvious data

- the locations and catchments of third party channel
- addresses (any groups or chains)
- specializations (market segment bias)
- alliances (biased to you, your competitors or neither)
- catchment area (size and shape)

- information on special deals or 'bundles'
- names of partners (yours and competitors')
- scope of agreement (estimated revenue and profit)

- market segment bias (yours and competitors')

- published statistics on:
  - sales of your products
  - sales of your competitors' products

- market research data on:
  - your marketshare
  - your competitors' marketshare

- third party data for segmenting your customers and prospects for companies
- standard industrial classifications (SIC) codes plus number of employees or turnover, etc.

- for consumers: geodemographics or psychographics (which classify people by where they live and what they do).

Much of this data is only published for groups or segments of the population. These segments can range from 'national sales of spreadsheets or graphics' to 'national sales through XYZ distributor'.

The marketing database must be designed to allow users to identify customers or prospects who may be matched to these segments. For example:

- Find all customers poorly served by XYZ distributor, i.e. not in target market or primary catchment areas.
- Find all prospects in geographic areas where your marketshare is above average.
- Find all relevant contacts in companies similar to those (using SIC or size) where you traditionally sell more spreadsheets or graphics.

Once you have all the above data, you can use the marketing database to hold the following 'modelled' information. This will help you to develop really powerful database marketing strategies and campaigns.

Modelled data

Knowing the facts, you can only see part of the picture. In order to build a complete picture, albeit flawed, you need to develop a top-down view of your market. These are some of the questions you need to address:

- What is my universe?
- What is the size and value of the total market available?
- Can I divide it into companies and consumers?
- Are my products/services relevant to all of them?
- How can I segment this market?

- What is my position within this universe?
- What is the size and value of my current marketshare?
- What is the size and value of my potential marketshare?
- What differentiates me from my competitors?
- Which segments do I best serve and have I saturated them?
- Which segments could I serve and what is the added sales value?

- How can I lever more sales?
- Can I identify more companies or consumers who match the profile of the ones I currently serve?
- Can I identify which products are most relevant?
- Can I identify the buyers and isolate some of the reasons they buy?
- Can I identify the best channel to reach and sell to these new customers?

A true marketing database will support decision-making in all of these areas, if populated with the correct data, including modelled data (Figure 28.3).

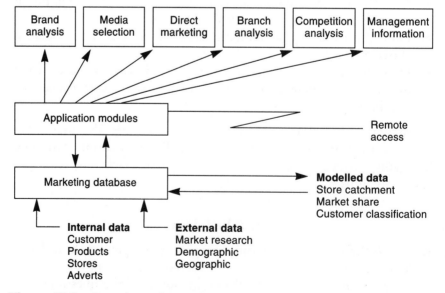

Figure 28.3 Overview of a marketing system.

This approach allows you to build a true customer-focused marketing strategy. You can aim your budget and resources at either your best customer segments, for customer retention programmes or loyalty building incentives, or your best prospects, in order to maximize acquisition amongst high response or high usage segments.

Having reviewed the ideal scenario, let us now consider some of the flaws within the data you have available. Of course, there are imperfections and holes and biases. But even so, powerful marketing databases may be built using such data, if correctly set into context by external and modelled data.

The sort of data you may hold in your organization are:

The 'installed base'

Companies which sell IT tend to talk about their 'installed base'. These are normally the segments of customers first captured, analysed and understood within the context of a marketing database.

Naturally, 'installed users' constitute a biased cross-section of customers. They are people who have registered for support. They may not even be the users but the 'technical representatives'. In the best of circumstances, these are only a biased sample of all customers.

Customers

Most IT companies rely on third party channels for all access to and communication with their customers. Not surprisingly, this has many drawbacks. Trying to build loyalty and strong relationships with customers through third party channels means that end-user needs and perceptions may be misunderstood and wrongly addressed.

Many manufacturers opt to incentivize the third party channel as a way of influencing the end user. Very often incentives are based on financial 'kick-backs' or promotions with a limited shelf-life. All very effective until the next manufacturer comes up with a newer or better incentive. In the meantime, customers are bounced from one recommendation to the next. Or are they?

In the case of PC software and packages, specialist research has shown us that most often the user has already decided what they are going to buy. If this is the case, how does the manufacturer influence the buyer?

Promotion respondents (on-pack, POS, direct mail, off-the-page, PR and exhibition)

Most companies now make an effort to collect and data-capture as many customer or enquiry names and addresses as possible. Sadly, few IT companies plan the 'back end' of the project as well as the glamorous 'front end'.

What do I mean by 'front end' and 'back end'?

In simple terms, most direct response campaigns (campaigns that generate an immediate call to action) fall into two parts. The first part is the hand-raising which involves the creation and implementation of an advertisement or promotion. The offer generates the consumer or business interest and excitement. This part is normally designed and implemented by an agency.

The second part starts from when the consumer or business respondent has raised his or her hand, 'I am interested in your offer'. At this point, you either have a sale to fulfil or an enquiry to manage. Most companies have adequate systems in place to manage the sale and thus the product fulfilment.

However, if the response is an enquiry which needs subsequent follow-up and management, companies do not seem to take the same care or allocate the same resources. Extra resources are rarely put in place and the administration goes wrong. In fact, there are specialist agencies who provide professional enquiry management and fulfilment for any response (postal or phone calls).

I have seen, in many companies, boxes of promotional response (coupons, etc.) which lay unopened and untouched in storage cupboards, waiting until someone has enough time to sort them out. Too often, the volumes are greater than can be data-captured by day-to-day administrative staff. By the time they are, and if ever, they are out of date and the respondent has given up waiting for an information pack or a sales follow-up. Sound familiar?

Third party customer or enquiry lists

Occasionally, IT manufacturers or suppliers seek to run direct mail campaigns by using the mailing files of their friendly channel (distributors). In many instances, this is because these mailing files are seen as a short-cut to reach end users through the mail.

In some situations, these lists turn out to contain an odd assortment of enquirers or, at best, buyers of competitive or complementary products and services; at worst, a poor and old file in need of cleaning or reactivation. The trouble is that using them is a bit like Russian roulette – you don't know what you've got till you mail them!

Third party rented lists

Many companies rush to third party list suppliers and spend large sums of money on rented lists. And why not? Lists are packaged and polished to sound attractive: hot exhibition attendees; contacts who have just purchased relevant hardware or software in complementary areas; or subscribers to specialist magazines and journals. The options are numerous.

Sadly, this is the area where database marketing is least understood. Where does direct mail start and database marketing begin? Well, renting lists and de-duplicating them with customer names and addresses held on a customer or marketing database is not database marketing. It is direct mail.

Practised well, direct mail is a technique which can use the data and knowledge held within the marketing database to identify your best chances for acquiring more prospects.

Renting or selecting good mailing lists is the most important part of any direct mail campaign. In all independent research, it is shown to account for at least 60% of the failure or success of any campaign. Good list rental relies on a detailed understanding of what makes a good and bad list, a good and bad contact and a good and bad set of addresses – all rather mundane and basic.

Most organizations find a decent list broker to help them and brief them with 'Find me some names because I want to sell this new product or service'. But how well does the list broker know your business, your customers and what segments perform well? Does your list broker analyse data from your marketing database? I doubt it.

The advice, which is undoubtedly better than amateur guesswork, is in no way a replacement for what a database marketing analyst from within your own organization will find to say about your best customers and what to look for amongst new prospects.

Some good principles to look out for are these:

- Regularly analyse what direct mail campaigns generate in terms of new customers or enquirers, by list.
- Track how these respondents convert into customers or users over time, by list.

- Measure how much new customers cost to recruit, by list (or other media).
- Measure how much these new customers spend over time (e.g. first three months, six months, one year or 18 months).
- Collect consistent information on all people who respond, e.g. list, size of company, SIC code, product interest, job title, etc. This information is critical for future list selection. Most organizations change the information they collect when they change their direct marketing agency or the department running the campaign. This breaks one of the key rules of database marketing, which is 'learn as you go, from the information you collect'.

Product usage and customer segmentation

Most IT manufacturers still think in terms of 'here's the product, where's the customer?'. At best, they are bundling products that hold a natural affinity. But the focus is still very much about technology and innovation first – the sales will follow.

In other, more mature industries, particularly fast-moving consumer goods, there is so little real product innovation and so little differentiation between leading brands that identifying customer needs and matching products to expectations and aspirations is all-important. This requires a very different sales and marketing focus – in fact a customer-led marketing strategy!

If IT manufacturers are to find customer solutions they first have to understand customer needs. Needs will vary by market segment. Most IT manufacturers need to consider a segmentation strategy which is more sophisticated than for large, medium and small businesses. For example, a strategy may be developed to target 'medium-sized businesses in the financial services sector' or 'large businesses in the energy industry'.

The needs of different customer segments will vary: by product, or combination of products, by factors influencing the buying decision, by the way they choose to buy, by where they choose to buy and, of course, by the 'before' and 'after' service they expect.

Edwina Dunn is the joint founder of Dunnhumby Associates (1989), before which she was Vice President of CACI Market Analysis. Projects range from data audits and market modelling to designing and building marketing information systems. She is a member of the Direct Marketing Association's Database Marketing Committee and is a frequent speaker at conferences.

29

DATABASE MARKETING, PRECISELY

Paul Stewart

> Our final objective, rather than mailing one standard message to 1000 customers, is to communicate 1000 individual messages to 1000 people, based on our knowledge of each person.
>
> VP Marketing, major US retail chain

Any successful salesperson who is a good listener (and aren't they all?) will tell you that the more they have knowledge about a prospective customer, the better they can tune their sales proposition to the prospect's situation – so they, too, can talk one-to-one with their customer.

These two would agree that knowledge is power.

In this chapter, we will explore the power of database marketing in the IT market, how it can be achieved and some issues.

Database marketing can be defined as **knowledge-based marketing** as opposed to marketing founded on ignorance. (This latter method of marketing is one that you may recognize in the IT sector.)

New Strategies for Marketing Information Technology.
Edited by Christopher Field
Published in 1996 by Chapman & Hall, London. ISBN 0 412 61520 7

Knowledge should be built into the marketing database (and be retrievable) so that informed decisions can be made about market segmentation, messages, marcom methods and timing as well as sales focus.

Sound too grandiose for a mere database? Consider this . . .

As we all know, in IT our targets for direct marketing need to be focused and precise; not for us the *Reader's Digest* approach of the mass consumer markets. Laudable and true. But what drives this approach?

For IT marketers in the 90s, the answer lies in three key influences that affect the thinking of all players:

1. Competition

Never in the history of the IT industry has competition been so tough. As a result, margins have dropped, not only in commodity product technology but also in services businesses. As a result of that, organizations have downsized and focused their efforts more sharply with more expected from those people who remain. Productivity is king.

Well-executed database marketing contributes to the productivity equation by allowing focused marketing and sales to be undertaken effectively, especially in the early stages of the sales/marketing process, i.e. market research, prospect identification, lead generation and continuous awareness.

Leading IT organizations are winning the productivity battle this way – as well as the hearts and minds of the customers. The competitive issue is this: if we're not doing it, someone else is.

2. Technology

Even the most technophobic among us appreciate the speed with which communications, processor and database technologies are developing and have spread to the heartland of 'professional' workers throughout industry and the public sector. Email is now a norm, PC usage is ubiquitous, relational databases are used and understood by many, ISDN and the information superhighway are phrases in common parlance.

These developments enable new and different approaches to information gathering and its dissemination as well as to the way we communicate with prospective customers for our products and services. How long can it be before we replace the archaic system of mailing letters and their handling by up to 8 people, 2–5 days turnround and wastage of mountains of paper? (A 'green' friend of mine once declared the experience of a visit to a Royal Mail sorting office for him as being how a vegetarian might feel visiting an abattoir!)

In particular, database technology has shot ahead to allow us to hold large datasets with many pieces of related information and to retrieve them with ease. The influence of Oracle Corporation on the development of relational technology has been staggering, whether we like their position of dominance or not.

If we're not doing it, someone else is.

3. Availability of information

The growth of the information services business has matched that of technology, with thousands of databases now available across national and market sector boundaries. Access through CD-ROM or public access networks such as the Internet or MCI makes all this information available in only a matter of seconds.

It is clear that we are now only in the first few degrees of the circle that is called the information revolution. We can expect increasingly specialized information to become accessible which will change our whole way of dealing with market and customer information.

This data together with our own in-house intelligence and customization will enable all those involved in the business or organization to make speedier and sharper decisions. Marketing has the opportunity to take the lead in realizing this potential.

Let's move on to how successful database marketing can be achieved. Other worthy textbooks deal with the practicalities of database design, information sources, software and so on. In the space available here, I offer you five principles of database marketing.

1. Segment

Of all markets that you could have chosen to market in, information technology is the most fragmented in terms of identifiable segments. There are vertical sectors and application segments within them, there are customers and new business organizations broken down by size, type (mainframe, distributed, open systems, networked, etc.), horizontal sectors and segments within them and, of course, vertizontal – one additional attempt to get some order into segmentation. It is the job of marketing to define, and get agreed, clear segments that represent the focus of the business. Database marketing asks very specific questions of the marketer about definition of the target market in precise terms – there is no room for woolliness.

2. Focus, focus, focus

Of course, as soon as we define segments and a clear focus in the marketing plan, someone, normally in sales, discovers a 'new market' based on a single success or opportunity. The attention is drawn away and focus is lost. Familiar?

This may be possible in sales, though not desirable, but it is not possible in database marketing. Although all marketers have to be responsive and flexible, we also have a responsibility to the business to maintain the defined and budgeted direction.

In database marketing, this means:

- creating the database to reflect the focus;
- NOT buying new 'lists' just because they are available;
- reinforcing the focus to everyone involved in the sales/marketing process, especially sales.

Above all, keep the faith and be consistent – successful database marketing is the work of a lifetime, not of one marketing 'season'.

3. Nurture the database

The marketing database is a living organism that needs careful tending, pruning and feeding. Someone, whether internal or external to the company, has to hold database management responsibility as a specific job, not just a Friday afternoon activity. In my experience, the principal cause of marketing database failure is lack of commitment and attention to the database.

Make no bones about it, the marketing database is at the very heart of IT marketing.

4. Measure and review

Once the strategy has been defined, the campaign planned, the suppliers briefed and chased and a mailshot goes out of the door (just on time), the temptation for the marketer is to fly away to a sunny spot for a spot of R&R. Wrong! This is the time to start measuring: goneaways, response rates (in what segments and over what time period), comparison with other campaigns and what we had expected, sales leads, quality, follow-up. Record these results and review with all parties to agree corrective action.

The beauty as well as the pain of database marketing is its measurability. By keeping score of key items in a successful campaign, you will help justification of a repeat exercise in the next budget round.

5. Be realistic

No matter how much you have to sell your soul to get the budget allocated to database marketing, never exaggerate the results that can be expected from the activity. It will come back to haunt you.

Quality database marketing may be new to some in the organization and for that reason there may be a false perception held of what is possible. Take advice from those with experience to predict the likely results, which should be cost-effective anyway without the hype. If they're not, do you really want to undertake that particular element of the campaign anyway?

Overall, database marketing has the potential to revolutionize your organization's marketing results and to make your own professional reputation in the process. The techniques are pure common sense, as summarized later in this book, and the application of quality is critical in order to avoid the 'junk' epithet justifiably applied to so much direct marketing. In other words, it can and does work for serious practitioners.

In the IT market, however, there is one overriding factor: database marketing is always only a part of the marketing/sales chain that ends with a satisfied customer. Every link in that chain must be strong for success to be achieved – a failure of marketing to deliver on time, a lack of sales follow-up or of management commitment to funding may be disastrous.

It is the job of marketing to take ownership of the chain, to champion and protect the process that, when executed well, will deliver for the organization. Database marketing is no longer just 'nice to have', it's a necessity. After all, if we're not doing it, someone else is.

Paul Stewart is Managing Director of Information and Research Services (IRS), a direct marketing services company that specializes in database management and telemarketing in the IT market. With a senior marketing and sales management background at IBM, Bull and in the software industry, Paul has spearheaded the use of quality database marketing in the IT industry.

PART TWELVE

IT'S GOOD TO TALK

Telephones

INTRODUCTION

The telephone is taken too much for granted. Although it is the most commonly used medium of communication with customers after the face to face meeting, people rarely consider its value. Moreover, many people who do not have good remote communication skills are expected to use it all the time.

Without a fundamental understanding of the use and value of the telephone, advanced telephone techniques such as telemarketing can seem like a black art.

There is another problem though. Telemarketing is often employed by companies that do not want to engage in first hand contact with customer and prospects, often out of simple shyness or because they do not know how to go about it effectively. The example that such companies provide gives telemarketing a bad name. Anyone who has been on the wrong end of a double-glazing company's telemarketing rep at home on a Sunday evening will claim it is richly deserved.

And yet there are also many examples of companies that have made a spectacular success of it. Some products lend themselves well to remote marketing, and provided that orders are followed up correctly using other forms of marketing, companies can surprise themselves at getting such good results without having to queue up for a personal sales call.

Greg Cooper says that, in the rights hands, or rather voices, telemarketing can be a key part of relationship marketing, the most personal form of promotion. He regards telemarketing not simply as a specialized function for a few chosen individuals but as a corporate ethos. Here he discusses the issues, the applications and how to control the costs.

New Strategies for Marketing Information Technology.
Edited by Christopher Field
Published in 1996 by Chapman & Hall, London. ISBN 0 412 61520 7

30

TELEMARKETING
The interactive edge

Greg Cooper

Consider for a moment the disadvantages of most advertising. It's wasteful – often it is necessary to blanket cover a market to make sure you hit your target prospects; then there is an in-built time lag, both in conception and preparation of a campaign and in analysing the results; and thirdly it's inflexible, so there is little or no ability to change a campaign once it has started. Telemarketing, in contrast, is personal, immediate and most important of all, interactive.

As the rate of change in IT accelerates, customers are faced with increasingly difficult business-critical decisions between not one but several new emerging technologies. Amidst the cacophony of marketing messages suppliers must find ways of rising above the noise and delivering their marketing messages quickly, accurately and responsively.

In an effort to deliver the right message to the right person at the right time many companies have started 'relationship marketing' programmes. New titles like 'Strategic Relationship Manager' are springing up in the recruitment advertisements, though few companies have achieved the level of integrated marketing that this implies. There is, however, an established and growing appreciation of the importance of the existing customer.

Figures from the Direct Marketing Institute put the cost of winning business from existing customers at 6–30 times cheaper than converting new business. As more marketing attention is paid to the

New Strategies for Marketing Information Technology.
Edited by Christopher Field
Published in 1996 by Chapman & Hall, London. ISBN 0 412 61520 7

customer base, the importance of the telephone becomes apparent. Syntegra, the BT-owned telecommunications consultancy, claims that 50% of all contact with customers is now conducted by telephone.

The telephone is becoming the key interface for relationship marketing. To understand why this is we simply have to look at the difference between telemarketing and direct mail. Like direct mail, telemarketing allows a strategic or tactical message to be delivered personally to a targeted decision maker. The crucial difference, however, is the opportunity for immediate interaction – the ability to listen and respond to the customer's opinions and circumstances in 'real time'. This is the interactive edge.

Having set a broader context for telemarketing I would like to now focus on a specific application and the place of telemarketing in the overall marketing plan. For the purposes of this article I make little distinction between outbound and inbound telemarketing activity.

Successful telemarketing must be part of an integrated marketing plan. To take an extreme example, there is no point in a telemarketer winning business from a customer only to discover that the company is on credit hold.

Some companies have taken the strategic position that all business will be conducted by telephone – First Direct, the personal banking service, is a highly successful example of this strategy. In the IT sector Dell pursued this strategy in the early days though now in response to increased competition in the direct channel the company has broadened its channel strategy to include dealers and retailers (e.g. Dixons) as well as having a large corporate sales force.

Whether or not the telephone is the main customer interface, the primary considerations when making the choice of campaigns on which to use telemarketing are:

- Will the use of the telephone generate additional profit on this campaign?
- Will the use of the telephone generate additional profit over the lifetime of this account?
- Are there good reasons for not using the telephone on the campaign?

Clearly there will be internal considerations which will also influence your decision, not least of which might be the capacity and availability of your telemarketing resource. In general, however, each campaign should be evaluated on its merits.

EXAMPLE

In this example a PC applications supplier wished to launch a popular stand alone product as a network version into English-speaking European countries. Advertising budget and internal resources were very limited, so the company considered setting up a small telesales team.

As a first step the company conducted a small test. From 150 calls:

66 contacts are made
15 units are sold @ £500
sales revenue = £7,500
G.P. = £7,500 × 90% = £6,750

This test took ten hours spread over several days. Using the following assumptions the company then worked out a projection of income.

Assumptions

- 46 working weeks in the year;
- a team of four telesales people spending seven hours per day on the phone;
- work load is split 70/30 between direct sales and awareness/appointment making;
- average sales conversion rate will be 8%;
- a contact rate of five per hour is achieved;
- cost of a telemarketing person including all overheads is £18 per hour.

Projected revenue from telesales

Four people will generate:

4 × 46 (weeks) × 35 (hours) × .7 (direct sales) × 5 = 22,540 contacts p.a.
Number of sales will be 1800 p.a.
Value of annual sales will be 1800 × £500 (Selling price of product) = £900,000
Gross profit @ 90% × £810,000
Telemarketing costs are 6440 hours × £18 = £115,920

This operation is now established and performing well. Here are some more examples of successful use of telemarketing in IT:

- A supplier of rapid application development tools used tele-marketing to overcome its low profile in the marketplace and win new customers by successfully marketing seminars on highly topical client server subjects.
- A retail IT consultancy used telemarketing to overcome the traditional difficulties associated with promoting consultancy by talking directly to key decision makers about topical issues. Skilled telemarketers, targeting top retailers, uncovered specific opportunities in one third of the retailers spoken to.
- A large systems integrator used telemarketing to penetrate corporate accounts and identify specific projects. Within weeks business opportunities worth hundreds of thousands of pounds were being negotiated.
- A chip manufacturer used telemarketing to rescue a prestigious industry forum that had failed to attract sufficient bookings. Over 100 last-minute bookings were obtained by the telemarket-ing team less than two weeks from the forum. This represented a conversion rate of 20%.
- A software company specializing in distribution and warehous-ing applications used telemarketing as a low risk, low cost way of exploring new markets and identifying sales potential. Dozens of sales opportunities were found and, armed with the wealth of information about the markets that was generated, the company has been able to successfully increase its penetration and develop a high profile in each market.

There is no space to mention all of the potential telemarketing applications in this short chapter before moving on, however, there is one very important and growing use of the telephone that we need to consider – customer service. Reflecting the greater appreciation of the customer base, the last three years has brought a shift from passive to pro-active customer care. Delivering goods on time is no longer enough. Companies must actively manage their customers to ensure long-term loyalty and maximize opportunities. Studies have shown that regular contact with customers (not sales contact) can by itself increase sales by three times.

This is a common-sense but often overlooked observation, and one which has an important lesson for marketers. A recent study of managers responsible for inbound telemarketing carried out for Syntegra found that one third of managers could not easily access customer information, whilst over 60% were not able to access accounts information.

Many companies are now following the examples set by consumer businesses and setting up helplines to provide a conduit for customer problems and suggestions. It is not so long ago that I remember speaking to managers at a major minicomputer supplier who boasted to me that they never returned customer calls. Unsurprisingly this same company is now deeply in the red.

One of the key customer service issues for software companies is support. Desktop applications are proliferating and at the same time becoming more complex; conversely both prices and margins are shrinking so that it is rapidly becoming necessary to restructure support arrangements. As well as reviewing charging policy many companies are now looking to outside companies to help them handle the increased volume of calls. Microsoft in the UK has contracted out part of its customer services operation to a tele-marketing agency in a deal worth £2m.

Any discussion of the strategic value of the telephone would be incomplete without reference to the marketing database. The tele-phone provides the live link between the marketing database and the prospect or customer. As differences between products become more subtle, competitive edge will come increasingly not from products but from the knowledge that a company has about its potential customers.

This knowledge can be used to differentiate the company's marketing message. Such information has to be painstakingly collected over time and cannot be substituted by the purchase of generic data externally, however sophisticated. In order to capture this information efficiently the database needs a marketing or telemarketing software 'front end' that enables data to be captured at the point of interaction with the customer.

There are numerous such packages on the market. Some caution needs to be exercised in the selection of a package and the following points should be considered:

- Is the requirement for a stand alone telemarketing package or a company wide sales and marketing system?
- Does information need to be exchanged across sites or with field salespeople?
- How will the system fit in with existing systems? What are the technical restrictions?
- What is the budget?
- Allow a sensible lead time. At least three months to select and install the system.

- Will the package cope with your needs in twelve months, two years, three years?
- Does the supplier have the expertise and the resources to develop and support the product over that period?

Suppliers often talk simplistically in terms of improved call rates; in many cases, however well-organized, telemarketers will work more quickly with a paper system. The real productivity gains are to be had in areas such as the enrichment of the database and consequent improvements in targeting, instant access to historical customer data and projecting a more professional image to the customer.

In the last three years a number of other new automation options have emerged which offer exciting possibilities for the marketer. For example, using 'interactive voice processing' or 'IVP' it is possible to completely automate the handling of simpler enquiries and orders using specially designed telecoms equipment. The ability to handle large numbers of calls quickly is important to IT companies experimenting with TV.

This type of system could also be used to handle first tier support calls, simultaneously reducing support costs and improving the level of customer service. Systems using voice recognition are also on the point of being launched.

In conclusion, as competition intensifies, the ability to develop and maintain an intelligent, two-way dialogue with the market is not only desirable but essential for survival. There is no more effective way to build and sustain this than the planned and controlled use of the telephone within your organization. Only companies which recognize this will be able to develop 'the interactive edge'!

Greg Cooper DipDM, M Inst DM is the Principal Consultant for Martrain, a Bristol-based telemarketing and database consultancy specializing in the marketing of IT products and services which he set up in 1990. Previously he ran his own telemarketing agency for seven years, designing and carrying out telemarketing, marketing and training programmes for IT suppliers. Clients came from both the software and hardware sectors including Apricot, IBM, ICL, CompuAdd, Dun and Bradstreet Software, Ross Systems, Symantec, and many other software companies and resellers large and small.

PART THIRTEEN

ALL THE FUN OF THE FAIR

Exhibitions

INTRODUCTION

If you know a company well, it will often admit that it dislikes exhibitions. Staff and managers alike don't want to go, don't want to spend the money and don't believe they are really worthwhile. If you don't know them well, they will tell you the exact opposite. Either someone is lying or they are just not clear about the real benefits and do not know how to go about getting the benefits. And yet they continue to go, not least because their competitors are there and they are terrified of missing an opportunity.

Exhibitions often paint a gloomy picture for the visitor. Staff on the stands avoiding contact with visitors and rushing around trying to look busy to keep their MD happy. The whole set-up seems to exacerbate the difficulties that many people have in making contact with strangers and when a visitor is ensnared, they will often turn out to be a poor prospect that ends up taking up valuable sales time.

And yet, exhibitions are more popular than ever. The grand do-it-all extravaganzas have given way to highly specialized exhibitions and seminars that, in theory, can attract only those companies that are currently in the market. However, exhibitors are faced with the same challenges as ever. How to attract attention.

Simon Daisley of Kerridge Computer Company and Hugh Keeble of Interactive Group say you have to get the objectives right first and make sure that those objectives are a core part of your overall marketing strategy.

New Strategies for Marketing Information Technology.
Edited by Christopher Field
Published in 1996 by Chapman & Hall, London. ISBN 0 412 61520 7

31

A NEW GENERATION OF SHOWS

Simon Daisley and Hugh Keeble

As a consumer of the marketing put out by exhibition organizers, it is easy to sympathize with Thomas Bonoma. He concluded over ten years ago that 'exhibitions are an inherently sloppy marketing problem'.

A great deal has been written over recent years about the exhibition industry, but the majority is from the perspective of the show organizer, who has a vested interest in selling space. It does not account for the view of the customer, who is constantly bombarded by direct mail claims about the quality and quantity of visitors to a particular show.

In pure marketing terms, the exhibition is often misunderstood, with definitions ranging from 'just another form of sales promotion' to 'three-dimensional advertisements'.[1] Motives for participating are often not clearly thought out; some organizations attend because 'they have always taken part'; others attend because all competitors would be present; some are simply sold space by well-rehearsed organizers.

Between 1981 and 1991, exhibitions and trade shows were the most dynamic of all major media types in the United Kingdom. During that time the UK's total spend on media and advertising rose from £2766 million in 1981 (Figure 31.1) to £7592 million in 1991 (Figure 31.2). The proportion spent on exhibitions rose from 4.7%

New Strategies for Marketing Information Technology.
Edited by Christopher Field
Published in 1996 by Chapman & Hall, London. ISBN 0 412 61520 7

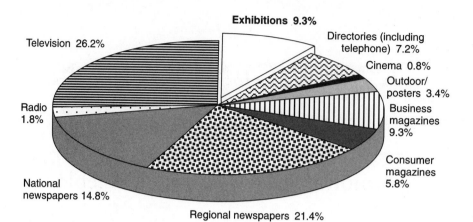

Figure 31.1 Total estimated media spend on all activities in 1981 (total market = £2766 million) (source: *EIF* (1992). *Exhibiting – The Facts*).

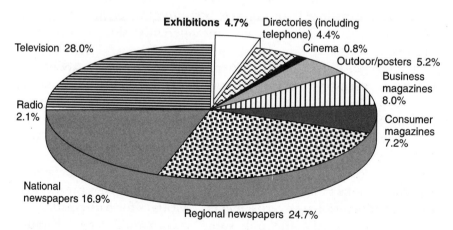

Figure 31.2 Total estimated media spend on all activities in 1991 (total market = £7592 million) (source: *EIF* (1992). *Exhibiting – The Facts*).

to 9.3%; an increase in real terms of over £575 million. The reason for this growth has been attributed to a change in emphasis on the part of organizers seeking to attract exhibitors to 'more tightly focused and targeted audiences'.[2]

If this is truly the case and all claims are true, it is unlikely that a single Managing Director or Financial Director in the country has spent more than a couple of days in the office over the last ten years; they have all been far too busy attending exhibitions!

Leon Kreitzman commented in 1988 that 'an independent survey would be more credible than direct mail claims about the show', and although the industry has grown by almost 1000% since 1981, little has been done to help exhibition participants a) to select which shows to attend and b) to evaluate the effectiveness of their participation.

DEVELOPING TRENDS IN EXHIBITIONS

Whatever happened to the giant computer shows of the 80s? Most exhibitors at these events remember the days of *Which Computer?*, *Compec* and *The PC User Show* with real affection. At the time the information technology market boasted over 80 events; in 1990 this has now been decimated, leaving 38 events. None of these exceed the 10,000 square metre mark – the threshold traditionally considered to be the sign of a 'successful event'.

Price Waterhouse[3] conducted a comprehensive survey of users and vendor trends in relation to their use of exhibitions as one of many media options. From the users' perspective the requirements were:

- keeping abreast of technology and trends in general;
- getting detail on specific areas of technical interest;
- understanding the implications for their business (i.e. its culture, organizations, personnel, systems and product).

For vendors the monolithic era is over. Customers are now pursuing a number of architectural transitions at a variety of places, hence the need for individualized marketing activities. Themes will tend to come and go. Accordingly, vendors will have to decide which events may be best for particular products and services to make contact with the right audiences – now and in the next 3–5 years. Price Waterhouse suggested the following audience segmentation:

- customers with discrete stand alone needs;
- the informed and decisive audience that knows what they need;
- the browsing audience building broad based awareness of what's available/possible;
- the fashion audience (responding quickly to hot topics and one-off needs);
- the sophisticated and discerning audience with a complex requirement.

In the context of an exhibition the vendor needs to consider the format of each event and deliver the right message or value added solution to the customer seeking to achieve substantial business benefits.

CHOOSING THE RIGHT EXHIBITION

In looking at shows it is worth looking at why and how events are launched. I am sorry to say that, more often than not, event and exhibition organizers find the right buzzword and rely upon vendors reacting impulsively by identifying themselves with that market or market strategy. Examples in the past include Open Systems, Workgroup Computing, and Workstations.

The market leaders having been identified, they are persuaded to option a space on the floorplan; the floorplan with ten or so companies is mailed to the 'followers' and you have another show draining your marketing budget. Both organizers' greed and exhibitors' naivety have to be blamed for the proliferation of these events.

WILL YOUR POTENTIAL CUSTOMERS ATTEND?

A more important question would be to ask what value those events offer to today's computer buyer of computer products.

Picture your customer receiving the mailshot – are they really going to take a day out of the office to come to Olympia? If they do, what value will they glean from the event? Will they know what will be at the event so they are in a position to visit the companies they need to talk to? Most importantly, will they buy?

CAN YOU EFFECTIVELY SELL YOUR PRODUCT FROM A STAND?

In many cases high-price information technology items are extremely complex by nature. One has to ask oneself whether one can demonstrate that product in the traditional exhibition environment.

These issues have spawned a new generation of event organizers, focused on the needs of specialist markets, providing highly niched events, with comprehensive pre-show information services, pre-booked meeting and seminar services, comprehensive directories and research reports for attendees. Examples include the Softworld Series (Software application markets) and the Canberra series (trade and niche markets).

The environment created by these types of event provide serious buyers with the opportunity to select and review product in an environment designed to show the product to best effect: at Softworld, seminars; on the Canberra, meetings.

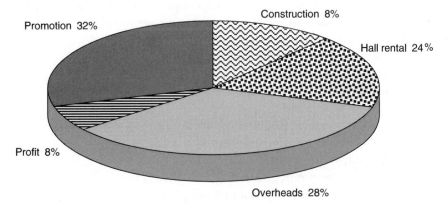

Figure 31.3 Breakdown of organizers' expenditure expressed as a percentage of turnover.

DISCOUNTS

Unlike many other forms of media, discounts for exhibitions are rarely budgeted when organizers write their business plans. The simple economics of an exhibition dictate that when an organizer is discounting, the show is in trouble. Not only is it selling badly but the reduced cost will be made up by reducing the funds spent on promoting the event. Exhibition costs are broadly divided as in Figure 31.3.

All of the costs in developing an event are fixed, with the exception of the promotional budget and profits. The latter are invariably protected in the interests of shareholders of the publicly owned exhibition conglomerates.

I would recommend asking an organizer for the breakdown of these elements of event management. Remember, if they are discounting there will only be one loser on the day.

MEASURING THE EFFECTIVENESS OF YOUR PERFORMANCE

The exhibition industry is no different from any other service industry and theories abound for measuring the effectiveness of services. It is just that, to my knowledge, no one has applied these methods to the marketing of trade shows.

Shipley, Egan and Wong, in research conducted in 1993, identified thirteen reasons for organizations to participate in exhibitions:

1. to meet new customers (which should include all components of a potential decision-making unit such as Management Consultants and other specifiers and professional purchasers);
2. to enhance company image;
3. to interact with existing customers;
4. to promote existing products (which should include all press and public relations functions);
5. to launch new products;
6. to get competitor intelligence;
7. to get an edge on non-exhibitors;
8. to keep up with competitors;
9. to enhance personnel morale;
10. to interact with distributors or suppliers;
11. for general market research purposes;
12. to take sales orders;
13. to meet new distributors or suppliers.

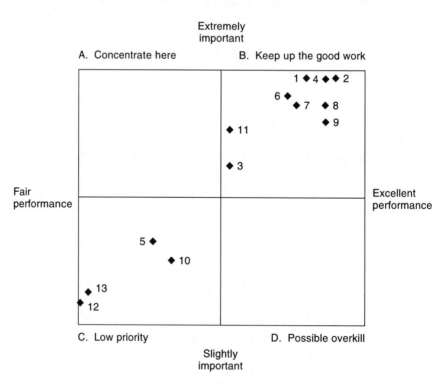

Figure 31.4 Martilla/James importance/performance matrix for exhibition A.

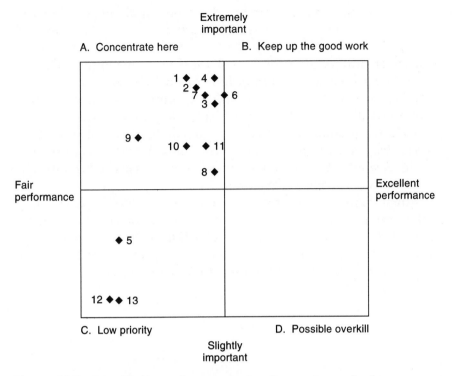

Figure 31.5 Martilla/James importance/performance matrix for exhibition B.

These components can be combined into an importance/ performance model: a framework devised in 1977 by Martilla and James for measuring service effectiveness. This allows meaningful statistical analysis to be conducted not just into the objectives both of exhibitors and visitors to trade shows, but also in the ability of the organizers to satisfy these objectives.

Participants are asked to allocate a score of between 1 and 7 to each of these thirteen attributes to determine how important each objective was in their decision to attend the show. Shortly after the exhibition, the same people can be asked to allocate a score of between 1 and 7 to indicate the extent to which each objective was satisfied.

These results are then plotted in a matrix to give a graphical illustration of the company's performance in each of its key areas.

In Figure 31.4 (taken from attendance at the *Softworld in Logistics and Distribution* Exhibition in 1993) the participating organization can be well-satisfied with their performance; those items which have a high relative score for importance also score highly in performance. At the other end of the scale, those attributes which are deemed unimportant do not receive good performance ratings. This shows that the organizers' objectives match those of the exhibitor and effort is not being wasted on issues of little or no concern.

In Figure 31.5, however, results for the same organization participating in a different exhibition which took place at about the same time clearly question the effectiveness of taking part. Only one of the factors flagged as important receives even a mediocre performance rating. A single company can now see quite clearly whether a specific show has worked for them or not.

If the organizers themselves take on responsibility for conducting this research, a completely new dimension can be added. Not only do the organizers themselves benefit by enhancing their own credibility, but they allow one participant to compare results with those collected from all other exhibitors at the same show.

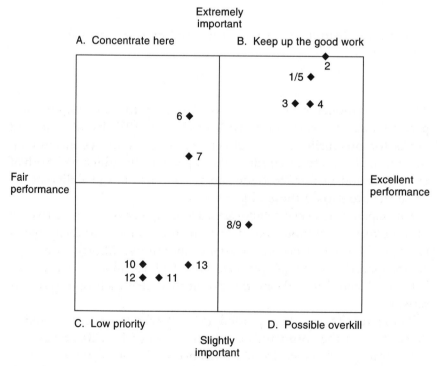

Figure 31.6 Martilla/James importance/performance matrix for exhibition B (competitors).

Thus by comparing the results in Figure 31.5 with those collected from a sample of other participants at the same show (Figure 31.6) it is possible to see how one company fared against its competitors.

It now becomes clear that the lack of success is not necessarily the fault of the exhibition organizer but brings into question the effectiveness of the company's own performance. In the eyes of competitors, the exhibition satisfied most (although not all) of their important objectives. At least the information is now available for an organization to make a valid judgement on such issues as stand location, design and pre- and post-show activity rather than simply saying 'we didn't get any good leads so the show was no use for us'.

Another way of adapting this framework enables organizers to match the objectives of exhibitors to those of the visitors. This can add objectivity to the views of exhibitors and can also help to highlight areas of conflict between exhibitors and those to whom they are trying to sell.

By transposing the objectives of exhibitors from active to passive actions, it is possible to establish whether they bear any resemblance to those of the visiting public.

1. 'Meet new customers' becomes 'meet new suppliers'.
2. 'Enhance company image' becomes 'reinforce perceptions about companies'.
3. 'Interact with customers' becomes 'interact with existing suppliers'.
4. 'Promote existing products' becomes 'reinforce perceptions about existing products'.
5. 'Launch new products' becomes 'evaluate newly launched products'.
6. 'Get competitor intelligence' remains valid from either viewpoint.
7. 'Interact with distributors or suppliers' becomes 'interact with distributors or customers' (those to whom you supply).
8. 'Take sales orders' becomes 'place sales orders'.
9. 'General market research' remains the same.

The three remaining categories of 'get edge on non-exhibitors', 'keep up with competitors' and 'enhance personnel morale' are primarily internal issues to the exhibiting organization and are not specifically influenced by individual visitors. They are therefore excluded from this process.

Since some of the categories are somewhat contrived, it is important to supplement this with qualitative research, questions such as 'which stands impressed you most/least?', 'which stands were the most/least professional?'. These questionnaires could be offered to each and every visitor on arrival for them to submit on departure.

This research may contain some unpleasant home truths, but in this new, enlightened age of 'openness' it is far more valuable for an exhibitor to know that the reason for their lack of success was due to the fact that no one knew they were there and that their stand looked like a building site. It would at least offer organizers a different excuse from 'blame it on the weather/traffic/bomb scare'.

Simon Daisley is Marketing Manager for software and software services company, Kerridge Computer Services, in the UK and overseas. Previously he worked in sales and marketing of industrial energy management systems and with software house MPSI on the development of marketing databases. He has an MA in marketing and is a member of the Chartered Institute of Marketing.

Hugh Keeble is a founder of Interactive Group. He used to be a director of Reed Exhibition Companies, part of Reed International, where he grew the *Which Computer?* Show into Reed's largest and most profitable event. He also conceived, launched and ran *Open Systems* for Reed. Interactive owns and manages a series of events including *Softworld* and organizes events for the British Computer Society.

PART FOURTEEN

LOOK BEFORE YOU LEAP

Research

INTRODUCTION

Most research in IT is used to validate a sales and marketing strategy before it is put in place – to find out how a market might receive a proposed new product, what it thinks about an old one, what the customer's long-term information strategy is, who the real decision-makers are, how future legislation may affect an industry and so on. Far less research is carried out after the campaign, to find out what the customers think about the product or service or the sponsor themselves. The sales figures are the only indicator and although they are clearly the ultimate proof that something has worked, there is no telling which parts of the campaign actually contributed.

One company's sales figures rocketed after a sales campaign because their only competitor had gone bust – the customers had no choice but to come to them. They were lucky. Another company spent all their venture capital cash on launching an expert system. They even did some research to show that there was a big market for packaged expert software. The product sold well but customers only took single-user licences and the product never got past pilot studies. However, the company did not ask its few buyers what had made them buy and why they were not buying again. They would have been told that the software was incapable of interfacing with the users' existing corporate data and that reinputting data to suit the package would have been uneconomical, not to say infuriating.

Honest, unvarnished feedback seems to frighten many companies which would rather guess at what their customers think about them than find out the unpalatable truth. The average customer satisfaction survey is undertaken merely to confirm what companies think they already know about themselves. The questions are not designed to get to the truth but to confirm the belief that customer satisfaction

New Strategies for Marketing Information Technology.
Edited by Christopher Field
Published in 1996 by Chapman & Hall, London. ISBN 0 412 61520 7

is high and that any changes required will be minor. Sponsors of research will often compound the error by trying to extract some small beacon of hope from the results and using this to send out a press release!

Peter Hutton of MORI urges research at every stage of the product life cycle.

Chris Kaday of Hi-tech Marketing argues that customer satisfaction research is the only way to protect the company from competitors, get closer to customers and to keep them.

32

RESEARCH THROUGHOUT THE PRODUCT LIFE CYCLE

Peter Hutton

Marketing research is already playing a critical role in the emerging IT markets. Its function is to provide objective information on what the customer really wants and the degree to which current or prospective products or services are able or likely to meet their needs.

And it has to keep up with an exploding market as multimedia becomes a reality in businesses and in people's homes. Within a few years most homes in the country could be able to link in to the 'information super highway'. Interactive technology could make supermarkets and high street banks a thing of the past. Potentially people will be able walk around a supermarket and select items to buy, transfer funds from one account to another and settle their bills, choose potential holiday destinations from a selection of interactive video 'brochures', check their symptoms with an interactive doctor and play roulette in Las Vegas without leaving the comfort of their computer screens. It is happening and now.

USING RESEARCH TO KEEP UP AND GET AHEAD

The traditional techniques of market research are as relevant to IT markets as to any other consumer or business-to-business markets.

New Strategies for Marketing Information Technology.
Edited by Christopher Field
Published in 1996 by Chapman & Hall, London. ISBN 0 412 61520 7

These can be broadly categorized into qualitative and quantitative. The former, as the name implies, is exploratory, being designed to probe in-depth the views of a small number of respondents rather than ask the same series of questions to a large sample of respondents for the purpose of quantification.

The two techniques are complementary. While the first will provide a lot more understanding of the thinking and processes underlying purchase decisions and other types of behaviour, the second will allow the marketer to say how many in the target market think or behave in a particular way. It can also allow limited probing of specific answers to provide further diagnostic information on why the market is behaving in a certain way. Similarly, qualitative research can be expanded to include some quantifiable questions although the small samples normally involved mean that the results can only be projected on to the market within very broad parameters.

Because the IT market is so broad there is scope for the full range of research techniques to be applied at each stage of the classic product life cycle: new product development, launch and growth, maturity and decline. Although they will be applied in quite different ways according to the product and its market, the applications will be similar whether one is researching a new computer, interactive games packages, home shopping services or videos on demand.

NEW PRODUCT DEVELOPMENT

New ideas are worth nothing in marketing if they do not find favour with the customer at whom they are targeted. Qualitative research techniques allow the researcher to explore potential customers' current needs and how they are likely to respond to new products or services. These can be examined at any stage from original concept through prototype and finished design.

So too can the marketing of the product. How the product is defined and presented to the potential purchaser, the image it has, and how it is perceived relative to consumers' identified needs, to competing products and to different segments of the market will be critical to its eventual success. Research is used to define these various parameters so that the marketer understands how their product is likely to be positioned in the market and to guide decisions on how a marketing strategy can be implemented.

LAUNCH AND GROWTH

If research has indicated that there is a viable market for the new product or service and has pointed the way to launching it, it can then be used to assist with the launch and growth of market share. Tracking research using surveys conducted at regular intervals can collect information which will not be apparent from simple sales figures, information such as propensity to purchase, reasons for purchase, and repeat purchase behaviour (where relevant) as well as measures directly related to the marketing campaign such as product and brand awareness, awareness of the advertising and recall of the key messages of the advertising. Integrating marketing surveys with media surveys research will also tell you which media, and which advertising slots within those media, will be most effective in reaching the targeted audiences.

As the product and brand becomes established the research can focus on more detailed information such as brand attributes and images. How the brand is positioned relative to the competition is critically important. How is it differentiated? What are its relative strengths and weakness? What underlies its position in the market? How vulnerable is it?

While in most markets the vision of the possibilities of a new product tend to arrive with the product launch, in IT often the vision is well in advance of the product's arrival. This can lead to early disappointment as early product releases often fail to meet customers' expectations.

MATURITY

In the IT market, product maturity is apt to come very quickly. By the time of their launch, the technology of most IT products is likely to have been superseded at least once. The 086 processor was soon superseded by the 186, and this rapidly by the 286, 386, 486 and pentium processors. The media is now abuzz with the possibilities of interactive electronic media with new developments being announced daily, even before such products have really begun to establish themselves in the market. Many products do not, therefore, have the chance to fully mature as the next generation of products quickly take over. Research then is useful in determining the degree to which a particular product still has life left in it. Is the market likely to move on rapidly or wait and see whether the new generation products are worth adopting first? A MORI survey conducted for Lotus Development in 1987, for example, found purchasers of computers and software reluctant to adopt the new IBM OS/2 operating system despite its extensive pre-launch hype. The reasons were largely to do with their substantial investment in, and therefore commitment to, the standard DOS operating system which they were not prepared to write off, but the expectations of alternative multitasking technologies such as the Microsoft Windows package just around the corner must have caused many to hesitate about embracing OS/2 too quickly.

DECLINE

Many IT products are based on enormous research and development costs. Businesses naturally wish to maximize their return on the investment, and research can be very usefully applied in identifying how this can most effectively be done. Can the product be repositioned to appeal to a different or wider audience? Can it be adapted to become acceptable in other markets? Or has the market already shifted on so radically that the best thing is to get out and move on as quickly as possible?

THE WIDER PERSPECTIVE

Technology is opening up possibilities for exchanging information, education, entertainment, shopping and financial management which have never been available before. How will society react? Is it the direction people really wish to go in or do the products only really relate to something in the imagination of the inventors? How far will technological change drive society forward and how far will society mould the applications of technology to its own needs? Are there certain patterns of work, leisure and lifestyle which will lay down the parameters in which technologically innovative products will have to operate?

In the 1990s technology is, and will continue to be, one of the critical determinants of social change. Its main impact has initially been in the workplace where the sharing of information through networks and the spreading of IT skills throughout organizations has facilitated the move towards much flatter, less hierarchical structures. Moreover, new computer driven technology is allowing producers to orientate themselves more and more towards meeting individual rather than mass consumer needs, giving greater opportunities for consumers to express themselves through their consumption patterns. Research has been used to explore these changing social patterns and to relate them back to the markets for individual products and services. In particular, such research is used to anticipate and identify new social trends which will help to define where the marketing opportunities of the future are likely to be.

Some research is specifically designed to understand the broader picture of how society is operating. Large IT companies are particularly vulnerable to using research to tell you the characteristics of yesterday's market rather than of tomorrow's. With new high technology products constantly being developed and brought onto the market, consumers themselves do not really know how they are likely to react to products which were not even conceived of a short time ago. How new products are received will depend on the values, motivations and lifestyles of different social groups each of which will need different market messages if the product is to be successful. The most forward thinking companies will therefore seek to keep pace with underlying social change since this will drive their new product development and their branding strategy.

Research can be used to identify groups in the broad population and business communities who are at the leading edge of socio-cultural change. In markets as fast moving as those related to IT, it is essential to focus on the leading edge rather than the mass market because the leading edge will become the mass market within three to five years.

OUTSIDE OF MARKETING

Apart from using research to aid marketing decision making, it is also used in a number of other areas. It has become increasingly common for companies to commission research with a view primarily for publication. Press releases which include a survey normally substantially increase their chance of being quoted by the media compared with normal company press releases which do not contain such readily quotable and credible information. IT companies, in particular, have seen this as a way of positioning themselves as spokespeople on particular issues in the industry, or on their products as being particularly relevant to an identified customer need.

Research conducted by MORI for WordPerfect, for example, found 62% of parents regarded computer literacy as important to their children in 'getting ahead in the world' and a third of those using computers for their children's education regarded it as 'more effective than books as a teaching tool'.

Research is also used to help guide the public relations activities of leading IT companies, whether this be aimed at the general public or specialist groups such as top businesspeople or journalists in the computer press. The chart shows for example, the fortunes of four major computer companies among Britain's computer journalists over a seven year period. It shows how the reputations of Olivetti and Tandon declined among this influential group of writers between 1987 and 1993 while that of Dell rose fairly consistently year on year. Commodore peaked in 1990 then declined. Such research is used to monitor the corporate reputations of IT companies with publics of importance to them and their relationships (e.g. press relations) with them. Research has shown how ratings of press relations are often highly correlated with overall favourability so that improving relationships with the media can result in an improved reputation which is likely to be reflected in better news coverage.

CONCLUSION

The IT markets are the most innovative and fast expanding of any and this will continue throughout the decade. The substantial investment involved in developing and marketing new products and services means reliable information on the market is critical. Market research has developed dependable techniques for evaluating customer needs and monitoring demand over time. As such it will continue to play a critical role in the development of the IT market for the foreseeable future.

Peter Hutton graduated from Cambridge University in 1974 with a degree in Social and Political Sciences and is now a director of MORI with over 20 years' experience of market research. He is also responsible for IT in MORI and research into IT and multimedia is one of his specializations. He is a frequent writer and speaker on research topics and the second edition of his book *Survey Research for Managers* was published in 1991.

33

GETTING CLOSE TO YOUR CUSTOMERS
Can you afford not to?

Chris Kaday

It is easy to think that revenue equals sales and some businesses even use the term sales revenue. Well, it doesn't. Revenue is certainly generated from the companies which the salesforce has acquired, but it also comes with far less effort from the companies which have continued to buy because they were satisfied with what they were getting. In fact, as fast as the salesforce is busy filling up the revenue bucket at the top, the customers are often draining out at the bottom. Although all IT companies have sales targets, how many have you encountered which have customer retention targets, let alone ones which are meaningful and closely monitored?

If the old maxim 'it takes five times the cost to get a customer than to keep one' is only half true, why is so little real attention paid to customer retention? There are a number of reasons for this which have to be understood if the satisfaction of customers is to be addressed with the same verve and vigour as achieving sales targets.

The IT industry is relatively young and was, in the early adopter phase, largely technology driven. This meant that customer loyalty had a low priority on the premise that 'there are plenty more where they came from'. Now, as the market matures, and there is a greater

New Strategies for Marketing Information Technology.
Edited by Christopher Field
Published in 1996 by Chapman & Hall, London. ISBN 0 412 61520 7

emphasis on standardization and open technology, the differential between products is reducing. This means that company performance, as well as product performance, is a significant factor in the purchasing decision. Also, as a company's installed base grows they will adopt new technology less frequently and with greater forethought, although the order value is likely to be higher.

Consider also the marketing implications of getting close to your customers and keeping them. Every company is barraged by the competitor's marketing with mail shots, seminar invitations and cold calls being received in volume every day. With companies adopting a more direct approach to their communications this will certainly intensify. In fact, through these processes, competitors can often establish a better relationship with a company before they get any business than can the supplier who already has the business. Like an opposition political party they can promise a better future, but do not have to deliver, yet! In this situation, the supplier had better beware as the account is at its most vulnerable to attack.

However, the good news is that companies tend to work on a trouble-shooting agenda, with the most visible problems being those which get tackled first. The likelihood of them considering a comparative supplier is greatly reduced, providing your level of service gives them no cause to. Even when they inevitably do look for their next upgrade, your relationship should be such that you are in pole position for the order. Unfortunately, in an enterprise where the existing customer receives the least attention, the salesforce has to work even harder to stem the attrition by generating new accounts.

One key reason why customer retention does not have the priority it deserves is that no one individual or department 'owns the piece' as the current jargon goes. It could rightly be argued that the initiative rests with marketing. In the past marketing placed the ads and sales got the business, but as marketing gets more direct, a close integration between sales and marketing is a necessity. But it goes further than this. Marketing should be concerned with the whole product adoption cycle which starts with the first sale rather than ending with it. The final stage of the cycle is where the customers are so happy with the company that they recommend it to others unprompted. This is an essential part of the sales process in such markets as financial services and the people businesses of consultancy and marketing agencies. It is less common in product led, as opposed to service industries. Remember that an enquiry as a result of a referral costs the company absolutely nothing. There is no doubt that the company which can get business through developing its existing customer base and generate more customers through referrals from them is extremely well placed. Indeed, in this situation the dependence on sales to create new accounts is greatly reduced.

So, having hopefully put forward a strong case for customer retention, how do you go about it? As a starting point, it is important to understand where you stand now in terms of keeping your customers. An essential calculation is the average lifetime value and retention timescale of your customers. This is not only essential from a customer satisfaction standpoint, but also essential when assessing the success of your sales and marketing efforts. You cannot evaluate the result from say a direct mail shot in terms of immediate business, but in terms of the likely lifetime value of that customer. This will be even higher if the customer retention programmes are working satisfactorily. Having established your customer attrition rate you now have one benchmark from which to measure the effectiveness of your future retention programmes.

The next stage is to establish a customer retention and development strategy. The very word 'strategy' throws some into a state of apoplexy and it is amazing how few companies have a well-developed and documented marketing strategy, let alone one for keeping and growing their customers. The most important thing is to start with your overall intention or objective. What do you wish to achieve as a result of this strategy and then what has to be in place to make it happen? It is also important to establish something which can be easily communicated throughout your organization; then staff can understand how it affects them and can play a part in the process.

Finally, there must be targets which are clearly measurable so that progress towards the objective can be assessed. All too often an individual or department is charged with achieving customer satisfaction, but their mandate is not sufficiently extensive. The drive for customer satisfaction should come from the top, but embrace the entire organization. We have used a facilitated workshop process very successfully to gain common 'ownership' across a company with everyone buying into what is required and offering their contribution towards making it happen.

All of this may seem a long way from research, but unless there is a clearly defined objective and strategy, it is impossible to measure against it. In other words, it is essential that one understands what management is trying to do; then research can demonstrate the gap between management intent and reality. Management can then make the closing of this gap the subject of their performance improvement programmes.

There are many ways of measuring customer satisfaction, but all too often companies use the ubiquitous customer satisfaction audit.

This very often uses a self-complete questionnaire which is sent out in the post. You have probably received these documents which usually resemble a pools coupon and ask you amongst other things to rate a supplier's responsiveness on a scale from 1 to 5. Many are carried out on a world-wide basis and seem to emanate from places like Geneva or the US. Usually a questionnaire is sent to one contact in the customer company although in a large organization, questions about say, software maintenance and administration, can seldom be answered by one individual. Clearly, this type of approach is far better than nothing and it does give the company something to work on, especially if it is benchmarked year after year. However, in our view, the customer's opinion of satisfaction is based on an accumulation of experiences, all of which add up to an overall perception. It is these 'moments of truth' which the customers experience every time they are in contact with a company which are important and the perception is often only as good as their last encounter. If the company can succeed in delivering positive experience after positive experience, then a strong level of belief in the company's performance is established. If the company delivers poor experiences time after time, then a situation can arise where the position is virtually unrecoverable.

These interactions between the company and its customer base can be effectively measured through what we call transactional based research. This aims to test the quality of every point of customer company contact, be it an enquiry, a service call and accounts query and so on. Not only does this succeed in generating feedback which is as close to the encounter experience as possible, but the information is also attributable to the company department or individual which provided the experience, thus making the work highly actionable.

A proven methodology for transactional customer experience monitoring is to regularly contact a cross-section of customers across all departments as close to the point of contact as possible. The point of contact more often than not is through the telephone, but it could be fax, letter, service visit and so on. With telephone for example, the process we use is to ring the customer within four hours of the original call being made. The call experience can then be monitored as near as possible to the time it was made.

The questioning is clearly exhaustive, but would for example include such topics as ease of contact, ability to satisfy requirements, the demeanour of the company contact and so on. Although the questions clearly revolve around the immediate contact experience, it is also possible to include questions on the overall level of satisfaction and therefore carry out a rolling satisfaction audit and transactional monitoring all at the same time. In this way it is possible to generate highly actionable feedback which can form the basis of performance improvement programmes, the effectiveness of which can be subsequently measured through further research.

Although transactional monitoring highlights customer experiences, there is one drawback to the process and that is that the customer does not know what should happen. The way to test if standards and procedures are being followed to the letter is to make a series of 'mystery' calls using well-developed scenarios and highly structured questionnaires to record the experience. An example of this would be to test the enquiry process where one would focus on the speed of response, as well as the ability to answer questions and record information accurately. By establishing mystery addresses it is also possible to test the company's ability to get the right material properly addressed into the enquirer's hands on time. In our experience this is a part of the process which often requires improvement.

An essential prerequisite in any customer satisfaction research is to understand what elements of service are most important to the actual customer and these can vary depending on the type of contact and market being addressed. Unless this is done the company can spend a large amount of time correcting something which to the customer is relatively unimportant when with a very small effort the company could correct something which would have a significant impact on the customer. All this sounds very obvious but it is amazing how little companies actually know about their customers' needs and desires.

The final requirement of any research programme is to action it, and unfortunately all too often research reports are sitting on the shelf gathering dust. An important way to ensure that results are actioned is to involve as many relevant staff in the company as possible at the start of the research in the setting of the questions. In this way, they will own the programme and, therefore, be far more committed to action the results. It is also important for there to be a session where an action programme is established as a result of the research and someone is responsible for monitoring that it actually happens. It is not the meeting that sets the action plan which is important, but the one after which monitors what has happened. All too often this is not convened and the initiative is lost.

Any IT company which is going to succeed in the future market has to get close to its customers and this does not mean getting research companies to tell you things which through your relationship you should already know. Most customer satisfaction pro-grammes and measurement processes are obvious but, like most things in business, talking and doing are poles apart. There is a long way to go, but we will know if we have won when the company employee is looking out over the Caribbean skyline because they played a major role in keeping and developing a customer rather than being rewarded solely for getting more.

From running a 300-strong salesforce for Kalamazoo, to Managing Direc-tor of Commodore Computers and main Board Director of PR company Burson–Marsteller, Chris Kaday, a recognized authority on channels management, now runs Hi-Tech Marketing, his own marketing consult-ancy which develops winning marketing and distribution strategies, delivers research in the areas of customer acquisition and retention, and uses direct marketing to generate bottom line results.

PART FIFTEEN

MARKETING GOES TO SCHOOL

Standards

INTRODUCTION

Sales and marketing people don't like each other; they are different personalities with different backgrounds. One resents the existence of the other and they will kick against working together whenever possible. Often the good they achieve together seems borne of conflict not co-operation. Whereas, the salesperson can validate their work based on a long heritage of methods, standards, strategies and not least of all hard sales, marketing personnel cannot.

Marketing has enough enemies. Its most important ally must be the one that is currently most against it. It needs to have the salesforce on its side.

The marketing strategy, if there is one, often just plays to the sales strategy and is based on delivering services within an existing sales structure rather than developing a life of its own. It does not have a long-term vision of what might be, merely a list of good ideas which may or may not please the salesforce and that are unlikely to have measurable benefits.

David Allenstein argues that marketers must develop and pursue qualifications and standards if they are to be taken seriously and if they are to work usefully alongside the salesforce.

New Strategies for Marketing Information Technology.
Edited by Christopher Field
Published in 1996 by Chapman & Hall, London. ISBN 0 412 61520 7

34

MARKETING AND SALES
Joint strategies for success

David Allenstein

Since the end of the 1980s, many IT companies have faced falling margins and falling profitability. Many have also faced failure and liquidation; in fact no organization, however large and apparently secure, has survived the last five years completely unscathed. Even the largest have had to make significant adjustments to the way they run and conduct their business.

Many IT organizations that grew up in the 1970s and 1980s developed and marketed products often via a team of relatively highly paid direct salespeople. For many IT organizations, the only real marketing function carried out was marketing communications, consisting in advertising, PR and promotional activities. Organizations flourished and the aggressive sales-oriented approach was apparently successful. In many companies, the salesperson ruled. Successful salespeople rose quickly through the ranks, with many achieving top positions in the corporate hierarchy.

But by the late 1980s the once predictable growth of the IT market was faltering. Technology was changing rapidly, but for the first time, for many organizations, the old and proven approach to marketing and selling was no longer reaping the expected and required results.

THE LACK OF PROFESSIONAL MARKETING SKILLS

Given the history of the IT industry, it is no accident that in both large and small organizations, the senior levels have tended to be

New Strategies for Marketing Information Technology.
Edited by Christopher Field
Published in 1996 by Chapman & Hall, London. ISBN 0 412 61520 7

occupied by either technical or sales-oriented personnel. The result is a culture where products are either developed or sourced with inadequate understanding of the market or marketing. Where this is true, product development is driven by technical staff with inadequate market research and knowledge of customer requirements. Many companies in this mould have developed great products, only then to wonder exactly who will buy them, and why.

The lack of professional marketing skills is widespread within the IT industry and results in many problems:

- Marketing is seen as marketing communications – the marketing department carries no real weight and is purely a 'support function' to undertake advertising, PR and promotional activities.
- The organization has no marketing strategy – it is unaware of exactly what it is trying to do in the marketplace. Is it trying to penetrate existing markets or develop new markets?
- There are no marketing objectives or planning – no detailed understanding of objectives or how to achieve them. The end result is often confusion and constant changes in direction.
- There is no marketing research, and therefore there is inadequate information on which to base important decisions relating to products and services, prices, marketing communications programmes and distribution.
- There is no market segmentation, which means failure to understand market segments and select target markets. In this mode, organizations will try to sell anything to anyone, resulting in a shotgun approach with little real penetration of any one market.

In the marketing naive company, the problems of revenue and profit instability may be easily seen by the management. However, in many cases, the lack of a marketing appreciation blinkers the management as to the problem causes and possible solutions.

SALES AND MARKETING – WORLDS APART

When growth started to slow in the late 1980s, it was common to blame marketing and, almost inevitably, marketing was seen as failing to deliver the goods. For many it is still a common story: marketing is seen as reactive, reacting only to market changes and not anticipating them; marketing is seen as failing to deliver quality leads; and marketing is seen as not delivering the programmes that salespeople require.

However, the problem runs deeper than a failure to come up with the right marketing programmes. Many sales departments appear to have a deep mistrust of the marketing function and the people within it. In many cases, and quite unrelated to the reality of the situation, marketing people are seen as mediocre – lacking the cut and thrust of sales; lacking in the go-getting aggression that is a hallmark of many a successful sales department.

Many organizations now appreciate and have committed substantial resources to professional marketing processes, but for many, problems still persist between sales and marketing. Although ideally the two should be difficult to separate in the real world, it is unfortunately common for the sales and marketing functions to be poles apart for a number of reasons.

Culture and people

In many organizations, sales and marketing people tend to be culturally diverse with different backgrounds and histories. Many marketing people have an academic background with either a technical or professional marketing qualification. Conversely, many salespeople have graduated from 'The University of Life' and are selected based on personality traits such as confidence and persuasiveness.

Tools and methods

The working methods of the two groups are different and tend to cause further alienation. The professional marketer may be office-bound and involved in analysis and planning. This is hardly a commendation to the salesperson for whom customer contact is the be-all and end-all. Conversely the marketing communications functions may deal with the glamorous side of the marketing process such as visiting venues, organizing advertising, and arranging seminars. However, the lack of face-to-face customer contact may often be a block to gaining the respect of salespeople.

Pressures and concerns

Although marketing will be involved in short-term and tactical issues, much of the workload of a researcher, planner or product manager will be concerned with medium- and long-term issues.

Conversely, the salesperson will often have monthly or quarterly targets that must be hit to pay the mortgage and survive in the organization. In many organizations, marketing personnel work under immense pressure, but often the lack of short-term targets means that this pressure cannot be perceived by the sales department. Too often, marketing is viewed as a 'cushy number', existing in a cosy world of its own.

The failure to communicate

Most important and underlying many of the problems is a failure to communicate between the two departments properly and adequately. Many organizations separate the two functions under different heads and even into different locations! With lack of communication, inevitable frustrations and misunderstandings appear, grow and go unresolved.

BRIDGING THE GAP

The difference between sales and marketing may be real, but even so, to achieve a close and mutually beneficial working relationship the gap must be bridged. Continual open communications are required in order to develop a culture of understanding, consultation and co-operation. Taken from a sample of IT organizations, the following represent a checklist of activities that underpin successful sales/marketing relationships and therefore underlie successful formulation and implementation of sales and marketing strategies:

- regular review meetings between sales and marketing and briefings on all activities;
- joint planning sessions;
- joint settings of objectives, marketing and sales strategies;
- joint agreement and specification of target markets;
- joint agreement of marketing programmes;
- regular feedback of customer attitudes and concerns from sales into marketing;
- regular feedback of perceived competitive activity from sales into marketing;
- regular briefings on product development and joint agreement of market needs.

However, achieving this level of communication and joint working between sales and marketing is not easy and may require training and coaching, along with organizational and cultural change. In particular, the following are seen as prerequisites to the process of achieving sales/marketing harmonization:

- board-level integration between sales and marketing under a single company director;
- developing professional marketing skills at board level;
- developing professional sales and marketing skills at practitioner level.

PROFESSIONAL DEVELOPMENT

To succeed in today's increasingly dynamic markets, IT companies must be committed to investing in training and educating their sales and marketing personnel on an ongoing basis. This will encourage the integration of the sales and marketing functions whilst providing personnel with the professional skills and knowledge necessary to operate effectively and competitively.

The Chartered Institute of Marketing is Europe's leading professional body for sales and marketing. The organization offers support to practitioners throughout their careers, i.e.:

- professional exam-based qualifications;
- National/Scottish Vocational Qualifications in sales, marketing and customer service;
- training in all aspects of sales, marketing, strategy and management in the form of:
  - company-specific programmes
  - residential courses
  - one-day seminars.

Professional development offers the opportunity for salespeople and marketers to gain theoretical knowledge and skills combined with practical application in the workplace.

To conclude, if IT organizations are to survive and prosper, they must re-examine their strategies to ensure that they adopt a customer-focused approach and encourage the integration of the sales and marketing functions.

Those who fail to do so will be faced with increasing attack from competitors who have adopted a marketing-led culture.

David Allenstein MA, DipM, MCIM runs his own consultancy, Allenstein Associates, which assists in the development of skills and strategies in customer service, sales and marketing.

PART SIXTEEN

MARKETING TO THE RESCUE?

Business process re-engineering

INTRODUCTION

Today, new ideas are received, understood, practised and discarded within a very short time. They are becoming commodities that only pay for themselves if they are picked up at the right time. Investment in an idea that proves unworkable or is overtaken by its antithesis is lost. Considering the rate at which new technology is introduced and becomes obsolete, one might have expected the IT industry to have become more sceptical and learnt the art of 'waiting and seeing' before jumping at the next big idea.

However, competitive advantage is now so hard to find that every idea, big or small, is leapt upon just in case there is some mileage in it. What companies have not realized is just how hard it can be to take on big ideas and how expensive it can be to get it wrong.

For instance, 1994 was the year that companies first read about business process re-engineering (BPR), tried it, by and large got it wrong, but at least ended the year with the certainty that their businesses had to undergo some sort of radical change, even if not on the scale that BPR's creator, Michael Hammer, may have envisaged.

One would expect the IT industry to have a better understanding of BPR and what it can achieve because IT is so central to its success. And because the main reason for re-engineering is the customer, marketing should be the discipline on which re-engineering is most closely focused. Businesses that re-engineer regard marketing not as a discipline practised by a few specialists but a philosophy that imbues the whole organization. In that sense, re-engineering can promote marketing to the level that marketers have always felt it belonged.

Dr Colin Coulson-Thomas shows how strategic client relationships can be built up through business process re-engineering.

New Strategies for Marketing Information Technology.
Edited by Christopher Field
Published in 1996 by Chapman & Hall, London. ISBN 0 412 61520 7

35

NEW RELATIONSHIPS, NEW STRUCTURES

Colin Coulson-Thomas

To effectively build an ongoing relationship with a customer requires an approach to marketing that is very different from traditional 'box selling'. The emphasis needs to be upon listening and learning, sharing vision and values, and the establishment of empathy and trust. The customer must be viewed as a colleague to work with, rather than as a target for one-way messages such as advertisements and direct mail shots. And the emphasis must be on capability and the compatibility of attitudes, approaches and processes, rather than products and services *per se*.

For the IT supplier facing pressure upon prices and margins, becoming a 'strategic partner', may be a means of breaking out of the 'commodity products' trap. Consider the added value chain from initial awareness of need to final implementation (Figure 35.1). The nature of both the profit opportunity and the competition faced will depend upon the point at which a relationship is established.

- Getting in early at the visioning or scoping stage or sustaining a relationship into a range of implementation, training, support and updating services can open up opportunities for an IT supplier to win high margin business.
- Companies that continue to operate as traditional suppliers of 'boxes' in response to competitive tender opportunities are

New Strategies for Marketing Information Technology.
Edited by Christopher Field
Published in 1996 by Chapman & Hall, London. ISBN 0 412 61520 7

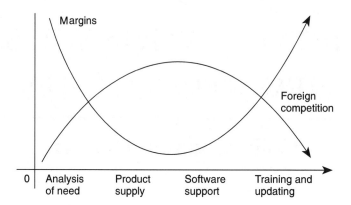

Figure 35.1   The added–value chain (source: Colin Coulson–Thomas (1992) *Creating the Global Economy*).

severely limiting their prospects. They run the risk of being confined to the stage of the added value chain at which the margins are the slimmest and the competition is the most intense.

Success as a 'preferred partner' comes from building and sustaining relationships with new and different sorts of people, beyond the ranks of technical specialists. For example, these people might include business unit managers and CEOs in addition to IT or business systems managers. Teams may be established to explore issues and opportunities, drawing their membership from customers, suppliers and business partners.

THE PERSPECTIVE OF THE CEO

It is important to understand the perspective of 'the other person'. As an example, let us consider a Chief Executive Officer. CEOs often have little interest in technology for its own sake. Their interest relates to what the technology may or may not be able to contribute to the achievement of business objectives and organizational goals. The key questions are:

- Can IT facilitate new 'network' relationships with customers, suppliers and business partners?
- Are investments in IT 'setting an existing departmental organization in concrete' or are they supporting those key cross-

functional and inter-organizational processes that add value for customers?

- Does IT support new patterns of group and distance working, and could IT enable new approaches to learning?

Although many CEOs have a neutral, if not negative, view of IT, there are some encouraging signs:

- While 'historic' IT is often viewed as part of the overhead cost of bureaucracy, efforts are being made to subcontract or otherwise reduce this 'cost'. The IT that is appropriate to the requirements of the network organization is more likely to be considered an 'investment'.
- The focus is likely to shift, as companies emerge from economic recession, from saving costs to transforming relationships with customers and suppliers and the support of cross-functional and inter-organizational processes and new ways of working and learning.
- Cynicism, resulting from an earlier generation of technology which has not delivered the hoped for benefits, is giving way to a realization that what is important is the use and application of technology, not the technology *per se*. In the main the major 'barriers' concern people, their skills and attitudes and the management of technology rather than the technology itself.

Technology is increasingly seen not as an end in itself but as a set of tools to be used, where appropriate, to support the way managers prefer to work and think, and enable more of them to move closer to their full potential. Technology needs to be applied to support those key processes that generate the value sought by customers.

High among the priorities of many CEOs is the transformation of their organizations to enable them to better cope with the challenges and opportunities of a demanding business environment which puts a premium on learning, flexibility and responsiveness.[1] Not all companies face the imminent threat of extinction, but more than incremental adaptation may be required to avoid a negative spiral of cutbacks and layoffs as internal resources are scaled back to match declining external competitiveness.

NETWORK ORGANIZATIONS

Boards are seeking to create more nimble, sensitive, 'horizontal' and team based organizations. IT is a crucial element of many of the

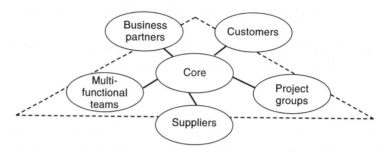

Figure 35.2 The aspiration international network organization (source: Colin Coulson–Thomas and Richard Browne, *The Responsive Organization, IM* (1989) and *Beyond Quality, IM* (1990)).

emerging models of organization. As fewer companies are able by themselves to deliver 'total value' to customers, increasingly, they are creating networks of relationships, with electronic links forward into customers, backwards to suppliers and sideways to business partners (Figure 35.2).

To become 'business partners', IT providers need to demonstrate their understanding of the form of organization being sought. They need to become 'insiders', people who share the vision, goals and values of the network rather than continue to behave as outside suppliers. Some suppliers will become key elements of certain networks and may seek a role in its management.

Networks and supply chains are becoming global, bringing together all those who share a common vision or a particular mission.[2] Managers, especially account managers, need to become enablers and facilitators, harnessing relevant expertise by all available means in such a way that it can be applied to 'add value' for their customers, irrespective of traditional barriers of location, function, time, organization and culture.

The desire for fundamental change could not have come at a better time. Due to the simultaneous availability of a number of complementary 'change elements', we have an unprecedented opportunity to transform the capacity of companies to harness the talents of people and deliver value to customers.

CORPORATE TRANSFORMATION

The findings of a programme of surveys I have undertaken suggest that all the individual change elements, from attitudes to processes, that are necessary to achieve the transformation of organizations have been identified. These are already in place in leading edge companies and their use has been demonstrated and documented. All that needs to be done is to think, select and relate their use to the situation and circumstances.

However, in many organizations the failure to question, anticipate and 'think things through' means that a wide gulf has emerged between expectation and achievement. Why is this?

A major problem area is that few companies have identified and manage their cross-functional and inter-organizational processes. These are the horizontal paths that cut across functional and organizational boundaries and deliver customer value and satisfaction.

In the past, expenditure on IT has too often been devoted to supporting departmental activities, rather than these key processes and the achievement of business objectives. This is why 'cost justification' has often been so difficult, and this is where the contemporary phenomenon of 'BPR' can help. It represents, for the IT industry, both an opportunity and a last chance.

BUSINESS PROCESS RE-ENGINEERING

As an element of corporate transformation, companies are increasingly turning to 're-engineering', either of one or more business processes or of their total organization.

Processes can be improved in various ways depending upon the degree of change required. Thus process simplification can yield significant but incremental improvements to what exists, typically by cutting out non-value added activities in order to improve throughput times and save on resource requirements.

In contrast, re-engineering involves radical change, the redesign or rebuilding of individual processes, or a whole organization, as a result of a 'blue skies' or 'vision led' examination of how the basic elements of people, processes, information and technology might be brought together in new ways to achieve a 'fundamental transformation'. For example, First Direct introduced home banking while 'lean manufacturing' replaces expensive stocks of components with deliveries from suppliers as and when they are required.

While many of the individual elements of BPR are not new, their combination under the umbrella of re-engineering concentrates attention on processes and their outputs. As most organizations are organized by 'vertical' function rather than 'horizontal' process, the potential benefits of such a focus are considerable.

Dramatic increases in productivity have been chalked up by well publicized BPR exercises in such companies as Ford, GTE, Hallmark, Pacific Bell and Xerox. Response times have plunged from months to days and from days to hours.

THE OPPORTUNITY FOR IT

Interest in BPR represents a 'lifeline' for IT suppliers, creating new sequences and combinations of activities to support and new flows and relationships to facilitate. With many approaches to BPR, IT is seen as the key to radical transformation.

The people of the network organization need to be supported by a communications network that is itself flexible and adaptable, and able to facilitate multifunctional, multilocation and multinational team working. The challenge, for both BPR and IT professionals, is to facilitate and support learning, adaptation and change, and the integration of learning and working.

A strategic window of opportunity exists:

- BPR can enable a 'first principles' review to be undertaken of what needs to be done to:
  - facilitate 'network' relationships with customers, suppliers and business partners;
  - support new patterns of group and distance working, and enable new approaches to learning.
- Management processes too need to be reviewed. If network organizations are to survive, they need to become learning networks, with the processes in place to ensure that both vision and capability continue to match customer requirements. The critical processes in the 'new arena' are those for continuing learning, adaptation and change (Figure 35.3).

Not surprisingly, members of the IT community are among the most ardent advocates of BPR, to such an extent that it could be viewed as little more than a cynical attempt to sell IT.

WILL IT SUPPLIERS STEP UP TO THE CHALLENGE?

Many IT suppliers do face a challenge in living up to the promise of their rhetoric. CEOs know this, and many are uncertain, even insecure, as to whom they can trust to deliver. As a consequence of the global aspirations of network organizations, the formulation and

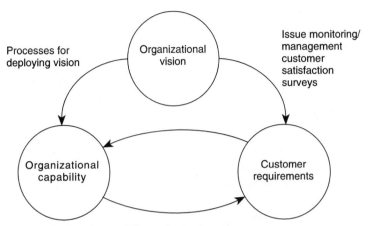

Processes for focusing on delivery of value to customers
Processes for harnessing talents of groups and teams to add value for customers
Processes for continuous learning and improvement

Figure 35.3 Organizational learning (source: Colin Coulson-Thomas (1992), *Transforming the Company*).

implementation of BPR strategy increasingly involves co-operation and collaboration across organizational and national boundaries. Yet many IT suppliers are still organized on the basis of national operating companies and cannot themselves do what their potential customers are seeking. This makes it difficult for them to be effective international partners.

IT suppliers should not take it for granted that re-engineering leads automatically to large investments in IT. The author has encountered some examples of radical improvements of performance that have resulted from the virtual elimination of IT. One operation was transformed by the introduction of a card index system! Instead of relating only to VDU screens, people started talking to each other.

There are dangers. BPR may be 'over-sold'. Well thought out programmes, even a variety of distinct initiatives that in themselves are worthy, may not be enough. They may fail the 'acid test' of impact upon attitudes and behaviour.

BPR: THEORY AND PRACTICE

Among companies, one finds an enormous variety of motivations for considering or embracing re-engineering. They include survival, differentiation, competitive advantage, and the desire for 'early wins' and 'quick fixes'. Some of the drivers may be negative, while others are positive. Objectives range from the modest to the ambitious. BPR initiatives can be relatively self contained or part of an overall transformation strategy.

In theory, re-engineering involves radical change, the redesign or rebuilding of processes as a result of a 'blue skies' or 'vision led' examination of how the basic elements of people, processes, information and technology might be brought together in new ways to achieve a 'radical transformation'. However, in practice many people are getting bogged down with incremental improvements to what is, rather than thinking creatively about what ought to be.

Very often what is referred to as BPR turns out to be process improvement or simplification and not process re-engineering. Such initiatives may result in worthwhile increases in performance, but they are unlikely to produce the radical transformation promised by advocates of re-engineering. While greater use may be made of project groups and teams, the departmental form of organization persists.

KEY SUCCESS FACTORS

The seemingly inextricable link between BPR and IT means that when a BPR exercise fails, the credibility and role of IT may be brought into question. Let us examine some of the more important success factors.

An organization needs to establish the scope of what it is trying to do. Is it engaged in BPR or wholescale corporate transformation? To answer this question, a company might need to undertake issue monitoring and management, or opportunity and competitor analysis, in order to better understand the business environment and identify the extent of the gap between actual and desired capability and performance.

Successful transformations can be identified by the extent to which:

1. the potential and capabilities of individuals and teams are harnessed;
2. corporate capability and commitment is applied to those activities that deliver value to customers and achieve business objectives.

To make an effective contribution, suppliers of IT need to:

1. understand and share clear overall transformation [or re-engineering] goals and strategy;

2. ensure that the resource and capability required for implementation have been assembled.

Too many BPR initiatives are self-contained rather than part of an overall transformation strategy.

A holistic approach is required that embraces all the elements needed to make the exercise happen in a particular context. Significant changes of attitude and behaviour are unlikely to occur while crucial change elements are not in place.

INADEQUATE APPROACHES AND METHODOLOGIES

The continuing absence of 'complementary' change elements is almost guaranteed by the limited nature of some BPR methodologies. Also, too many approaches are insufficiently tailored to the situation, circumstances and context.

Applications of BPR are frequently mechanical and procedural rather than creative. Excessive amounts of time are devoted to documenting and understanding current organizations rather than thinking about alternative models.

Methodologies need to be introduced with care and a sense of balance needs to be maintained. Too detailed and extensive a methodology can result in people 'going automatic'. The importance of sensitivity and feel cannot be overstressed. At the same time, how can people work together without an agreed framework?

Both methodologies and supporting IT are only elements of what needs to be done. Neither should be allowed to take over. Internal ownership should be maintained. Some organizations become so drawn in to heavy and protracted investment in IT, and so exposed to the risk of non-delivery, that the 'tail ends up wagging the dog'.

THE NEED FOR AWARENESS AND SENSITIVITY

Many IT people put an excessive focus upon the 'hard' and quantifiable, such as document flows and supporting technology. Insufficient attention is devoted to the softer people issues because these are perceived as 'difficult' or 'intangible'.

Organizations are communities of people with feelings and sensitivities. In view of the attitudinal and behavioural changes that are likely to be required, particular attention should be paid to internal communication, involvement and other people issues.

Success is dependent upon the effective management of fundamental change. It is ultimately all about feelings, attitudes, values, behaviours, commitments and personal qualities such as being open-minded. Techniques, methodologies and supporting IT are only elements of what needs to be done.

Many IT suppliers would benefit from either employing more people with an understanding of the 'people' issues or forming partnership links with those who do understand them.

Given the total process scope of BPR reviews, the demanding goals which tend to be set, and the fundamental nature of the issues and choices which may emerge, sustained and intense involvement of appropriate members of a senior management team is usually needed. Account management and support needs to be in the hands of those who can operate at this level. Mutual trust, especially between senior management and change and support teams is critically important.

FORMULATING BPR STRATEGY

Suppliers that wish to work as 'partners' and 'colleagues' of senior management in the formulation of transformation strategies need to understand their caution. Radical transformation is an inherently risky activity.

Most boards have little if any experience of corporate transformation and they and their individual members may need to be equipped with new skills and supported by new management processes that begin and end in the boardroom.[3,4] Major transformation challenges tend to be cross-functional or multi-functional. 'Experts' and those who head functional departments may be barriers to, rather than facilitators of, change.

To develop an effective strategy for re-engineering, and before agreeing transformation vision, goals, values and objectives, it is necessary to: (i) understand the challenge and the risks; and (ii) assess and understand 'stakeholder' expectations. People need to be challenged as to whether they want or need radical change with all the risks inherent in BPR initiatives.

The next step is to understand the various helps and hindrances, and obstacles and barriers, that are present. The elements of a programme need to be related to what is necessary to tackle the hindrances, obstacles and barriers. For dramatic breakthroughs in managerial performance these must be identified and overcome.

Clear roles and responsibilities and a few vital priorities can ensure that resources are applied where they are likely to have the greatest impact. The review process must address any gaps and deficiencies. Upon completion of a review an action programme of recommendations should be drawn up, detailing the next steps to be taken, any missing elements and the tools and techniques that could be used to overcome implementation barriers.

Those who advocate BPR need to consider what, if any, value it can provide in the context of transforming organizations. Successful transformation can and is occurring. It depends critically upon a strategy that results in the selection, combination and application of relevant change elements at each stage of the change process.

To participate in the strategy formulation process, IT suppliers need to broaden their perspective to embrace the full range of change elements and pay particular attention to the 'people' aspects.

Colin Coulson-Thomas, Chairman of Adaptation and leader of COBRA, the European Commission's pan-European survey of BPR experience and practice, is a counsellor and advisor to top companies and other organizations on the achievement of corporate transformation. He holds a portfolio of company directorships, is a member of the European Commission's Team Europe, and is regularly called upon to review corporate change programmes and approaches to BPR.

REFERENCES

CHAPTER 9

1. Gibson, C. and Nolan, R.L. (1974) Managing the four stages of EDP growth. *Harvard Business Review*, **52**(1), January/February.
2. Galliers, R.D. and Sutherland, A.R (1991) The revised stages of growth model. *Journal of Information Systems*, 1991(1).
3. Pascale, R.T. and Athos, A.G. (1981) *The Art of Japanese Management*, Penguin, Harmondsworth.

CHAPTER 14

1. O'Neil, Tip (1994) *All Politics is Local*, Random House.
2. Quinn, Professor James Brian, Professor of Management, Amos Tuck School (1994) Intelligent enterprise: a knowledge and service based paradigm. Cited in *The McKinsey Quarterly*, 2, p.83.
3. Sanders, J. (1993) From here to eternity. *PC Magazine*, Ziff Davis UK, August.
4. Smith, A. (1776) *The Wealth of Nations*.

CHAPTER 31

1. Alles, Alfred (1988) *Exhibitions: A Key to Effective Marketing*, p.3.
2. EIF (1992) *Exhibiting – The Facts*.
3. Price Waterhouse Survey of IT vendors and users (1992).

CHAPTER 35

1. Coulson-Thomas, C. (1992) *Transforming the Company: Bridging the Gap Between Management Myth and Corporate Reality*, Kogan Page.

References

2. Coulson-Thomas, C. (1992) *Creating the Global Company: Successful Internationalisation*, McGraw Hill, Europe.
3. Coulson-Thomas, C. (1993) *Creating Excellence in the boardroom*, McGraw Hill, Europe.
4. Coulson-Thomas, C. (1993) *Developing Directors*, McGraw Hill, Europe.

FURTHER READING

Ansoff, H.I. (1968) *Corporate Strategy*, Penguin Books, UK.

Argyle, M. (1974) *The Social Psychology of Work*, Penguin Books, UK.

Christopher, M., Payne, A. and Ballantyne, D. (1993) *Relationship Marketing*, Butterworth-Heinemann, UK.

Cowell, D. (1991) *The Marketing of Services*, Butterworth-Heinemann, UK.

Davidow, W.H. (1986) *Marketing High Technology*, Macmillan, USA.

Davidow W.H. and Malone M.S. (1992) *The Virtual Corporation*, Harper-Business, USA.

Davis, S. and Davidson, W.D. (1991) *20:20 Vision*, Business Books (Random House Group), UK.

Deal, T.E. (1988) *Corporate Culture*, Penguin Books, UK.

de Rouffignac, P.D. (1990) *How to Sell to Europe*, Pitman Publishing, UK.

de Rouffignac, P.D. (1990) *Packaging in the Marketing Mix*, Butterworth-Heinemann, UK.

Drucker, P.F. (1994) *Innovation and Entrepreneurship*, Butterworth-Heinemann, UK.

Drucker, P.F. (1994) *Management*, Butterworth-Heinemann, UK.

Drucker, P.F. (1994) *Post Capitalist Society*, Butterworth-Heinemann, UK.

Fallon, I. (1988) *The Brothers: The Rise and Rise of Saatchi and Saatchi*, Hutchinson (Random House Group), UK.

Fraser-Robinson, J. (1994) *Total Quality Marketing*, Kogan Page, UK.

Galbraith, J.K. (1969) *The New Industrial State*, Penguin Books, UK.

Grindley, K. (1991) *Managing IT at Board Level*, Pitman Publishing, UK.

Hammer, M. and Champy, J. (1994) *Reengineering the Corporation: A Manifesto for Business Revolution*, Allen & Unwin, Australia.

Harvey-Jones, J. (1991) *Making it Happen*, Fontana (HarperCollins), UK.

Heller, R. (1991) *Culture Shock*, Coronet, UK.

Huczynski, A.A. (1992) *Management Gurus*, Routledge, UK.

Kanter, R.M. (1985) *The Change Masters*, Routledge, UK.

Keen, P.G.W. (1991) *Shaping The Future*, Harvard Business School Press, USA.

Kennedy, C. (1993) *Guide to the Management Gurus*, Business Books (Random House Group), UK.

Lawson, M.K. (1988) *Going for Growth*, Kogan Page, UK.

Leiderman, R. (1990) *The Telephone Book*, McGraw Hill, UK.

Maciuba-Koppel, D. (1992) *Telemarketer's Handbook*, Sterling, USA.

Maisonrouge, J. (1989) *Inside IBM*, Fontana (HarperCollins), UK.

McCormack, M.H. (1986) *What They Don't Teach You At Harvard Business School*, HarperCollins Publishers, UK.

Moore, J.I. (1992) *Writers on Strategy and Strategic Management*, Penguin Books, UK.

Naisbitt, J. and Aburdene, P. (1991) *Megatrends 2000*, Pan Books, UK.

Ohmae, K. (1992) *The Borderless World*, HarperCollins Publishers, UK.

Ohmae, K. (1991) *The Mind of the Strategist*, McGraw Hill, USA.

Pearson, B. (1991) *Common-sense Business Strategy*, Mercury Business Books, UK.

Peters, T.J. (1994) *Liberation Management*, Pan Books, UK.

Peter, T.J. (1989) *Thriving on Chaos*, Pan Books, UK.

Pugh, D.S. (ed.) (1971) *Organization Theory*, Penguin Books, UK.

Pugh, D.S., Hickson, D.J. and Hinings, C.R. (1977) *Writers on Organizations*, Penguin Books, UK.

Rapp, S. (1990) *The Great Marketing Turnaround*, Prentice Hall, USA.

Scarborough, H. and Corbett, J.M. (1992) *Technology and Organization*, Routledge, UK.

Sculley, J. and Byrne J.A. (1994) *Odyssey, Pepsi to Apple*, HarperCollins Publishers, UK.

Steinfeld, F. (1990) *Organizations and Communication Technology*, Sage Publications, UK.

Sveiby, K.E. and Lloyd, T. (1988) *Managing Knowhow*, Bloomsbury, UK.

Taylor, B. and Sparkes, J.R. (1977) *Corporate Strategy and Planning*, Butterworth-Heinemann, UK.

INDEX

Page references in **bold** refer to figures and page references in *italic* refer to tables.